Carl Fisher takes a drive around the new Indianapolis Motor Speedway during construction.

Carl Fisher

He Loved To Make The Dirt Fly.
He Conceived and Built The Indianapolis Motor Speedway and The Indianapolis 500.
He Is Considered The Father of The Lincoln and Dixie Highways. He
"Carved A Great City From A Jungle," When He Developed Miami Beach, Florida.
Carl Fisher Sold Candy, Books, Magazines, Bicycles, Motorcycles, Automobiles.
He Tried To Sell Travel Trailers, Diesel Engines, Sand Impregnated Tires, Life-Boats,
Solar Refrigerators, Normal Refrigerators, Display Mannequins Whose Eyes Rolled.
He Created With Partner Jim Allison, Allison Engineering and The Prest-O-Lite Firm That Supplied
Motorists With Marvelous Headlight Illumination.
He Flew A Car Over Indianapolis, Indiana
He Built A Wooden Race Track That Held The World's Fastest Race.
He Tried To Convert Montauk, Long Island, New York Into The Miami Beach of The North.
He Soared In Gas Balloons, Played Polo, Raced Bicycles, Cars and Boats. He Read Continually and Swore A Lot.
He Made Millions.
He Made Friends.
He Died With No Money and The Same Spirit He Had When He Sold His First Magazine.

By Carl Hungness

I Love to Make the Dirt Fly

A Biography of Carl G. Fisher
1874-1939

Carl Hungness Publishing
P.O. Box 225
Madison, IN 47250
USA
e mail: carlhungness@frontier.com

Copyright 2015
First Edition

Layout & Book Design By Ron Smith
Tucson, Arizona

Edited by Greg Max

Indexed by Dan Connolly

ISBN 978-0-915088-86-7

Dedication

To Those Who Put Themselves
In Position Of Judgment:
Your Courage
Furthers Us All

Author's Note

In order to fully appreciate the world Carl Fisher knew as a young man the author suggests the reader does not begin reading this book with Chapter One as you would normally expect.

I would much rather see you turn to the back of the book (Page 156) and read our two chapter Historical Background Section: 1. Rolling Over The Land and 2. Pedal Power. The first chapter relates origin of the wheel, the engines and the men who were responsible for taking the horse off the road and replacing it with the self-propelled vehicle.

The second chapter is a brief and entertaining history of the bicycle. After reading both chapters you will have a very good understanding of the state of transportation Carl Fisher entered although you will admittedly have to plow through some tedious history.

Because our subject was born in 1874, his generation experienced the most drastic change in transportation the world had ever seen. By the time Fisher was 26 in 1900, the first New York Auto Show was held and Carl attended. The Madison Square Garden exhibition introduced the new mode of transportation to America.

Fisher could have ridden in a buggy pulled by a horse on his way to the train station in Indianapolis and shared the road with bicycles. Upon arrival in New York his days of looking at a horse's tail while driving were over.

After leaving the New York Auto Show, Carl Fisher and the other attendees would never again refer to horse-power as they had previously.

As you will see, Carl Fisher became a man in his element when he entered the world of wheels. They carried him far.

Table of Contents

Preface

My journalism career path led me from running a weekly newspaper titled "*Speed Wheels*" in 1968 while I was a senior in college to convincing the United States Auto Club (USAC) the most prestigious automobile racing organization in the world at the time, to allow me to start another weekly paper appropriately titled *USAC NEWS*. I made a presentation to the USAC board a few weeks after graduation and introduced the new paper in January of 1969.

USAC sanctioned four divisions of race cars: Stock Cars, Midgets, Sprint Cars and Championship, or Indianapolis 500 cars. This was the club that set the rules and specifications for the famed Indianapolis 500 and was known as The Club of The Stars. The Sprint Cars and Midgets were considered feeder routes to the the Indianapolis 500 cars. Their Stock Car division was respected as it held races on both dirt and paved tracks. At the time the now popular NASCAR circuit was considered a regional, Southern circuit famed for its super-speedways.

Becoming editor of the USAC NEWS landed me squarely in the midst of professional automobile racing. I would be a part of the press covering the Indianapolis 500. Driving in the Memorial Day Classic was considered to be the ultimate goal for a professional race car driver. I was in awe of the Speedway's size and all it represented. What was once farmland had been transformed to hallowed ground in the mind of a young auto racing reporter. The Indianapolis Motor Speedway was the Yankee stadium of the auto racing world.

As the years passed my knowledge of the environment surrounding the facility grew and by 1973 Al Bloemker, the vice-president of the 'Speedway' as it had become known, gave me permission to publish an annual titled *Carl Hungness Indianapolis 500 Yearbook*. My yearbook was published a few months after each '500' and detailed all activities of each race and usually included historical features as well. It was 224 pages, published in hard and softbound.

Along the route I became interested in not only the history of the track, but of the men, machines, factories who made it possible. Consequently I began studying the history of the motorcar in general because in the beginning, many wanted to prove their vehicles at The Speedway.

When I researched Carl Fisher's biographical background it became evident, to me at least, a movie should be produced on this man's life and times. Through research, I was introduced to another one-of-a-kind automotive man, Billy Durant and I became fascinated with he and Fisher's achievements along with those of many of their peers.

Billy Durant had risen from cigar salesman to found with his pal Dallas Dort, the Durant-Dort Carriage Company. It became the largest carriage manufacturer in the world. Billy went on to establish what was to become the world's largest and richest corporation, General Motors. He was forced from management of GM, whereupon he took his main race car driver with him and said, "Louis, I love this car business, you design me a car and we'll put your name on the radiator shell."

Louis Chevrolet did design a vehicle and Durant's Chevrolet Motor Car Company amassed enough stock to retake control of General Motors, but Billy was ultimately shuffled out of GM only to try a rebound with his own Durant Motors as the Depression loomed near. Ultimately he died broke and his tale facinates me as well.

Carl Fisher had entered the workforce after completing the sixth grade, then managed to open a bicycle shop by the time he was a teenager, became Indianapolis' first and most successful automobile dealer, made a fortune by installing gas burning headlamps on automobiles. He conceived and built the Indianapolis Motor Speedway, started a successful campaign to build the first trans-continental highway (The Lincoln Highway) and literally invented Miami Beach, Florida from what was a jungle. He also spearheaded the construction of the Dixie Highway and envisioned the success of products from refrigerators to travel trailers and Recreational Vehicles.

I compiled enough information on Fisher and Billy Durant to write a movie script. I envisioned a movie that would intertwine the lives of both men and the 1900-1930's era.

As my credibility and contacts grew I was able to sit down with famed actor Paul Newman for nearly an hour to explain my proposed movie project to him. Newman sat in a lawn chain with sunglasses covering his publicized baby-blue eyes while I spoke, uninterrupted for about forty-five minutes. All the while he stared directly at me, and I had no idea what he was thinking because all I saw was my own reflection in his sunglasses.

At the end of my presentation I said, "Well, what do you think? Is that movie material?"

He stood up and said: "Jesus-Christ, that's the most amazing goddamn story I have ever heard. How in the hell did you ever remember all of that? A movie? Hell, it would take forty-seven mini-series to tell that story. It's phenomenal."

Basically, that was it. Nothing came of my meeting other than Paul Newman treated me like a long-lost friend thereafter and removed his sunglasses each time I saw him. I did not know anyone else in the movie business so set the idea aside..

There had already been two very good biographies written about Carl Fisher. One by Jerry Fisher a relative who researched his subject matter thoroughly and wrote a fine book titled *The Pacesetter*. Then Mark S. Foster a professor of history at the University of Colorado turned out another well-researched book titled *Castles In The Sand*. Previously, author Polly Redford had written a book titled *Billion Dollar Sandbar* centering upon Miami Beach as its main topic, that told much of Fisher's basic story as well.

An hour long documentary titled "Mr. Miami Beach" was produced for the American Experience series on PBS by Mark Davis of MDTV Productions that did a credible job on Carl's life.

A documentary film on Billy Durant's life has not been made yet, but he has been the subject of three competent biographies. I want to produce a heavily illustrated book on Durant in the future. Each man left indelible marks on our country and my goal is to assist in preserving their accomplishments. Consequently, what started out to be a movie of Fisher and Durant has transformed into two separate books.

Armed with a suitcase full of Carl Fisher documentation and over 250 photographs I decided to write the book you are now holding. It differs from previous work inasmuch as the story has been told from the perspective of an automotive and auto racing historian. You can expect to meet people, places and circumstances not previously visited in prior work.

Carl Fisher was a grand example of those turn-of-the-century men who were not expected to go to college directly upon graduation from high school. He was one, like so very many others of his era who never set foot in a high school, yet left impressive accomplishments behind.

Today we would call him an entrepreneur. Growing up and as a young businessman he was probably referred to as being a hustler. In the world of pool-playing the term hustler signifies a gambler who manipulates a situation to his advantage, most often taking advantage of a lesser player.

After spending thousands of hours living with Carl Fisher's dreams and deeds this reporter can say with certainty he was an honest man, trying to make an honest buck. He held life-long friendships, was articulate in speech and writing, and must not have had a lazy bone in his body. If he had, he could have quit as a rich man. Instead, as he said himself, "I love to make the dirt fly."

Any dirt that Carl Fisher made fly was moved around so you and I would enjoy life more.

To me, Carl Fisher's legacy is he accomplished. He didn't always win, but he was swingin' for the fences every time he took a cut. He had a memorable journey and the fruit of his Crazy Carl schemes are being enjoyed today.

Chapter 1
The Greatest Race Course in the World

"I don't care how much it costs, we are going to have a track surface the world's fastest race cars will run on, so to hell with the cost."

"They're dead, Carl."

"Oh for christ's sake. We don't need this," noted the man who had envisioned the facility that had just claimed its first pair of victims. Carl Fisher's dream of constructing the finest auto-racing track in the world had just turned into a nightmare as it demonstrated how peaceful land where corn and beans once grew could reap horror in all its finality.

On August 19, 1909 race car driver William Bourke and riding mechanic Harry Holcomb became the first fatalities of Carl Fisher's new race track, the Indianapolis Motor Speedway. The next day another riding mechanic, Charlie Kellum, was thrown from Charlie Mertz's speeding vehicle after catapulting over 100 feet and plowing into a cluster of spectators who were standing in a prohibited area. Kellum along with spectators James West and Homer Jolliff were pronounced dead. [1]

Thus began the coronation of what was to become the most famous automobile racing track in the world. Its inventor had perceived a place where the automotive manufacturers of the world could not only test, but also race their creations in what was supposed to be one of the largest, safest and purpose built racing facilities in the world. Fisher had made a comprehensive study of the world's auto racing tracks and he and his partners believed they had accomplished their goal. The place that would hold the world's largest single day sporting event was vomiting blood.

Carl Fisher's dream child had entered the world with an explosive internal combustion engine roar that first excited, and then extinguished life. Some 35,000 fans were expecting to see a 300-mile dash for what was called the Wheeler-Schebler Trophy Race at the glorious new facility but now many had to wonder if the track had a future at all.

The Indianapolis Motor Speedway had been in business for three months prior to the first fatalities. Since Fisher himself was a licensed illuminating gas balloon pilot, the 18th so registered in the U.S.[2] he and his three partners (who will be detailed a bit later) decided to introduce the press to their 500 plus acre facility on May 1, 1909 with balloon races. Carl

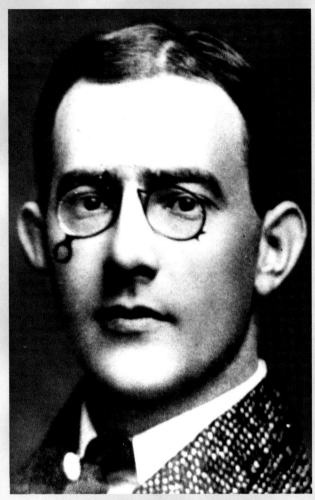

Sporting the popular pince-nez glasses, a thirty-something Carl Fisher was a successful businessman whose greatest accomplishments were yet to come. [2]

Fisher's race track wouldn't produce any noise for its first few months of operation as crews readied their silent transport for tranquil flight.

Nine balloons that ranged in capacity from 40,000 to 110,000 cubic feet of gas were launched on June 5, 1909 at five-minute intervals. While an estimated 40,000 spectators watched the tulip shaped bags rise, about 3,500 had actually paid admission to the grounds. They saw a greenish-yellow New York, a chocolate colored University City, a golden Cleveland, brown Ohio, and pearl white almost transparent Indianapolis. Two more locally named units followed, the Hoosier, and the Indiana. The St. Louis III and the the Chicago followed. The latter was the world's largest, containing 110,000 cubic feet of gas and standing nearly eight stories tall.

A military atmosphere prevailed when it was noticed over 100 uniformed members of the Army's Battery A were on hand to enforce the No Smoking Near The Balloons rule. All were successfully launched and the Chicago unfurled a huge silk American flag that brought cheers from the throng. Fisher himself displayed half a dozen American flags as his balloon, the Indiana, became airborne and brought cheers when he dropped red roses to the crowd below. With Fisher was "Colonel" George Bumbaugh a parachute and balloon enthusiast who would partner with Fisher on many flights. [3] Once out of sight participants occasionally dropped notes to those they could see on the ground. The St. Louis III with a sleepy H.B. Lambert aboard earned the distinction of staying aloft for 45 hours and 59 minutes to establish a new endurance record. [4] *The Indianapolis Star* reported:

Race car driver Lewis Strang surveys a chalk outline of the new Indianapolis Motor Speedway where he would win a race in 1910. He raced in the first "500" in 1911 and completed 109 laps. [4]

Just watching gas balloons take off was a treat in 1909. [2]

"The sight was so beautiful and the balloons made such perfect starts that, not withstanding, the trouble getting to and from the grounds, there were no "knocks" to be found after the races."

The Indianapolis News said "The fame of this race course is now a matter of history. House tops groaned under the weight of hundreds."

A footnote to Fisher and Bumbaugh's journey was their initial claim of being in the air for over 49 hours but they "did not land, on land" previously. They did admit to dropping down after 24 hours when Fisher said,

"The Indiana's water supply was contaminated with oil and this made the water unfit to drink. We came down for water. It was brought to us from a spring. We came down regardless of being disqualified and rested the balloon on crossits (sic) where it did not touch the earth. However we concede all time and distance prizes to the other contestants without argument."

At a party afterwards supporters sang:
"Fisher and Bumbaugh, they're the stuff
Fisher and Bumbaugh, they're no bluff.

George Bumbaugh, Fisher's balloon expert, ties excess covering while Carl, in full business suit, talks with an official shortly before take-off. [2]

Sure they landed before they oughter, but just to get a bucket of water."

It may have transpired Fisher and Bumbaugh discovered the contaminated water and decided to land on saw-horses or some other stick-style device that actually kept their balloon from touching Mother Earth. We can just hear Fisher complaining:

"For crying out loud. How in the hell did the water get oil in it? Now we have to land this damn thing."

Distance winner was John Berry in his Universal City who traveled 382 miles to land near Fort Payne, Alabama.

There is a tribute still in effect at the Indianapolis Motor Speedway that actually pays homage, whether the promoters know it or not, to the early balloonists. Before each Indianapolis 500 thousands of helium filled balloons are released prior to the call for, *"Gentlemen, Start Your Engines"*.

Although they really had nothing to do with the automobile races that were to ultimately make the Speedway's reputation, Carl Fisher and his balloons achieved their publicity mission for introducing the track to the public. Fisher was, by the time his race track opened, accomplished at gaining publicity as we shall soon see.

Motorcycle races were scheduled for the July 1909 meeting and set a portent for the future. The track surface itself, which had actually been painstakingly and expensively applied, was termed unsatisfactory by the two-wheel racers. It wasn't as smooth as the designers had hoped. In contained in fact, jagged edges of rock that had been rolled into what was supposed to have been the finest racing surface ever created. Talk of not competing in the races circulated. Of the 46 contenders scheduled for the 10 Mile amateur event only the quartet of J.F. Torney, John Merz, E.G. (Cannonball) Baker and H.R. Bretney appeared. Torney blew a tire and was pitched off

his machine, thus making Cannonball Baker the first man to take a checkered flag at the new track. The featured 25 Mile event on the new two and one half mile rectangular oval for the professionals was canceled for lack of entries, as were the scheduled races for the next day.[5] Motorcycle racers of the day were used to dirt tracks, often deeply rutted, but the jagged surface presented was clearly unacceptable.

Nevertheless, interest in the upcoming automobile races, (two weeks after the motorcycle event) still captured the public's attention and the two main grandstands were filled to their 15,000 capacity. After the fatalities, the nation's premier auto racing sanctioning organization, the AAA (American

Our colorized photo probably doesn't depict the track's true surface, but it still looks menacing for the first motorcycle race. [4]

Automobile Association) said it would not sanction any future events at the track. This is the same AAA that is familiar to Americans today.

Fisher responded immediately by saying:

"The track will be paved and guardrails constructed on all of the turns before another race is scheduled. We definitely will have the world's finest and safest race course." [6]

Fisher's interest in creating the finest facility in the United States was stated in his long letter to the respected Motor Age publication in 1905, four years before his own facility would open.

Dear Sir:

I note with considerable interest that you are taking up individual opinions regarding the advisability of racing on large tracks. As you are probably aware, a large track of 3 to 5 miles in diameter (sic) with a width of 100 to 150 feet has been a hobby of mine for the past three years and I have done a great deal of work toward a track of this kind. The proposed track at French Lick (Indiana) fell through, for the reason that enough ground could not be secured for a track of sufficient size. After considerable time and investigation, arrangements were made with our Fair Board in Indianapolis for the ground for a 3-mile track, but after a careful survey it was found impossible to put more than a 2-mile track on it.

Very few people understand what an immense difference there is between a mile track and a 3-mile track and to do this it will be necessary to have a drawing of 1, 3, and 5 mile tracks in order to convey properly to the average driver the respective sizes. I have been an interested spectator in most of the big track meets and road races in this country—and France—including the Vanderbilt and the Bennett-and in my opinion that the only successful racing course, and the one which will ultimately find favor

The banking at the Speedway is not very high as evidenced in this photo. Carl Fisher negotiates the new course in a beautiful Stoddard-Dayton a technologically advanced vehicle of the day. [4]

go down the road. There is no accommodation for the public of this kind, and the thousands of dollars spent in advertising for special privileges that go to private individuals could well come into the purse of a 3 or 5-mile track. The American manufacturers annually spend thousands of dollars in building high speed racing cars to compete with French cars and without possible chance of winning, and I think this is largely due to the fact that American drivers do not have a chance to thoroughly test their cars continuously at high speed for weak spots in construction or to become entirely familiar with and have their car under perfect control at very high speeds.

There is no question in my mind that it takes weeks and months of practice handling a car to 75, 80 and 90 miles an hour to be able to properly gauge distances, numerous road conditions, and the response of the car to such conditions. It has been my experience that quite a number of racing cars when tested on the best roads we had in this country seemed to have wonderful speed. There was no accurate way to time them for any distance, and the best anybody could do was to guess at what the cars were doing.

It seems to me a 5 mile track properly laid out, without fences to endanger drivers, with proper grandstands, supply stores for gasoline and oil, and other accommodations would net for one meet,

with both drivers and the public, will be a 3 or 5 mile circular course.

There is no question in my mind that track racing on mile tracks is doomed. The average horse track is narrow, has fences that are too dangerous, and is always dusty or muddy and with high speed cars, where wide skids are necessary, racing becomes so dangerous that frequently the fastest car, from a slow start or other temporary delay, gets off in the rear without chance of gaining the front on account of continuous seas of dust and skidding cars ahead that would also make it too dangerous to attempt to pass. This condition would not exist on a 3 or 5-mile track.

To the spectators there is very little enjoyment in seeing a 25 or 50 mile road race, where immense crowds throng the course where only fleeting glimpses can be had of the cars as they come and

The finished facility depicted in postcard form. [11]

Artist rendering of the oval and proposed road course. [19]

such as the Vanderbilt Cup race, a sufficient amount to pay half of the cost of the entire track. With the present record of 52 seconds on a mile track, I am confident a 3-mile track 100 feet wide will stand a speed of 100 miles an hour, and that a 5-mile track will stand a speed of two miles a minute.

In diagrams I have seen of a 5-mile track it is possible at any point of the curve to see in a direct line 800 feet ahead and a curve of this kind when gradual and continuous is not nearly so severe as some of the short, choppy curves of Ormond Beach where a speed of almost 2 miles per minute was made by a couple of contestants in the meet in the south last winter.

Signed: Carl Fisher

Fisher's Indianapolis Motor Speedway creation

was a two and a half mile rectangle. A road course in its interior was originally designed to be another two and a half mile layout, thus giving him his five mile track. He had discussed the possibility of building such a track with his main real estate investment broker and adviser, Lem Trotter. Trotter had encouraged Fisher to construct the track himself rather than calling for others to undertake the project . They considered the resort town of French Lick, Indiana but didn't find enough suitable flat land. Trotter located the Pressley farm, owned by a Kevin Munter and the Chenoweth family. There were four 80-acre tracts of land that had both the Ben Hur Traction line and the Big Four railroad running next to it. Along with Carl's partner Jim Allison they convinced friends Arthur C. Newby of the National Motor Vehicle Company, Frank Wheeler of the Wheeler-Schebler Carburetor

The picket fence entrance suggests tranquility. [4]

Company and Indianapolis banker Stoughton Fletcher to join the venture.

The land was located about five miles west of downtown Indianapolis and was considered out in the country. Their total outlay for the property was $72,000 but banker Fletcher backed out at the onset for fear his investment in such a promotional activity would be looked upon as unacceptable by financial associates. Their initial name for the new track would be "Indiana Motor Parkway Grounds". [7] The articles of incorporation showed the name to be the Indianapolis Motor Speedway Company and it was capitalized at $250,000. Fisher was president, with Newby first vice-president, Wheeler was second vice-president and Allison was secretary-treasurer.

Their finished product would result in a race track that would have 50' wide straights, each one being 3,301' long; 60' wide curves that are technically described as being 16 degrees, 40" and were not of the spiral easement variety utilized by railroads, and the glorious wooden speedways of the era. The spiral

Suits, ties, fedoras and straw kadys along the front stretch. [2]

A fair damsel wishes Godspeed to the speedsters in this 1909 promotional piece. [11]

Before a race was held, Fisher called his new creation "The Greatest Race Course In The World" and built it accordingly. [3]

easement curve featured an ever decreasing series of radi that allows for a smooth entry and exit of the turn, thus the reason railroad trains don't fly off their tracks when rounding a bend. Fisher's track was so flat the designers used practical judgment for the sweep of the curves.

Chief Engineer Park Talifero Andrews ordered a sandwich of materials consisting of two inches of crushed limestone as a base compacted by an eight-ton roller. It was topped with two inches of creek gravel leveled by a 15-ton three-wheel roller. Two gallons of taroid (sic) to the square yard and one-two inches of crushed stone chips filled the voids along with another 8-10 gallons of taroid to fill gaps. Then an additional 1-2 inches of crushed stone finally compacted by another 3 ton roller. The crushed stone did not result in the smooth surface hoped for.

Undoubtedly Fisher had met with engineer Talifero and said, "We're going to build the fastest, smoothest race course in America and I'm trusting you to do it. Don't spare any expense, this has to be the best track in the world."

The original grandstands, handsome in their green and while livery, consisted of a main covered seating area 500' long and 82' wide plus two bleacher sections of 500' x 60' and 350' x 65'. There was also a huge aerodrome building that was 300' x 50' with a 35' high roof. Three miles of board fence 8' high, 25 suspension bridges for spectators and a truss bridge

Speedway founders, from left, Newby, Wheeler, Fisher and Allison. [1]

Successful bicycle mechanics and manufacturers, the Wrights tested air-pressure effect on the wind vanes attached to the horizontal wheel mounted above the front tire of this 1898 bicycle, a St. Clair made by the brothers' firm.[4]

Although the Wright brothers, Orville (left) and Wilbur (right) did not appear at the Speedway's 1909 air show event, their accomplishments helped fuel the interest. The life long Fisher friends could already claim having flown around the statue of Liberty.[7]

for vehicles were installed. Overall it was evident the promoters were building a world-class facility to stage their racing events.[8]

After the initial motorcycle and auto racing events were held, it was evident Fisher and friends had to extensively modify their racing surface which may best be described not as smooth, but consisting of an endless series of jagged rocks protruding from the surface. The huge facility itself impressed all attendees and the general consensus had to be,

"This place will be great if they improve the track surface." Fisher and his partners would soon pony up additional investment to provide a surface no one could complain about.[9]

No record exists of what Fisher said after he found out the original track surface was not suitable, but we can well imagine most of his language wasn't fit for print.

Chapter 2
The Salesman

"I know I can sell your bicycles but you have to give me a whole bunch of them so I can keep the price down. I can't afford to buy them all at once, but I promise I'll pay you if you give them to me on consignment."

By the time the official shocked him with report of the deaths at his new race track in 1909 Carl Graham Fisher was 35 years old and his name, along with his automotive achievements and entrepreneurial business practices were well known to not only residents of Indianapolis, Indiana, but he had received some world-wide publicity for his stunts and achievements. Fisher had risen far by 1909, after having joined the work force at age 12 in 1886 like many of his peers of the day. Across the world compulsory education was often finished by age 14. By 1897, Indiana made it mandatory to finish the eighth grade, so Carl had an adequate apprenticeship in the basics.[1]

"Carl, I don't think you ought to quit school," his mom said to him.

"Well dad's gone and someone has to bring the money in. It's Ok mom, I can read and write and add and subtract. I'll get a job, make some money, you watch."

After researching through the voluminous material on Carl in the Historical Museum of Southern Florida and seeing the vast number of books Fisher requested for his own personal reading, this reporter concludes Carl Fisher had an inner drive to become conversant about a phenomenal range of topics. He continually requested long lists of books be sent to him and was in the habit of sending books to friends whom he thought would benefit from their content.

Carl Graham Fisher was born on January 12, 1874, to Albert and Ida Fisher. He would mature to see his visions become reality, a wonderful spiritual

experience for a boy whose actual sight was extremely poor. He had acute astigmatism but no mention has been located as to why optometrists were not able to give him a prescription until much later in life. He had two younger brothers, Earle and Rolly, neither of whom distinguished themselves as having Carl's temperament, drive or gregariousness.

Carl's father Albert was descended from a line of Fishers who emigrated from Berlin, Germany in 1770.[2] While Albert was actually termed a lawyer, the title did not hold the educational respectability that was to come later. It appears as though he was able to provide at least a good middle class existence for his family for the first few years of his marriage. Albert Fisher was afflicted with alcoholism in a severe enough condition causing the resolute Ida to leave

Ida Fisher presents a bundle of joy and energy to the world, son Carl. [2]

Ida Fisher as a mature woman. [2]

Patriarch Albert Fisher presented an imposing image. [2]

him when the three boys were youngsters. The family had lived in Greensburg, Indiana, a typical Midwest courthouse square town southeast of Indianapolis (now famous for having a tree growing out of the courthouse spire) and about halfway to the Ohio River city of Madison. Ida moved her brood to Indianapolis. She obtained a residence and was able to keep the proverbial wolf from the door by taking in boarders.[3]

"That alcohol has got a grip on your father," Ida told her boys. "The stuff is just no good for you."

Carl's lack of an exemplary father figure did not seem to hamper his integrity or drive toward success. Nevertheless, in her biography *Fabulous Hoosier* about Carl, his first wife Jane says her husband bemoaned his parents' separation and was emotionally scarred by his upbringing. Overall, this reporter gives significant credibility to Jane Fisher's biography although some of it has to be taken as hero-worship and biased. Records prove many of her historical facts are less than accurate but we trust nearly all of her personal emotional recollections.

Her immediate access to Carl's personality gives us the best overview extant.

As is happily often the case, Carl's mother was an encouraging woman who set a standard that held her boys in good stead. Of course we don't know precisely how Albert Fisher treated his three sons but Carl displayed an emotional attachment to his dad throughout his life. Records show Carl gave him financial assistance and seemingly longed for a close relationship. He maintained a measure of respect for the man as is evidenced in a letter

Appearing as though a child of privilege, young Carl was nattily attired. [2]

Carl wrote to rental car magnate (and Chicago cab company owner) John Hertz where he quoted his dad as saying, "My father was a lawyer and he always told me that if I would stick to doing what I thought was right, I would never get in very serious trouble." [4]

The society Carl Fisher entered as a work-a-day 12 year old in 1886 is difficult to comprehend as we write this tome in the first decade of the 21st century. Maybe most significantly, the horse and buggy was the normal mode of transportation so one's immediate world was limited to a point we find difficult to imagine today. However, the bicycle was gaining in popularity and Carl intended to sell a lot of them. The old three to five mile walks into town became a joyful adventure balanced atop a pair of wheels. The population began to realize just how much they desired easy mobility.

We know young Fisher was a gregarious enough type to have garnered a nickname (Skipper) from his friends and would actually be referred to as such by close acquaintances for the rest of his days. John Oliver LaGorce, Vice President and Associate Editor of the famed National Geographic Society, a life-long friend (after Carl began his Florida investments) referred to Carl as Skip in his continuing letters as did famed automobile racer Tommy Milton. [5]

"Hey Skipper, I'll race you down to the apple tree."

"Hell, I can beat you running backwards."

A dozen years after Carl entered the work force in 1896 the nation was interlaced by thousands of miles of railroad tracks, but the East had only met the West in 1869 when rails were joined at Promontory Point, Utah. This was the era of Robber Baron control. J.P. Morgan's railroad trust controlled more track than any other combination of interests. Between 1865 and 1900 national railroad mileage grew from 35,000 to 260,000. Labor unrest was common and over 100 rail strikers were killed during 1877. Over 60,000 struck in defiance of Pullman rail car company's policies. John D. Rockefeller's Standard Oil would literally control the nation's oil flow. One Samuel Gompers organized skilled craftspeople into the powerful American Federation of Labor (AFL) in 1886. The Civil War ended in 1865 after over 600,000 Americans had died fighting one another and in 1886 Abraham Lincoln's name was still fresh in the minds of U.S. residents.

The electric light bulb had come into existence in

Ida and her brood as adolescents. [2]

1883, seven years after both Alexander Graham Bell and Elisha Gray applied for patents on the telephone in 1876.

Carl Fisher did not enter an apprenticeship in a trade. We find reports telling us he worked in a grocery store, then a bank, and began his salesmanship career hawking newspapers and candy on passenger trains in a capacity known as a butcher boy. One of the most influencing experiences Fisher obtained during his teenage years came as a salesman for the book sets authored by famed orator of the day Robert

The world Carl Fisher entered and spent his youth in was surrounded by the horse drawn vehicle. [3]

Ingersoll. We know from the Florida Fisher Files Carl was an ace salesman for the Ingersoll books and won a prize for selling more copies than any other news "butcher" on the B & O railroad. At the time the word 'drummer' was also utilized for being a salesman and his trips up and down train aisles hawking his wares had to give him a base education about human nature. Given Carl Fisher's appetite for digesting knowledge, we have no doubt he read every word in the volumes he was selling and became an articulate disciple of Ingersoll. He sold by parroting what was already successful; Ingersoll's words. He must have been an impressive and articulate kid in order to be successful at book sales. He wasn't afraid of rejection. While his vocabulary was not scholarly, Fisher's letters as an adult were fluent, expressive and perceptive. His sales pitches probably sounded like the following:

"Yes ma'am, every word in these books was written by Mr. Robert Ingersoll. He would never copy

A typical big city photo from 1901 depicts an American Main street.[3]

anyone else's work. Look what he says here about writers. He says, 'Every article in a newspaper should be signed by the writer. And all the writers should do their best to tell the exact truth.'

"I can get you this whole set of books delivered by next week and you can have them on the easy-payment plan. What he says makes good sense, doesn't it? See what he says about women, listen to this: In my judgment, the woman is the equal of the man. She has all the rights I have and one more. She has the right to be protected. If there is any man I detest, it is the man who thinks he is the head of the family-the man who thinks he is the boss.'

Carl would continue, "Why Mr. Ingersoll is famous and these books will be a wonderful addition to your library. My mom has a set."

Robert Ingersoll's name is all but forgotten to modern society but his popularity couldn't have been more pronounced than it was in the late 1800's. Known far and wide as The Great Agnostic, Ingersoll was able to claim significant credibility among the most respected and famed people of the day. A Darwin advocate, he was of the opinion there may or may not be a God. His respectability even among church regulars thus becomes all the more impressive.

He was invited for example, to address the January 15, 1892 Unitarian Club dinner in New York City. His after dinner speech has been preserved and reprinted in one of his books and it is easy to understand why he appealed to the masses. Ingersoll, a learned student of the bible, does not preach that everyman should not believe in a supreme being. Ingersoll questions the savagery of religion throughout the ages while simply stating "that there be a church in sympathy with the best human heart and human brain."

In Ingersoll's opening remarks to the churchgoers he said:

"You have shown that you are not afraid of a man

*The carriage without a horse was
a spectacle to see* [1]

simply because he does not happen to agree entirely with you. You know, I presume you know, that I have no religion-not enough to last a minute-none whatever-that is in the ordinary sense of that word. And yet you have become so nearly civilized that you are willing to hear what I have to say; and I have become so nearly civilized that I am willing to say what I think. "

He skillfully questions time-honored beliefs in such a manner that the rank and file listened to him as though he was a thoroughly reasonable man. Carl

Fisher was most likely captivated, as were throngs of others by Ingersoll's writings. Ingersoll said about religion:

"Religion and morality have nothing in common, and yet there is no religion except the practice of morality. What you call religion is simply superstition.

"Real religion means the doing of justice. Real religion means the giving to others every right you claim yourself. Real religion consists in duties of man to man, in feeding the hungry, in clothing the naked, in defending the innocent, and in saying what you believe to be true.

"Let us judge each other by our actions, not by theories. Not by what we happen to believe-because that depends very much on where we were born."

No less a personage than the inventor of the electric light bulb, Thomas Edison, said of Robert Ingersoll: "Ingersoll had all the attributes of a perfect man, and in my opinion no finer personality ever existed. Judging from the past, I can not help thinking the intention of the Supreme Intelligence that rules the world is to ultimately make such type a man universal."

Author Mark Twain said: "He was a great and beautiful spirit; he was a man, all man from his crown to his foot soles. My reverence for him was deep and genuine. Of all men living and dead I love Ingersoll most! And lastly: Except for my daughter's, I have not grieved for any death as I have grieved for his."[6]

Steel magnate Andrew Carnegie: "Ingersoll and Lincoln were cordial friends. To have known both is one of the satisfactions of my life. As all the world knows they thought alike on political and religious subjects. If there is another world they live in bliss; if there be none they made the best of this."

Evidence of Ingersoll's monumental popularity was displayed at Chicago's Interstate Industrial Art Exposition Building on October 20, 1876. The

COLONEL ROBERT G. INGERSOLL
He quenched the fires of Hell and planned a Heaven on Earth for all Mankind! The Ingersoll League offers you the Key to his Earthly Paradise!

"I GOT Ingersoll's books and never lost an opportunity to hear him speak. He had a tremendous influence upon me. He liberated my mind. Freedom is what he preaches. He wants the shackles off everywhere. He wants men to think boldly about all things. He demands intellectual and moral courage. He wants men to follow wherever truth may lead them. He was a bold, heroic figure!"

—ROBERT M. LA FOLLETTE,
("Fighting Bob") famous Wisconsin Senator.

Ingersoll's Victorious Life Gives You The Secret of Happiness and Power!

ABRAHAM LINCOLN fought to free the slave, Robert G. Ingersoll to free the soul. Lincoln ended physical bondage. His friend, Ingersoll, is ending mental bondage with fearless philosophy couched in matchless language.

The writings of Ingersoll attack the tyranny of social, political and religious prejudices. He found the facts, and exposes the frauds. When the history of these centuries is written, he will stand out as the beacon light of reason who swept away the menacing shadows of superstition, ignorance, fear and intoler-

Ingersoll delivers you from your fears, superstitions, doubts, dreads, anxieties, hatreds and resentments. They are poisons that destroy the man who harbors them. He liberates you to express your best, achieve your utmost, ennoble your outlook, and enjoy the consciousness of personal power and the happiness of victorious living.

Most people trust to luck to "get by" amid the perpetual series of emergencies which confronts every one of us. But why do that?—when you can have the rock-solid support of Robert G. Ingersoll, a wise, sane, fearless fighter who mastered the Secret of Victory early in life, taught it to thousands, and is only

Adopt Ingersoll's Attitude Toward Life and You Can Live Victoriously

A REVOLUTION in thought has occurred, brought about mainly by one individual," writes Elbert Hubbard. "The world was ripe for Ingersoll's utterance. A hundred years before we would have snuffed him out in disgrace. But crowds hung upon his utterances and laughed with him at the scarecrows that had once filled their daydreams, made the nights hideous and the future black with terror. On the urn that encloses his ashes should be these words: Liberator of Men."

He wrote what he LIVED—what had WORKED in his life—what was PRACTICAL. From the village of Dresden, New York, where he was born to his niche in the Temple of Fame, his life is a triumphal record of growth and progress. He was a success from the outset. He had the temperament for it—happy, exuberant, revelling in existence, marching to the front in every fight.

That spirit is in his books. Your response to their appeal will probably amaze you. You will be carried away by them. Your heart will leap with joy as you turn over the pages. His thoughts have an effect like that of Spring sunshine on trees and buds and birds.

You Too Can Lead the Victorious Life

Through his writings Ingersoll has organized the Victorious Life for thousands. He can do as much for you as for these others. Life-power pours out of every phrase. In every page and paragraph there is information, inspiration and infectious vitality.

With his aid you will bid farewell forever to envy and hostility—just as he did. You will stop feeling frustrated, inferior to other people. He gives you Self-Confidence, Poise, Self-Assurance. Through him you will discover that the world is after all YOUR world. At present you may merely be living in it. Through reading him you will learn to feel AT HOME in it!

Arm Yourself with Ingersoll's Humor

Into your hands Ingersoll puts the mightiest weapon in the arsenal of the gods. His own favorite weapon—Humor! Fighter that he was, he never lost his sense of humor. He faced the evils of this world and fought them to a standstill with easy, fearless, sunshiny humor. Learn to do it with him!

Ingersoll's immortal writings enable people to live ruggedly, comfortably, sanely. Look at the world from his viewpoint, adopt his attitude, and you will find yourself equipped to deal with all life's emergencies, major and minor.

So infectious is his gay, humorous viewpoint that you will adopt it before you have read a hundred pages of his singing, buoyant, fighting prose! His attitude is so sensible, so attractive, so rewarding—so certain of VICTORY!

The twelve handsome volumes of his immortal writings give you superb equipment for the kind of life that is lived victoriously, the kind he lived himself, and has taught so many others to live. With his books at your elbow you will proceed with his powerful aid to create your own Heaven for yourself here and now!

Send To-day for Ingersoll's Writings It Costs You Nothing to Examine Them

What The World Thinks of Robert G. Ingersoll

He was a great and beautiful spirit; he was a man all man from his crown to his footsoles. My reverence for him was deep and genuine.
—*Mark Twain.*

His works are an inspiration to the whole earth.
—*Luther Burbank.*

I love him, I respect him, I venerate his name. For the name of Robert Ingersoll and True Manhood are the same.
—*James Whitcomb Riley, the Hoosier poet.*

He has done more than any other man this world has ever produced, in any age, to improve the condition of common humanity and to leave the world happier, better and brighter than he found it.
—*Eugene V. Debs, much-beloved, radical leader.*

Robert Ingersoll was "brother to the mountains"! Writer of lines that leaped with laughter, of pages that were wet with tears, orator, dramatic artist, lawyer, glittering man of affairs, master-builder of home, poet, philosopher, dreamer, genius—where, among the great men of America may we find the match of the many-sided Ingersoll?
—*Minnie Maddern Fiske, America's great actress.*

Ingersoll and Lincoln were cordial friends. To have known both is one of the satisfactions of my life. As all the world knows they thought alike on political and religious subjects. If there is another world they live in blue; if there be none, they made the best of this.
—*Andrew Carnegie, steel magnate.*

Colonel Ingersoll will stand forever as one of the historic figures who from Socrates to Milton and from Milton to Lincoln, have battled fearlessly for human rights.
—*Senator Albert J. Beveridge.*

Ingersoll was one of our noblest Americans. No man stood on a higher summit. He was a prophet in his advocacy of the clean individual life, in his insistence upon reason in religion, and in his demand for social justice and a court for international arbitration. Let

Colonel Robert Ingersoll was a famed and highly regarded orator whose positive attitude influenced Carl Fisher[8]

length of this structure was one hundred feet less than three football fields laid end to end, two hundred feet wide and its three domes were one hundred and sixty feet tall, the equivalent of a seventeen story building. It was erected where today's Chicago Art Institute stands, a facility which could have been put inside the Exposition Building. To cover Ingersoll's speech the Chicago Tribune devoted its front page to coverage and said, "an immense crowd of at least fifty thousand," attended.[6] For Ingersoll to have attracted such a throng in those days before public address systems, and jumbo television screens is almost beyond imagination. His magnetism was unequaled.

Hoping my readership will bear with me to dwell on Ingersoll's attitude and teachings a bit

longer, research shows an impressionable Carl Fisher adopted a good deal of Ingersoll's attitude. If Fisher's father were absent it seems to follow Carl would be highly susceptible to such a convincing role model as Ingersoll. We can imagine by the time Carl was selling the Ingersoll books, he was probably 17 years old and gained enough in commissions to open his first business, his bicycle shop. Then as now, the commissioned salesman had an opportunity to make more than an hourly wage earner. It would be hard to imagine Carl Fisher was able to actually save enough cash from his menial jobs to open a retail establishment. Successful salesmen have long had the attitude of 'the sky is the limit' when referring to commissions.

While Carl Fisher sold a goodly number of Ingersoll books and went into the bicycle repair and selling business he could easily identify with Ingersoll's attitude that "happiness is the only good, the way to be happy is to make others so and the time and place to be happy is here and now". [7]

Ingersoll died in 1899 and was lauded by no less a journalistic leader than the *Chicago Tribune* which said: "Splendidly endowed as he was he could have won great distinction in the field of politics had he so chosen. But he was determined to enlighten the world concerning the '*Mistakes of Moses*'. That threw him out of the race."

Ingersoll had written a book with the Mistakes of Moses title challenging biblical tenants seemingly set in stone, and it gained wide recognition but assuredly ended any hopes he may have had for a political career. Ingersoll's popularity of the era cannot be underestimated nor can his influence on Carl Fisher's life.

Fisher's entry into the bicycle business came at an opportune time, as proven by the number of clubs and spectators dedicated to the vehicles throughout the world. In 1870 some 4,000 fans turned out in England's Birmingham Aston Cross track to watch John Henry Palmer and John Prince battle in a one-mile heat, won by Prince at a time of 4:25.5 [8]

Carl Fisher's introduction to the world of cycling came atop a high wheeler, a most appropriate description for the machines that regularly had front wheels of 36" or more in diameter. One James Moore gained notoriety in France and England utilizing a machine with a 48" front wheel. The four-minute mile record was eclipsed by an E. Shelton of Wolverhampton on a machine with "nearly a fifty inch front wheel." [9]. Such machinery was completely tractable as four members of the Middlesex Bicycle Club were featured in a beautiful full color illustration in The Graphic publication of July 1873. The quartet were featured as they rode seven hundred miles from London to John O'Groats an outpost at the tip of England. [10]

By the time Carl started selling bicycles the familiar high-wheeler was being phased out and replaced by what became known as the safety bicycle. As one can imagine, flipping over the handlebars of a high-wheeler, commonly referred to as "ordinaries" and "Penny Farthings" resulted in "taking a header". Henry J. Lawson's Bicyclette of 1879 led the way to machines having equal height front and rear wheels. [11]

By 1888 horse veterinarian John Boyd Dunlop had experimented with installing air-inflated rubber tires on his son's bicycle and devoted himself to the inflatable tire A Belgian named Dietz had experimented with the idea as far back as 1836 and by Englishman Robert W. Thompson in 1845, but Dunlop is the one who wound up with a patent thereby changing the world of tires forever, and adding to the desirability of the oncoming safety bicycle. [12]

Carl was a member of the popular Zig-Zag Bicycle Club of Indianapolis, a group of young men whose numbers climbed to nearly 200 in the early 1890's. It is said the veteran riders preferred the high-wheeled ordinaries to the new user-friendly low-wheeled machines and both were part of Fisher's formative years. Although the reportage is not documented with dates, we take author Al Bloemker's word when he tells us in his *500 Miles To Go* Carl became a barnstorming bicycle racer in towns throughout the Midwest along with a man who would become a life-long friend, and one of the most famed race car drivers of all time, Barney Oldfield.

Fisher's entrepreneurship was in its apprenticeship stages after he, undoubtedly aided by his brothers. opened the C.G. Fisher Bicycle Co. in the last decade of the century. The earliest ad we find is from an 1899 newspaper offering new machines for sale at 112 N. Pennsylvania Ave. in downtown Indianapolis.

My own research has failed to turn up any significant details of a man Carl himself gives significant credit for his success, one George Erland, a bicycle manufacturer in Columbus, Ohio. Given Carl's future performance record, we can easily imagine Fisher convincing Erland to give him bicycles on consignment as has been previously reported many times.[13] Jane Fisher recounts Carl as being nineteen at the time of convincing Erland to give him several thousand dollars worth of bicycles on consignment.

High Wheelers or Ordinaries as they were termed, were a common sight on America's roads during Fisher's youth. [3]

She describes Carl's first bicycle shop as the finest in all of Indianapolis. We don't doubt her word, for she claims to have first seen, and become enamored with Carl when she was 15 and Carl was 35.

"Mr. Erland, I have been working on bicycles for a long time now and every one I have fixed has been sold. Now if you'll give me a load of new machines everybody in Indianapolis is going to see them. I know I can sell 'em. Your machines are beautiful and they'll be just perfect for my new shop. I

" I promise, I'll pay you for them as I sell them. It'll be a good deal for both of us, you'll see."

The young man who has just opened his first business featuring a worthwhile, appealing, fascinating, thrilling, product has to be one proud human being. Besides, bicycles were fun. You can race 'em. Carl Fisher had the heart of a racer in every definition of the word, from the physical to the mental. He would ultimately prove the ideas he conceived and received were valuable in and of themselves, even if you couldn't see it. He had looked around and said to himself, "This place needs a great bicycle shop. I can sell bicycles here, lots of them." It was as simple as that.

As a teenager Carl was utilizing his considerable prowess in having a gift of the gab. Convincing a manufacturer to give him product on consignment was in reality a monumental accomplishment. From what we can glean Carl was a very physically active youngster who was dubbed "Crip", short for Cripple, due to the number of mis-calculations he experienced. It is noted he practiced running backwards so diligently he could still outpace friends well into mid-life. His wife tells us he built a pair of stilts so tall they had to "be mounted from an upstairs window." and became the best ice skater in Indianapolis.[14]

The accomplishment of Fisher opening a retail establishment as a teenager cannot be underestimated. After being in the workforce for just a few years years, we imagine he and his brothers repaired, bought and sold bicycles as a way to raise extra cash, Carl's entrepreneurial spirit brought the adventure to its natural conclusion. His shop in Indianapolis was on one of the city's main streets (Pennsylvania Ave.). Carl worked as a nominally paid employee from age 12 onwards [15] and he had to exude an honest, hard-working spirit that impressed adults. While there were no shortages of bicycle manufacturers in the U.S. in the 1890's (at least 25 were in business in Chicago during this period) Fisher must have been a self-assured, persuasive salesman to convince a manufacturer to stock his store. Can you, gentle reader, imagine a teenager approaching you with a business proposition to stock him with product? Eventually his shop sold many different brands as displayed in the newspaper ads we were able to locate.

Fisher was a young man no different than vast numbers of his kind throughout the world who fell in love with bicycles. The daredevil spirit he had displayed as a youngster kindled the flame of competition in him when he became a bicycle racer. As a member of the local Zig-Zag bicycle club, and another named by Jane Fisher as the Flat Tire Club. Although obviously mechanically oriented he did not show an interest in working with his hands in a machine shop setting as did many of his friends. He most likely performed some of the necessary maintenance on bicycles and his own

Zig Zag Bicycle Club members numbered about 200 in their heyday,[3]

early vehicles, but did not make working in a shop one of his priorities.

Time and again we find the bicycle enthusiasts went on to become the men who crafted the upcoming automobile industry. While we do find several newspaper ads for Carl's bicycle shop dating from 1899 onwards, we haven't located any actual newspaper reports that solidify some of the stories told about young Fisher's promotional stunts. Even if memories have faded in the re-telling of these incidents, most are believable given his future exploits that are amply covered in print.

For example, most sources claim Fisher strung a tight wire in-between two downtown buildings, and while wearing a padded suit along with safety guide ropes tied to the handlebars, actually traversed the multi-story height on a two-wheeler.[16] He is reported to have constructed the "world's tallest bicycle," that had to be mounted from a second story window. Your author has seen two bicycle frames bolted together vertically to raise the rider several feet off the ground, so we can imagine Fisher and friends erected a similar model . He announced he would throw a bicycle from atop a building (and reward the one who returned it to his shop with a new machine).

After ruining a perfectly good bike by tossing it off a roof he concocted another scheme to attract customers.

This time he was aided by his new pal, the previously mentioned George (Colonel) Bumbaugh, a young man who appears in photos to be about the same age as Carl. Bumbaugh was a balloon enthusiast who performed at county fairs and was known to have thrilled audiences with a parachute drop from one of his elevated baskets. Fisher had Bumbaugh glue together 1,000 tiny toy balloons that were to be dropped as Bumbaugh sailed over central Indiana. A hundred of them were tagged and redeemable for a new bicycle.

Possibly ready for a little sprint race, this well-dressed group of young men look eager to get started atop the popular safety bicycle.[3]

[17] The anticipated reports of farmers shooting at the toy balloons could also be well imagined. Carl's early antics remind us he may have been one of the nation's first wheeled-vehicle hawkers we have come to know and love through radio and TV.

After gaining an inventory from the afore-mentioned George Erland, Carl approached one of the most famed manufacturers in the industry, Colonel Albert A. Pope a Civil War veteran. Pope had become a well-to-do producer of shoe parts and air pistols. Pope was enamored with bicycles in the late 1870's and became a leader in the industry. Initially he had invested heavily in the popular high-wheeler. It is estimated about twenty five-hundred

bicycles were in use in American in 1879 and Pope was one of its leading proponents.[18]

"Colonel Pope, if you will sell me your machines at a little lower cost, I'll buy ads in the newspaper advertising the Pope bicycle. When I sell one, we'll sell another one. Every guy in the neighborhood will see the new bike and they'll want one too. But I need a whole bunch of them right in the store. The worst thing that could happen is if someone comes in and we don't have anything to sell him right away. That makes sense to you, doesn't it?"

Fisher approached Pope and convinced him to part with a significant number of bicycles (250) at near cost. Fisher's reasoning was Pope had a fine machine that wasn't selling in his shop as well as it could and with enough advertising dollars Carl could promote the brand.

From his involvement in the Zig-Zag Club, Carl became friends with Art Newby. Newby would go on to become a young manufacturer in the bicycle industry, creating the Indianapolis Stamping Company. Later he was associated with the Hay & Wilhite Manufacturing Company which made the Outing brand bicycle. The long-tenured Diamond Chain Company grew out of Newby's first manufacturing effort. Newby also founded the National Motor Car Co.[19]

What turned out to be a very influential organization, the National Wheelmen were able to hold a national championship race in Indianapolis at Newby's new race track designed specifically for bicycles. The Wheelmen were credited for their efforts in lobbying to build America's roads, an endeavor Fisher would become deeply involved in. The first race at the Newby Oval was held in July of 1898 and the track was an impressive wooden velodrome with a capacity for seating 15,000. It was built at the intersection of what are now Central and 30th streets in Indianapolis The bicycle craze was in full steam when Carl Fisher was advertising his wares a couple of years before the turn of the century. Nevertheless, it is reported the Newby Oval actually had only one good year and was torn down a little over a year after its introduction. Newby would later be called the Father of The Six-Day Bicycle Race.

"Hey Art, everybody is racing. Why don't you build us a real race track? Everybody would come and watch. You'll probably make a fortune from it."

Indianapolis was a thriving city in the late 1800's. In 1880 its population was 75,000, it grew to 105,000 in 1890 and by 1900 the population had risen to 169,000.[20] Consequently, the Fisher bicycle

Fisher pal A.C. Newby's wooden bicycle velodrome in Indianapolis featured extremly high banking and provided exciting races. [2]

Carl in front and brother Rollo aboard a two man racer. [2]

emporium was generating enough revenue to give our subject the feeling that only success can provide.

Carl purchased a deDion-Bouton motor tricycle, one of the first successful internal combustion engined vehicles to appear in the U.S. He also bought a powerful Mobil Steam wagon. More than likely he was impressed after he saw the machine churn its way up the two-story ramp outside of Madison Square Garden where he saw the first automobile show.

Carl was fairly financially stable by late in the century. His newspaper ads show he sold not only bicycles but motorcycles as well by 1901 although we haven't been able to ascertain the precise motorcycle brands he represented. The now legendary Harley-Davidson would not be introduced until 1903 and the Indian was introduced in 1901. It was a natural progression for him to travel to New York City to see the first well-organized exhibition of horseless carriages.

Traveling from his Indianapolis home was nothing new to Fisher as shown by a letter dated Nov. 13, 1925 we found from Howard Ruggles, President of Ruggles & Brainard that stated in part:

"You will remember me when I tell you that I knew you when you were a "twenty-five dollar a week salesman" for the Mobile Company of America of Chicago. I was the Western Manager of Cosmopolitan Magazine and it used to be my duty to hand you your paycheck every week…. I spent a few days at Coral Gables and looked over Miami Beach. I'll say you started something down there boy!" [21]

Fisher replied he recalled how difficult it was to live in Chicago on twenty-five dollars a week. The Mobile Publishing Co. was not connected to the Mobil Steam Carriage firm Carl would later represent.

The Madison Square Garden automobile show Carl attended began on November 3, 1900 and was referred to by some as "the horseless horse show."

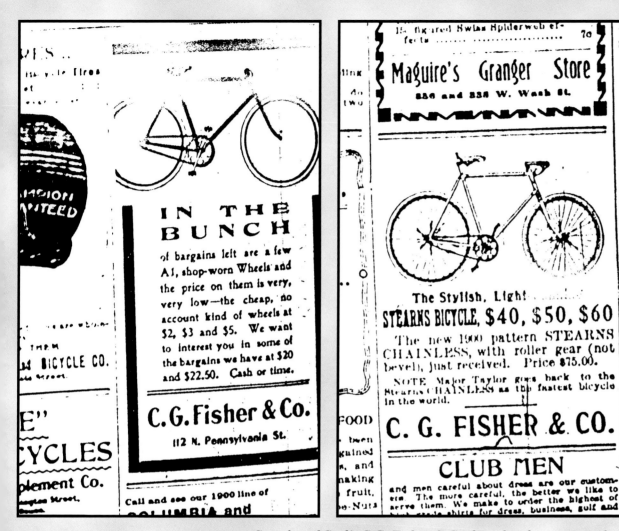

Samples of Carl's C.G. Fisher & Co. bicycle advertising in the late 1890's.[2]

Forty brands made up the three hundred vehicles that were exhibited in the center of the arena ringed by a wooden eighth-mile oval. Steam, electric and gasoline powered contrivances with model designations such as Brougham, Surrey, Victoria, Phaeton, Cabriolet, Trap, Brake and Spider competed for attention. Demonstrations were the highlight of the show and more than one driver knocked over a straw-filled pedestrian as he, or she, attempted to negotiate a course riddled with bar-

rels. A two-hundred foot ramp was erected that shot upwards toward the roof and the Mobil steam carriage thrilled onlookers several times per day as it made its way up the incline.[22] Carl borrowed the promotional idea later on when he built a similar ramp to the top of his dealership from the street and Jane Fisher recalls he drove a vehicle skyward regularly to attract buyers.[23]

"I want you to build me a ramp all the way from the

top of the building down to the street so I can drive a car up it."

"Why Carl, that'll be kind of dangerous."

"I'm not going to drive off the damn thing. You should have seen everybody look at the car driving up the ramp at the New York Auto Show. If they can do it, so can I. And some of them will stop and buy a new car. Now let's get started."

The word automobile was not a part of the Ameri-

From left, brothers Earl, Rollo and Carl Fisher as young men.[2]

can vocabulary in 1900. The French derived it from the Greek autos meaning "self" and the Latin had moilis meaning "moving". The great promoter P.T. Barnum and his traveling circus took an automobile on tour in 1896 to display the oddity to the mostly agrarian population of the day. [24]

Volumes have been written reporting the condemnation of the newfangled vehicles by the general population, the clergy, lawmakers, economists who claimed increased use of leather and rubber would raise the price of boots and shoes and of course the farmer who could not sell it oats or hay. Initially the automobile could be afforded only by the upper class and that fact made it an unacceptable invention to most, especially the farmer who considered city slickers the enemy. Soon it would be lauded in song and on stage. Jane Fisher says the Gus Edwards and Vincent Bryan tune of, "In My Merry Oldsmobile" became their official courting song. The tune had been preceded by "Love In An Automobile," "Let's Have A Motor Car Marriage," "Our Little Love Mobile," "The Automobile Honeymoon," and "The Automobile Kiss," to name a few. [25]

Carl Fisher the salesman was set to look at a field of dreams when he went to the Madison Square Garden auto show. The thought of transporting yourself from here to there without a horse had to create an inner excitement in the year of 1900 such as we cannot imagine today. Just seeing one of the vehicles on the street was awe inspiring. Carl Fisher loved to make people say "Wow!"

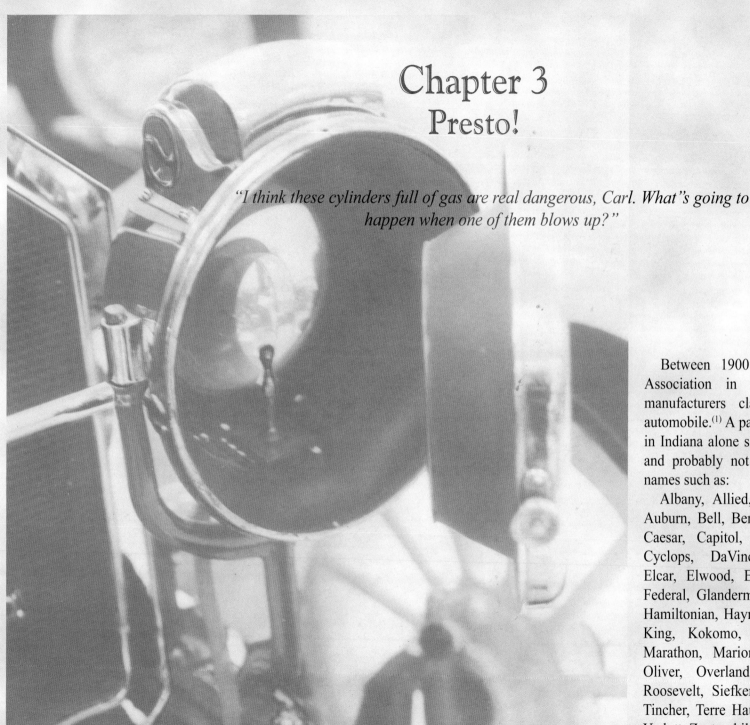

Chapter 3
Presto!

"I think these cylinders full of gas are real dangerous, Carl. What"s going to happen when one of them blows up?"

Between 1900 and 1908 the Motor Vehicle Association in the U.S. listed 502 various manufacturers claiming to have produced an automobile.[1] A partial list of automobiles produced in Indiana alone shows us 76 cities producing one, and probably not very many more, dreams with names such as:

Albany, Allied, American, Amplex, Anderson, Auburn, Bell, Bendix, Birch, Black Crow, Brazil, Caesar, Capitol, Champion, Columbia Electric, Cyclops, DaVinci, DeSoto, Dolly Madison, Elcar, Elwood, Excellent Six, Empire, Famous, Federal, Glandermobile, Garrett, Gillette, Goshen, Hamiltonian, Haynes-Apperson, Ideal, Imp, James, King, Kokomo, LaPorte, Lexington, Madison, Marathon, Marion, Muncie, National Octoauto, Oliver, Overland, Pan, Pilot, Real Cyclecar, Roosevelt, Siefker Steam, Senator, Stanley, Star, Tincher, Terre Haute, Union, Washington, Wizard, Yarlott, Zentmobile, Zimmerman [2]

Our photo of the first auto show at Madison Square Garden in 1900 does not do justice to the many multi-colored vehicles that were on display but at least gives us an idea of what Carl Fisher saw when he attended. [2]

The horseless carriages Carl saw at the 1900 New York Auto Show represented the best technology the world had to offer at the time. As noted previously, the internal combustion method of utilizing fuel would bark its way to being the preferred choice. The rumble and waca-waca of an exhaust note can be symphony to many appreciative ears. The silence of an electric or steam car never brought a "Boy, does that sound great," from an enthusiast who grins at the sound of an engine being revved up. The tone of an exhaust depicts the personality of its source. Fisher had heard the low drum and high scream of a gasoline engine and was drawn to its voice. The silent bicycle would play second fiddle to Carl's new seat in an automobile. He set about building Indianapolis' first automobile row after his visit to Madison Square Garden. You could race cars just like you did with bicycles, only better. His dealerships would provide an engine-firing symphony for eager ears.

"He sold so many makes of cars that his garage resembled a motor show. At it newspapermen interviewed tourists who dared cross the continent from New York." The *Indianapolis News* said[3]

Carl Fisher would promote the automobile as no other before or since. If you think you have ever seen a real car salesman on television, compare him to Carl. He would perpetuate his "Crazy Carl" image and make those who encountered his world smile, and spend. He may have been living on the second floor of his first dealership with his mom, but soon he would build one of the most coveted homes in the city.[4]

To promote the sale of his bicycles he basically said to his ballooning buddy Colonel George Bumbaugh, "OK, George. You stitch me up a thousand tiny balloons, put a tag with a number on one hundred of them, and drop 'em all over the place from your balloon. I'll buy ads that tell the finders of the tagged

Imagine being a resident of Indianapolis, Indiana and looking skyward to see the city's most famous car dealer commanding your attention in an effort to advertise his wares.[2]

balloons they can come to my shop and trade it for a brand new bicycle."

His most memorable promotion to sell cars was unique in the history of automobile promotion. He told Bumbaugh:

"George, we're going to tie a balloon to one of my cars, fly the goddam thing clear across town and out into the country. Then we'll untie the balloon and drive 'er back home."

Of course he and Bumbaugh 'flew' the car.

Carl Fisher's daily speech didn't appear to have contained curse words relating to sex, but was peppered with a continuing flow of goddams, jesus christs, christ on a bicycle, etc.[5]

Jane Fisher gushingly tells us the first time she ever saw Carl Fisher was on October 30, 1908," as he sat in the automobile attached to a balloon gliding over Indianapolis."[6]

Between the time Carl visited the first auto show in 1900 and the clear October day in 1908 when he and Bumbaugh sailed over Indianapolis in a new Stoddard-Dayton automobile, Carl had become well known and well-to-do. He had proven publicity worked for selling bicycles and applied all of his energy toward promoting the cars he would sell. The Stoddard-Dayton was one of his favorites.

John Stoddard of Dayton, Ohio could soon see photographs of the balloon with the name of his

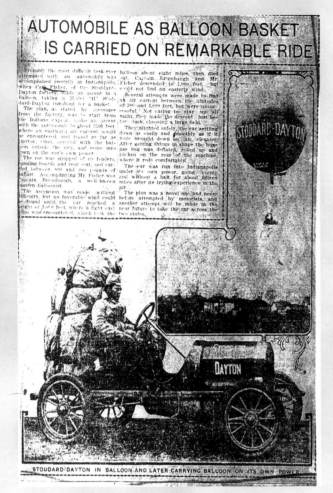

STODDARD-DAYTON IN BALLOON AND LATER CARRYING BALLOON ON ITS OWN POWER

The publicity value of Fisher's floating automobile stunt was immense as evidenced by the two unmarked newspaper articles. [2]

Stoddard-Dayton emblazoned across it in newspapers throughout the country. One of his cars was hanging from the balloon itself. Stoddard was the proprietor of one of the nation's top ten auto manufacturers in the country employing over 2,000 people. His firm would reach a peak production year selling duplicates of the car Fisher was flying as they sold 1,600 units in 1909. The company would survive another few years as John and brother Charles consolidated it into the United Motors combine formed by automotive pioneer Benjamin Briscoe who had gathered together the Maxwell, Columbia, Brush, Sampson, Courier and Crestmobile in an effort to make a glorious automotive corporation appealing to the masses. The idea of a huge automobile combine was finally brought to the public by Billy Durant who organized General Motors in 1908. Overall, there were about 4,000 Stoddard-Daytons manufactured of which approximately 34 survive.

Stoddard knew wealth early on as his own dad was a successful manufacturer of paint and varnish. John entered the manufacturing business with farm machinery such as discs, harrows, plows, cultivators and a side rake that acquired a worldwide reputation. He then became, what else, a bicycle then automobile manufacturer. His vehicles initially used engines supplied by a specialty manufacturer, but by 1907 was producing his own power- plant. The Stoddard-Dayton, says no less an authority than automotive expert John F. Katz, can probably be considered as America's first hemi.[7] It takes a gear-head to know what a hemi is, but in 2007, the Chrysler corporation still held so much esteem for the word they featured it in their ads with a cheeky, "Yeah, it's got a hemi" tagline. The hemi (short for hemispherical) cylinder head design is proven to be an efficient design. The Stoddard-Dayton engine was considered technically advanced for its day, and it is a brilliant work of engineering to look at with all its exposed mechanisms. It would have smiled at Carl Fisher and he couldn't have resisted its elegance.

Fisher didn't bother to tell John Stoddard he had removed this gleaming example of mechanical craftsmanship, along with its attendant transmission and anything else that looked heavy before the flight. He didn't notify the pubic either, and when he came roaring back into town, balloon stuffed into the backseat, it was in a duplicate vehicle that had chased the balloon. No reporters bothered to follow the crafty duo. Fisher, probably with Bumbaugh's urging, decided to lighten up the massive vehicle that had taken more than a little of its body design from the majestic Mercedes-Benz. The car they were flying couldn't drive its way out of the driveway.

He said of the promotion, "It was simple, yet no one seemed to figure it out."[8]

Fisher's floating car trick brought him coast-to-coast publicity and undoubtedly, customers to his showroom. Milking the stunt for all its worth, Carl announced he and Bumbaugh would make an Atlantic crossing for their next venture. *The Pittsburg Dispatch* reported in their Christmas day edition of 1908:

"The plan is to make the trip in a gigantic balloon attached to which will be 20 smaller supply balloons, the gas from which may be fed into the large balloon as the leakage makes necessary. Instead of a basket a specially built boat will be used."

The same basic story appeared in *The New York Evening Post* the day before. [9]

Carl's fertile imagination was on full tilt during the first decade of the new century, and his hormones were keeping pace. The comely 15 year-old Jane Watts snapped his senses so completely that he married the girl barely a year after his automobile flight. On October 23, 1909 a newspaper headline said *Carl Fisher Becomes A Benedict* [10] A benedict is a newly married man who has long been a bachelor.

Fisher had announced to the young lady, "I'm tired of traveling alone. If we marry now you can come on this trip with me. I've got to cut out this courting business and get back to work." Jane adds Carl telephoned and abruptly said, "If you want to get married, you'll have to get the preacher. I don't know any preachers."

Jane recalls she was awakened at six in the morning of her wedding day by the blaring of a German band who played relentlessly despite a downpour until they completed their final tune, "Ach, Du Lieber Augustine".

The day before, Carl's servant Galloway had visited Jane and informed her mom, "Mister Fisher ain't much for fuss and feathers, Maam," and the wedding was to be just a family affair on the quiet side.

Carl did keep the upcoming nuptials from a certain Gertrude Hassler, his former lover who was so rocked by the circumstance she made headlines, and money after the marriage by bringing a breach-of-promise suit against the fertile Mr. Fisher. The October 6,

The BEST PLACE to STOP

WHEN IN

INDIANAPOLIS

Never Closed

Fisher's Garage

330 NORTH ILLINOIS STREET

Three Squares North of Claypool Hotel

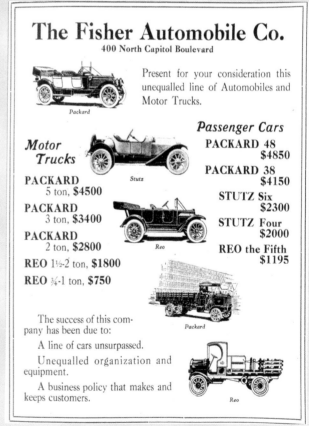

Carl not only put together a proper automobile dealership but had to be one of the first to offer 24 hour service. [2]

Look closely and you can see eight men working on a variety of brass era vehicles in the Fisher shop. [2]

The girl who finally stole Mr. Fisher's heart, Jane Watts poses with her man. [2]

1909 Indianapolis Star headlined "Singer Asks Half-Million: Gertrude W. Hassler, concert singer, charges capitalist with breach of promise."

Carl was hassled properly by Ms. Hassler who in court documents said Fisher had brought prospective customers to her home where she sang to them; how he promised her a winter home in the South and a summer home in the North; "then we will build us a castle up in the mountains, and we will have our ponies, our saddle horses, our automobiles, our boats, our dogs and guns, a grand piano and you can sing and I will lie before the fireplace and listen… and thus we will go down into old age happy, joyful, loving each other until the grave." [11]

The lady won her suit and was awarded $55,000 but eventually settled for $25,000. Fisher is also reported to have attempted to deduct the expense as a legitimate expenditure to the Bureau of Internal Revenue (forerunner of the IRS which was named in 1913) but the deduction was not allowed. Fisher was a very wealthy man by the time Gertrude Hassler sued him.

During the first decade of the new century Carl was literally flying as high as his balloon ascensions. His Fisher Automobile Company at 330 North Illinois had to be one of the city's first 24 hour per day operations. He advertised "Never Closed". He reported in his advertising, "The success of this company has been due to: A line of cars unsurpassed; Unequaled organization and equipment; A business policy that makes and keeps customers." No doubt his early yearning for folks to buy bicycles taught him the ways of the business world and he was eager to deliver. Evidently, the promises he made to his customers varied from those spoken to Ms. Hassler.

The impressionable Jane took the settlement in stride and seemed to be comforted when Fisher told her, "Why you little wench, I love you. I wouldn't trade you for two skunks."[12] Carl's attitude toward women was summed up by a pillow in his apartment embroidered with the slogan, "A woman is just a woman, but a cigar is a smoke."

Jane received an immediate indoctrination of Carl's attitude toward women hours after their marriage when she claimed he cut the gold braid off her wedding dress and said, " That's the way I like my women, little wench, unadorned, the way God made her." Jane says she was quick to forgive the act because Fisher charmed her once again with his deep, dimpled grin that never failed to turn her heart. He promptly left her alone with a copy of the Ladies

The new Mrs. Carl Fisher looking serene and properly outfitted. [2]

Home Journal while he went to discuss the building of a new boat with one Clement C. Avery who had boarded the couple's honeymoon train for the express purpose of dealing with Carl about the new vessel.

By the time Fisher married he had success in not only the bicycle business but his automotive exploits reached beyond the showroom floor.

As expected, he became an automobile racer and was a proficient one. Fisher purchased a vehicle to barnstorm from a young man who had a very similar background to his own, Alexander Winton. Winton had started a bicycle repair business in the late 1880's. He was a Scotsman whose significant accomplishments in the automobile industry are detailed in a labor of love book titled, *Famous But Forgotten* by Tom Saal and Bernard Golias, required reading for any serious automotive historian. Winton became a master machinist and, you guessed it, a bicycle manufacturer before turning to automobiles. Winton was another who was enamored with the internal combustion engine. He drove one of his creations from Cleveland to the 1900 Madison Square Garden show in New York in just over 38 hours.[13] Fisher was undoubtedly impressed with the machine. Winton had previously gone mostly unpublicized for his distance journeys. In 1897 he had driven from Cleveland to New York in 79 hours. [14]

Fisher could see Winton had a remarkable vehicle and rightly believed he could astonish and entertain Midwestern county fair attendees with exhibitions. Fisher is said to have banked $20,000 during the summer season racing his motorized steed against the four legged creatures the spectators had utilized for power to attend the events. The horse would grab the lead at the beginning of each contest only to be overtaken by Fisher's Winton. Rides to the bib-overall set were offered at a nominal figure as well.[15] Alexander Winton's creative genius resulted in the manufacturing of one of America's finest motorcars that saw its production end in 1924. His work on the diesel engine was recognized by General Motors as being superb and the automotive giant merged Winton's products into their firm.

Flushed with the success of his initial outing into the world of motorcar racing, Carl teamed with champion bicycle racers Barney Oldfield, Louis Chevrolet and drivers Tom Cooper, Walter Winchester and Earl Kiser in 1902 to stage exhibition races throughout the Midwest. Although Carl proved proficient enough at his new craft to be called a "driver of national reputation" by *The Columbian Magazine* [16] he couldn't equal the national fame garnered by the

An eight- cylinder engine, a pair of skinny frame rails, and a slim Carl Fisher became record setters at the Harlem Speedway in Chicago in 1904 when he covered two miles in just over two minutes. [17]

cigar chomping Barney Oldfield. In 1903 Oldfield astounded the industry by setting a one-mile record at the Indiana State Fair Grounds with a speed of 60.4 miles per hour becoming the most recognized auto racer in the country.[17] Carl's 2:02 time for covering two miles in 1904 at Chicago's Harlem track was considered a world record and gave him enough credibility to be named as a back-up driver for the American team which would compete in France's James Gordon Bennett Cup races that same year. [18]

Carl's European trip wasn't one he cherished. He preferred steak and potatoes as a daily diet and didn't harmonize with either the food or the language barrier. He had been promised he would be given a chance to drive one of the Pope-Toledo entries if a relief driver was necessary. His old friend Colonel Pope would, as we expect, become a force in the automobile business.

Barney Oldfield became one of the most publicized racers of early day competition. This is a photo of the self-promoting driver later in his career. [4]

After driving about the 85 mile Circuit De l'Auvergne, Fisher wrote later, "The possibility of an American victory was so remote that I lost interest completely because I valued my life far more than the little prestige and honor I might have gained by finishing behind the leaders.

"The course was the most hazardous ever selected for any race. It twisted its way through the most mountainous part of France. In many places the roadway was so narrow it was impossible for one car to pass another. Several of the turns were protected only by low stonewalls, on the other side of which were chasms many hundred feet deep.

"Only the French and Italian drivers, who had covered the course two or three times a day for at least four months prior to the arrival of the American team were sufficiently familiar with the dangerous route to travel it at maximum speed. Certain death awaited the inexperienced driver who failed to gauge his speed exactly right or who made even the slightest error on one of the sharp turns cut into the side of a mountain wall."

Carl was duly impressed by the advanced technology of the European vehicles as the French and Italian entries swept the first four places. He railed to American manufacturers,

"You are being outdistanced so rapidly by your rivals across the ocean, that they can take over the entire American market any time they decide to export cars in sufficient quantity to meet the demand. If you don't start building cars the public can buy with confidence, you won't even be able to give 'em away. The only way to gain the public's confidence quickly is to prove the dependability of your products on the racetrack. You'll learn ten times as much racing against each other, as you will from listening to the complaints of your customers.

"Road racing is doomed. The farmers will fight

you every inch of the way if you try to test your cars on the open highway. What this country needs is a big new racetrack designed for automobiles instead of horses. Until somebody builds such a track, the only thing to do is use the dirt tracks which are available. We can't continue to sit on our rumps and do nothing."[19]

Thus began Carl's campaign in earnest to establish a proper automobile racing facility in the United States. Carl's voice was heard, and printed as we have seen previously, but his stature could not come close to matching one of America's richest men, Willie K. Vanderbilt, Jr. who was echoing Carl Fisher's words.

Willie K. was the grandson of a man who had once taken a job as a ferryman on New York Bay, the collective term for the area surrounding the entrance to the Hudson River and the Atlantic Ocean. He saw steam was overtaking the sail and invested in one small steam-powered vessel that would ultimately multiply into dozens and made the first family fortune in shipping. He ventured into the railroad business and developed what would become the New York Central, an American colossus. He was known throughout the land as Commodore Vanderbilt who left his own son a fortune of some one hundred million dollars in 1877. His son William K. left a two hundred million dollar estate in 1885, of which Willie K. inherited something between seventy and a hundred million for himself.

Willie K. had no interest in running the family enterprises. His brother Harold would shoulder that responsibility. Nor was he interested in politics. Motorcars became his passion and he displayed enough inherent bravado to become an accomplished driver. Willie too had ventured into the European racing scene and upon return announced establishment of a prestigious event called the

Vanderbilt Cup Race. The cup itself was to be designed by Tiffany's which in itself represented a commitment to quality for the event. Willie noted,

"I felt the United States was far behind other nations in the automotive industry, and I wanted the country to catch up. I wanted to bring foreign drivers and their cars over here in the hope that Americans would wake up."

His first event in 1904 was held on Long Island, home to America's society leaders and while the event was won by a French Panhard its driver was American George Heath.

Fisher had already commissioned the building of at least three race cars we know of: the Premier he set a record with in Chicago and a pair of machines named Mohawks for he and his brother.

It was in one of the Mohawk machines at Zanesville, Ohio that Fisher gained a report in the September 10, 1903 edition of *The Zanesville Signal* which haunted him for years thereafter. The paper says Earl Kiser was "steering" but refers to a riding mechanic.

"The large 3,000 pound machine driven by C.D. (sic) Fisher of Indianapolis with Earl Kiser of Dayton steering, became unmanageable, owing to a defective tire, and dashed through the fence and into the crowd, hurling human beings right and left. From its path while scores of other people frantically rushed over each other in the efforts to get away from the monster.

"The car was moving at a rate of about 40 miles per hour when the tire exploded, but the driver succeeded in reducing the speed to about one half before the machine became entirely unmanageable.

"Both Messrs. Fisher and Kiser were more or less injured.....

"C.D. (sic) Fisher the driver of the auto, had his ankle severely sprained while his companion, Kiser

He ordered a monstrosity of a vehicle from the Premier Company especially for the Vanderbilt race. The car exceeded the 2,204 lb weight limit and still couldn't qualify after Fisher ordered the frame to be swiss-cheesed full of lightening holes. Carl did not compete in the event that drew some 50,000 to watch 18 entrants compete in the 30-mile road race.

Fisher and Vanderbilt were correct in their assumption Americans were enamored with automobile racing, as the 1905 race brought out over 100,000 spectators and the following year a quarter of a million were on hand. The events were, as predicted, dominated by the Europeans. By the time the Americans caught up in 1909-1910, Willie's interest had waned, but not before 300,000 had witnessed the last race in 1910. [20] Willie K. and Carl would remain life-long friends.

The Vanderbilt road race-course did not come close to fulfilling the idea Carl Fisher had of holding an event. He had been a circle track bicycle and car racer and wanted a permanent oval facility that would capture both fans and competitors alike. After a series of successful races at the Indiana Fairgrounds in October of 1905, (where Fisher's obese Premier was again denied entry and allowed only a match race) he penned the letter to Motor Age magazine we printed in Chapter 2 calling for the construction of a three or five mile race track.

He was Indianapolis' leading auto merchant by 1903 and it wasn't beyond conception he could wheel and deal his way into building a race track. An event held in the spring of 1904 brought the fountain of hope, which gave him the means to make the dirt fly.

The story goes, and he seems to have told it himself more than once, that he was late for lunch one day at his usual haunt of Pop Haynes' restaurant.

"If I don't get there in time there isn't anything

Sprint car racers sometimes say, "I stood up and drove 'er like a milk truck." Carl Fisher's Mohawk racer surely evokes the same kind of description. It was in this car, or a duplicate that he and Earl Kiser were involved in an accident that caused death at Zanesville, Ohio in 1903. [1]

had his leg badly wrenched. Kiser's shoe was caught in the sprocket chain and had his shoe not been torn from his foot he would have been thrown out and under the car.

"John Goodwin, known all over the city, who was acting as special policeman at the fair, was directly in front of the machine and was struck fairly by it, and was thrown under it.

"Hamilton Shutts of Roseville, an old soldier, aged about 61 years was severely crushed by being caught between the machine and the wire fence."

On the same day, September 10, 1903, the *Zanesville Times Recorder* also headlined: "At Detroit Tires Exploded on A Racing Auto Breaking Down The Fence And Bringing Death to Frank Shearer, a Spectator—Accident Similar to That on Our Own Fair Grounds."

Fisher pal Barney Oldfield had suffered a similar accident at the Grosse Point, Michigan track and mowed down a spectator to gain the front page headline.

Neither accident immediately stopped Carl's own

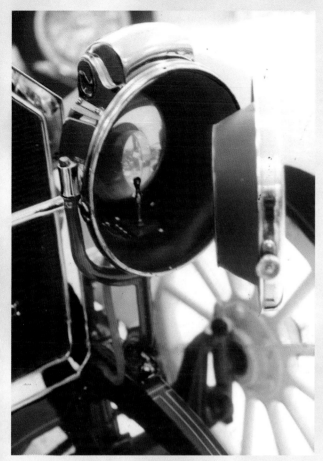

The motorist popped open his headlight door and lit the small gas jet we see standing vertical. The light's reflector can be seen behind the jet. [13]

flame somewhere inside the Fisher garage without explaining the device's purpose to Fisher personally.

Avery finally explained the cylinder contained compressed acetylene gas that when burned in front of a reflector provided light enough to drive an automobile at night. The idea was to mount the cylinder on the running board of a car, run small hoses to the headlamps which would contain on/off valves that could be lighted, thereby providing superior lighting.

Fisher was impressed, as he should have been. The standard lighting of the day for an automobile consisted of either kerosene lamps, or carbide pellet generators that produced acetylene. The kerosene lamps contained wicks that provided poor lighting and the carbide generators were finicky in their operation. The carbide generator worked on the same principle as the miner's lamp whereby carbide pellets were inserted into a running-board canister that contained a water drip supply. The dripping water mixed with the carbide produced an illuminating gas that was piped to the headlamps The carbide generator looked for all the world like a one-gallon paint can with another quart can on top of it. They were however, handsome as most were made of polished brass. Neither the kerosene nor the carbide generators were user-friendly.

Research has not turned up any significant details of Fred Avery who obtained the rights for a French patent to compress acetylene gas into a cylinder. The basic process seems to have been invented by a man whose spirit Carl Fisher could have easily loved. The Frenchman Louis Bleriot "made a fortune making acetylene headlamps for automobiles". Acetylene gas was discovered in 1836 by one Edmund Davey and rediscovered by another Frenchman named Marcel in 1860. Bleriot is credited with perfecting and patenting a process to compress the highly

The key to the Fisher-Allison fortune was this Prest-O-Lite cylinder that ultimately gave motorists excellent headlight illumination. [13]

volatile substance into a cylinder. Avery evidently obtained US rights to the patent and attempted to sell the idea to various manufacturers when he approached Fisher.

Bleriot gained worldwide recognition and awakened the isolated English when on July 25, 1909 the Frenchman piloted his low wing monoplane from the shores of Calais to a field just south of Dover Castle, thereby making him the first man to fly across the English Channel. He covered the 22 miles in 37 minutes and said afterward of a portion of his flight:

left for me to eat," he said and related if he had not been tardy in his schedule he would have missed the man who was loading a short cylindrical tank into his vehicle.

"I've left this tank burning in your shop for weeks and you haven't even taken the trouble to look at it," said one Fred Avery.

"Why, the boys were afraid to touch it, they said they were afraid it would blow up. What's it for?" [21]

Evidently, Avery had stationed the tank along with its attendant tube protruding from it that held a burning

Frenchman Louis Bleriot was the first to fly across the English Channel. He is also the man who perfected the method of filling a cylinder with acetylene thereby making the Fisher-Allison Prest-O-Lite company possible. [1]

Although not highly publicized, Fisher friend and eventual Indy 500 winner Ray Harroun was also an aviation enthusiast and successfully flew his own plane a few years after Bleriot's channel crossing. [1]

"I am alone. I can see nothing for ten minutes. I am lost."

Bleriot, who had to hobble to his plane on crutches due to a prior accident, claimed the thousand pound prize offered by the prestigious *London Daily Mail* for the accomplishment and went on to gain recognition as an aircraft manufacturer. He literally astounded the English government who had previously believed their isolated island was impervious to attack and was given a hero's welcome in London. [22] His flight stunned the conservative British who had for centuries built the world's strongest naval defenses never considering anyone would ever fly into their island.

Carl would have undoubtedly known of Bleriot's achievement through the attendant publicity it received. Fisher himself was the subject of an unsigned newspaper ad (relating to flight) located in the Florida Fisher files dated October 31, 1909 with a headline of:

"Fly Fly Fly
Buy An Aeroplane
An Aeroplane Properly Constructed Is Safer Than An Automobile
We have just placed our order with the Fisher Aeroplane Co. for a demonstrator to be delivered early in the spring. These planes are designed by Mr. Carl Fisher who owns the big balloon "Indiana" and who has just completed the second largest dirigible in the world."

A photograph of the bi-wing aircraft along with a drawing of Fisher himself was included in the ad purchased by the McDuffee Motor Co. located at 1626 Broadway in Denver, Colorado. We did not locate any other documentation relating to Carl Fisher the airplane manufacturer in his files so we can offer no speculation as to why this individual ad appeared. [23]

Jane mentions in her biography that while Carl loved aircraft, he himself did not harbor any

How and why this ad for a Fisher aeroplane came about remains a mystery as no data has been located to infer Fisher ever contemplated manufacturing aircraft. [2]

Look closely at the running board on this brass era car and you will see a carbide generator used to provide illumination for early day headlights. The devices worked but were no match for the easy to maintain Prest-O-Lite cylinders. [2]

aspirations of becoming a pilot especially after his initial flight with pioneer aviator Walter Brookings. She gives us the impression he was fairly shaken by the experience in the spindly machine. As we have seen, Carl was comfortable in a gas filled balloon, but the aircraft of the day must not have appealed to him personally.

While Louis Bleriot was enjoying the fruits of his aeronautical exploits (he did not invent the monoplane wing design, but is credited with its initial perfection), he is also responsible for making Carl

Fisher and his pal Jim Allison exceedingly wealthy men through the compressed acetylene venture.

Fisher and Allison gathered enough cash to entice Fred Avery to part with the secrets necessary to manufacture the product. Almost. Although papers of incorporation were filed on September 6, 1904, "for the purpose of manufacturing, assembling, handling and selling lamps, reflectors, receptacles and gas for automobiles, carriages, mines, buoys, and all other machines and things in which artificial gas is necessary or required to be used," [23] the precise method-

ology wasn't perfected.

The conversation of just how the new company was titled is lost to another day, but it is conceivable one partner said to another, "Well, presto, we have lights." Consequently, the new firm of Prest-O-Lite was formed and it would ultimately lead the way to death, destruction, construction and illumination

The story goes Fisher had immediate interest in Avery's gas holding cylinder and naturally showed it to one of his best friends, Jim Allison. Allison was another bicycle fanatic who hailed from the other side

The Prest-O-Lite system worked so well the company was able to run un-retouched photos of the actual illumination headlamps would provide as shown in our night-time ad. Dependability was a natural selling point as well. [2]

Jim Allison was also involved in the Allison Perfection Pen Company. We know by his later involvement with Allison Engineering Allison was a man who appreciated precision machine work and the manufacture of fountain pens required precise component control.

His friendship with Fisher steered his life and fortunes away from coupons and into the world of wheels. Given Carl Fisher's prior performance record in the bicycle and automobile sales business he himself must have been at least adequate at handling the mundane day-to-day paperwork of running his operations, but Jim Allison proved to be the anchor for taking care of the oncoming paper load they would encounter while building the Prest-O-Lite concern.

Legend has it Jim Allison was afraid the two-foot long cylinder would blow up on the running board of a car so he tested the device by chucking it off a bridge over Indianapolis' White River. Little did he know once the cylinder was successfully filled with the volatile gas there was not much chance of it destructing itself even if abused.

"Listen Jim," Carl probably said to Allison, "every damn car out there can use better headlights. These cylinders aren't going to blow up. We can sell so many of these things it'll make your head spin. We can sell them in every town in the whole country."

While Mr. Avery may very well have had legal title to the production of the gas cylinders, it was soon proven there would be many a slip between the cup and the lip and manufacturing the product was a very dangerous proposition. If acetylene is pumped into a hollow cylinder in what is known as a free state, and the pressure reaches just over 29 lbs. per square inch, the cylinder will explode. The cylinder has to have a core of fiber material combined with asbestos, Portland cement, emulsified earth and acetone to maintain stability. Combining the proper chemical

of the tracks. Of Scottish descent, his father had risen from a salesman for the National Surgical Institute to forming his own knitting and hosiery firm Allison and Nixon. He conceived the American Creditors Association, to aid businessmen in collecting bad debts, as credit had become an American way of doing business. He went on to become a publisher with a successful journal titled *Indiana Trade Review*.

He invented a system whereby workers could purchase an Allison book containing coupons, which would be traded for goods, such as groceries. Workers found the system desirable as a self-induced way of

not squandering all their ready cash and merchants gladly supplied the books, at a small discount and redeemed the coupons for merchandise. Thus the merchants received cash in advance, and the work force took to the system en masse. James became a vice-president of the firm while his two brothers became directors. The plan became so successful workers on the Panama Canal between 1904 and 1914 were paid in part with Allison coupons. The coupon books were also incorporated into Army use and by the early 1920's the new General Motors Acceptance Corporation utilized the method. [24]

MONDAY EVENING, JUNE 8, 1908.   SIXTEEN PAGES

A PLAIN CASE

TWENTY-FIVE PERSONS KILLED; FIFTY INJURED

PREST-O-LITE PEOPLE IN MORE HUMBLE MOOD

This June 8, 1908 Indianapolis News page one story depicted the volatility of the Prest-O-Lite process and public sentiment toward it. [2]

balance between all these ingredients turned out to be a challenge that resulted in many explosions for the new firm.

That the end product was desirable was never in question. Light shone brightly from the tiny gas jets that were installed in automobile headlamps. The motorist had only to flip his headlight's door open, turn on the gas valve, light the flame and drive carefree into the darkness. Later advertising featured un-retouched photos showing the bright path provided in a pitch-black situation. Unless the reader has actually witnessed the brightness generated by the Prest-O-Lite product you will find it hard to believe the photo shown in this book is un-retouched. Overall illumination was fabulous as long as a perfect reflector was used. Fisher and Allison

"could sell a million" of them if they could deliver.

Jane Fisher tells us a youngster by the name of Jack Noble made-up the production team at first, getting himself a good case of tennis elbow by filling the cylinders with a hand operated pump. Jane also tells us that one of the early explosions blasted apart a nearby sauerkraut factory that was located next to a hospital that soon found itself and its patients covered with wet kraut. [25]

Jane had her stories slightly mingled. There had been a couple of explosions, the second one killing a worker named Elmer Jessup, but the one she refers to happened on June 6, 1908 and later was the cause of a finger-pointing page one *Indianapolis News* story headlining: 'Prest-O-Lite People In More Humble Mood". It seems Fisher and Allison (Avery had left the company in 1906) had churlishly challenged city officials when it was suggested they move their

operations outside city limits. After the blast the News reported:

"The force of the blast shattered windows in buildings half a mile distant. Pieces of iron weighing several hundred pounds were hurled into the air and landed hundreds of feet from the plant. Incredibly nobody was killed, even though the explosion occurred during working hours when about thirty employees were in the building. One workman suffered a broken leg when he jumped from a second-story window. Several others were burned, although papers reported that none of the injuries were serious. Most of the damage occurred outside of the Prest-O-Lite plant. St. James Infirmary, located nearby, was badly damaged, and numerous patients were in shock. " [26]

City council hearings were held and it was discovered one local resident of German descent did

The huge Prest-O-Lite factory located just across the street from the main gates to the Indianapolis Motor Speedway. [1]

in fact have the lids blown off three of his barrels of sauerkraut. It is said Fisher grinned at the circumstance and paid the man two dollars for the inconvenience. An ordinance was passed prohibiting the firm from performing certain operations within city limits. They would ultimately construct a massive plant about five miles west of the town center.

In addition, they added branches in at least, Atlanta, Baltimore, Boston, Buffalo, Chicago, Cincinnati, Cleveland, Dallas, Denver, Detroit, Jacksonville, Kansas City, Los Angeles, Milwaukee, Minneapolis, New York, Omaha, Philadelphia, Pittsburg, Providence, St. Louis, St. Paul, San Francisco, Seattle and constructed charging plants in fourteen cities. Their foreign agencies could be found in Honolulu, Manila, San Juan, Toronto, Vancouver, Mexico City, London, Berlin and Australia. Their advertising was able to state "Exchange Agencies Everywhere" [27]

We estimate a full tank of the Prest-O-Lite product would last the average motorist at least a month or better as it had to contain many hours worth of fuel necessary to power a couple of headlights. Thus the invention was a most worthwhile one until the automobile manufacturers began producing generator-equipped cars that would power self-contained light bulbs. Jim Allison explained the efficiency of their recharging process when he said:

"In the evening at eleven-thirty we would go to the post office and pick up the orders that were mailed to us as late as four o'clock in the afternoon from such cities as St. Louis, Terre Haute, Cincinnati, Dayton and other places within two hundred miles, and fill orders that night. For some time the customers couldn't understand when they mailed an order in the late afternoon how their goods could be on their steps the next morning." [28]

When one considers the towns Allison spoke of are within a four hour train ride from Indianapolis it is easy to see they could pick up cylinders, refill them and have them back on a train dock within a few hours.

In 1910, the renamed Prest-O-Lite Storage Battery Company was worth six million dollars. Three years later in 1913 the Union Carbide Company bestowed the duo with a nine million dollar cash and stock buyout of the firm recommended by poor old Mr. Avery. [29] He had provided the bicycle buddies with a virtual monopoly on the acetylene headlight business that although lasted only a brief time, was extremely lucrative. Daredevil pilot Louis Bleriot would have been proud we're sure. The U.S. Department of Commerce statistics show us a gallon of gasoline cost seven cents in 1910 while a loaf of bread or quart of milk was three cents. The average college graduate could expect to earn about $750 per year, or $14.42 per week. The 1910 dollar is worth $23.10 in 2013 dollars. Consequently the Prest-0-Lite buyout was worth over 207 million dollars in 2013 money.

When the Indianapolis Motor Speedway official walked up to Carl Fisher in 1909 and told him, "They're dead, Carl" in 1909, our bicycle salesman was already a rich man from his annual Prest-O-Lite and auto dealership earnings. He had not cashed out of Presto-O-Lite at this time, but he had to have been pulling down an annual income that put him far above the average. An official was basically telling this upper income individual his new race track wasn't worth a damn and something had to be done about it.

Both the motorcycle and car racers had previously said the same thing. He and his partners knew it would have to be resurfaced; they had to decide how much money they wanted to pour into this patch of Indiana farmland. Race car drivers were going to kill themselves through regular competition with one another. They had enough to worry about and didn't need to endanger themselves on an unacceptable surface. Fisher and friends did not need any more convincing.

It was ultimately decided names the race fans and drivers would never see such as W.C. Culver, Poston, Knobstone Block, Wabash, Marion Paver, Veedersburg Paver, Dunn Patent, Brazil, Terre Haute Block would provide 3.2 million paving bricks to cover the two and a half mile track. Beginning right after Labor Day in 1909 and continuing for sixty-three consecutive days, the bricks were placed on their sides, not flat as one might expect to give the facility the now time honored title of The Brickyard. [30] The decision to line the track with bricks was made after a test was done. A strip of bricks were laid and driver Johnny Aitken spun his wheels over the surface. He accomplished the feat by having his National racer held stationary by ropes fore and aft anchored to concrete supported posts. At full throttle he burned rubber on the bricks in an attempt to break them loose, or actually destroy their baked surface. It had been estimated the track could be covered with concrete at a cost of $110,000 and to do the job with bricks would require twice the amount of money. The backers wanted proof their investment would literally hold up. [31]

The ceremonial last brick, that a publicist may have called gold, and more than likely made partially from melted down from Wheeler-Schebler carburetors [32] was placed on December 17, 1909 a date previously made famous by the Wright Brothers first flight in 1903. The date also marks the beginning of the festival of Saturn in ancient Roman history known as saturnalia, an unrestrained often licentious celebration associated with orgies, excess and extravagance. Anyone who witnessed the "Snake-Pit" activities by the crowd in the infield at the Indianapolis Motor

The Indianapolis Motor Speedway track with its new brick covering. (3)

Speedway throughout the 1970's would agree with the Festival of Saturn descriptions,

Carl convinced Indiana Governor Thomas R. Marshall and his private secretary Mark Thistlethwaite to become masons for a minute or two as they placed the last brick in position.

The first vehicle to make an official lap around the rectangle was an Empire automobile. Partners Fisher, Allison, Art Newby and a fine engineer named Robert Hassler (no relation to Carl's girlfriend Gertrude) had a significant interest in the production of the vehicle and had formed a company to manufacture it. Art Newby knew the car (and bicycle) business well. His National Motor Car Company was a mainstay in the industry. There were high expectations for the Empire but the vehicle didn't succeed. It was cute enough and had a catchy name of "The Little Aristocrat" but in reality it was just a 20 horsepower motorcar that couldn't compete with those producing more muscle. Its performance at the Speedway was disappointing during the December 1909 events although for its size it was at least an acceptable vehicle that did offer some technological twists ('the power plant is not dependent on the frame for alignment,' said *Cycle and Automobile Trade Journal*). Engineer Hassler's talents were considerable, but he couldn't have been expected to promote the car. (33)

Lack of an intense interest by the founders probably caused the demise of the vehicle, as all were probably just too busy with other projects to devote the time it would take to see it through to success. By 1912 there was a re-organization of the firm, production was moved to Greenville, Pennsylvania and the originators moved away from the day- to- day operation. The brand held on for a few more years under new ownership and passed from the American scene by 1918.

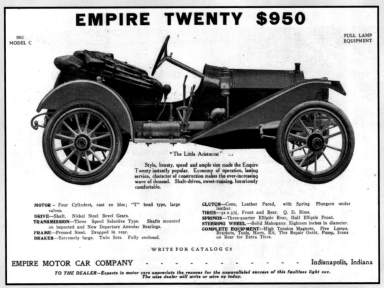

EMPIRE TWENTY $950

1911
MODEL C

FULL LAMP
EQUIPMENT

"The Little Aristocrat"

Style, beauty, speed and ample size made the Empire
Twenty instantly popular. Economy of operation, lasting
service, character of construction makes the ever-increasing
wave of demand. Shaft-driven, sweet-running, luxuriously
comfortable.

MOTOR—Four Cylinders, cast en bloc; "T" head type, large valves.
DRIVE—Shaft. Nickel Steel Bevel Gears.
TRANSMISSION—Three Speed Selective Type. Shafts mounted on imported and New Departure Annular Bearings.
FRAME—Pressed Steel. Dropped in rear.
BRAKES—Extremely large. Twin Sets. Fully enclosed.

CLUTCH—Cone, Leather Faced, with Spring Plungers under leather.
TIRES—32 x 3½, Front and Rear. Q. D. Rims.
SPRINGS—Three-quarter Elliptic Rear, Half Elliptic Front.
STEERING WHEEL—Solid Mahogany. Eighteen inches in diameter.
COMPLETE EQUIPMENT—High Tension Magneto, Five Lamps, Brackets, Tools, Horn, Kit, Tire Repair Outfit, Pump, Irons on Rear for Extra Tires.

WRITE FOR CATALOG C5

EMPIRE MOTOR CAR COMPANY   Indianapolis, Indiana

TO THE DEALER—Experts in motor cars appreciate the reasons for the unparalleled success of this faultless light car.
The wise dealer will write or wire us today.

Left and above:"The Little Aristocrat" manufactured by the Fisher group's Empire Motor Car Company was jaunty enough looking, but did not enjoy commercial success. [2]

The founders of the Indianapolis Motor Speedway naturally had to be more interested now in their race track than ever before as they saw the bricks appear. The organizers boldly proved their faith in the future of airplanes, gas balloons and dirigibles as they erected the world's largest aerodrome after grading a landing strip 105 feet wide and half a mile in length in the infield. The building to house the aircraft soared to 100 feet tall, 60 feet wide and was 300 feet long with sliding entry.

Although the re-christening of the track took place in that cold December of 1909, a series of speed trials were held that displayed the viability of the new surface and all awaited the 1910 season.

1910 was the first year the track could be called The Brickyard and featured auto races in May, July, August and September with an aviation week set for June and another balloon meet in August.

During the first meet there were 24 races and Fisher

pal Barney Oldfield set a pair of new records for the one kilometer and one mile distances. Johnny Aitken started in six consecutive events and the racing world gave the facility the unofficial title of being the best in the world.

The aviation meet began just two weeks after the opening races and while there was ongoing litigation brought by the Wright brothers over the licensing of aircraft regarding a patent the Wright's had obtained, Fisher was able to convince the brothers to permit rivals to compete. Eleven entries were received, six of which complied with the Wright's demand. All except Lincoln Beachy piloted the bi-wing models. Beachy flew a monoplane, said to be his own creation. Exhibitions, pursuit races and attempts to establish altitude records were featured, and the early events were attended by only a smattering of spectators. Attendance climbed as records were broken and by mid-week 19,000 were on hand to watch the

pioneers. Walter Brookins had soared to 2,093 feet to set a world's record and Orville Wright closed out the successful event with a ten minute display that was considered the most memorable of the event. [34] While Orville is not reported to have performed any acrobatics, the mere fact he and his machine stayed aloft for such an extended period of time was momentous to most in attendance.

Seating capacity was expanded for the next series of auto races from 35,000 to 50,000 and once again the audience came away satisfied. The next event was scheduled to be a 24-hour grind but the organizers decided to cancel it, possibly due to a lack of entrants. The track claimed another life as Tom Kincaid was fatally injured while testing a couple of days after the July races. Controversy and disqualification of the Marquette-Buick team gained publicity throughout the automotive world and may have angered the entrants, but did demonstrate the Speedway and the sanctioning AAA were upholding rigid standards.[35]

The Fisher group had lived up to their promise of providing an excellent surface for their races, and for the most part staged a successful season ending with the balloon championships in September. Thus far the track had claimed a total of six lives. The 1910 season ended much better than the previous year when the powerful *Detroit News* had penned an editorial calling for the elimination of auto racing across the board. They ended their diatribe with the sentence, "The blood of the Indianapolis Motor Speedway has probably run the death knell on track racing in the United States." [36]

We have previously seen Fisher was taken with the idea of holding a long race, preferably a 24-hour marathon. At the end of the 1910 season the founding quartet set precedent for the auto-racing world by announcing there would be a 500 mile race at the Speedway. They were granted two race dates for the year but as events transpired only the 500 Mile International Sweepstakes would be staged on Decoration Day for what was then a phenomenal purse of $25,000. Remembering our 1910 monetary conversion, $25,000 would be five million in 2013 dollars.

The 24 hour automotive enduro had gained significant popularity in the U.S. Initially, the Packard company announced it would attempt to cover 1,000 miles in a 24 hour period and attempted the feat on the Grosse Point, Michigan track. The car's headlamps failed one after the other and driver John Boyd wound up amidst the pine fencing encircling the facility. The company tried again and managed to average 33.5 mph for 29 hours, 53 minutes and 37 seconds to achieve the 1,000 mile goal.[37] Then the Peerless company, Packard's rival, went to Brighton Beach in New York and lowered the record to 25 hours, 40 minutes. Finally, a French Deauville piloted by Guy Vaughn covered the 1,000 mile distance in 26 minutes and 40 seconds less than 24 hours to claim bragging rights. [38]

The natural progression of things brought about the first 24-hour race and it was held in Columbus, Ohio in 1905 before 12,000 spectators. Basically stock automobiles with everything but the essentials removed competed and a Pope-Toledo claimed victory. Colonel Pope had seen his firm switch from the high-wheelers to the safety bicycles that made his Columbia brand become a household name. He also produced the Pope motorcycle. Once again, we could not locate any direct quotes from Colonel Pope relating to his dealings with Carl Fisher but we have no doubt the pair shared respectability for one another.

The era of 24 hour races would last for five years. Their stage was nation's dusty one-mile horse tracks. Tent cities served as garages located in front of the grandstands and provided the numerous spectators a front row seat for watching the mechanical prowess of these automotive pioneers. The attendant publicity gained from success in these grueling events sold automobiles as reliability was not claimed, but proven. The term wasn't utilized then, but spectators were watching stock cars.

The Indianapolis Motor Speedway promoters had appropriately decided a 500 mile race, one that could actually be watched from start to finish was the way to go. The timing was perfect for a 500 mile event and the announcement of the race "broke the record for sustained newspaper space" across the country.[39]

We see eight vehicles here and get a glimpse of the smoke generated just by the front-runners.[4]

Carl Fisher in one of his signature floppy hats surveys the activity during the 1912 Indianapolis 500. [2]

As you can see by some of our early photographs, the early day internal combustion engines visually let the spectators, and drivers know beyond a doubt that gas was being burned under the hoods by watching the belching storm clouds of white smoke. It had been decided 40 cars would start the 1911 race and an impenetrable smoke screen would have been created if they had been made to begin from a standing start. It is claimed Fisher himself came up with the idea of a rolling start and he would pace the group in his trusty Stoddard-Dayton. Since it would take just under two minutes to encircle the two and a half-mile oval the scoring, the organizers believed, could be handled efficiently. Russ Catlin, one of this reporter's professors of auto racing knowledge in my youth tells us:

"One hundred men would operate four Burroughs adding machines, two Columbia Dictaphones, a Warner Harograph (whatever that was), and four complete scoreboards, one in front of each stand. All of this was tied into a Telautograph, a machine that would duplicate handwriting from the scoring stands to twelve places on the grounds. Just like building the Titanic, nothing was left to chance." [40]

We learn the start of the first 500 was, "electric and beautiful" and at 25 miles into the fray S.P. Dickinson, riding mechanic with Arthur Greiner in a Simplex crashed fatally as a result of both rear tires blowing out.. Then near the halfway point, at 240 miles Joe Jagersberger's Case racer broke a steering part and careened into the pits, scattering mechanics and officials. It was a horrendous pile up that left at least one car upside down and took out three others. Although C.L. Anderson was thrown to the track, surprisingly there were no serious injuries. Later events would prove scoring records may have been the subject of the most damage.

In a well-researched article titled, *"Who Really*

Old time photography resulted in giving Indy winner Ray Harroun's Marmon Wasp speedy looking eliptical wheels in this 1911 photo. Ray's innovative rear view mirror can clearly be seen. He had the only car in the race without a riding mechanic. [4]

Ray Harroun, innovative engineer, is credited with winning the first Indianapolis 500.[1]

Won The First Indy 500" Catlin outlines the scoring problems that plagued the birth of this famous event and finally quotes the chairman of the sanctioning organization, Sam Butler of the AAA as writing: "Mechanical devices for scoring should be avoided at major contests. They can break down and at best are only as good as the operator."[41] In 1969 Catlin found the man who many claim actually won the first "500", Ralph Mulford, who related: "Mr. Harroun (Ray Harroun, winner of the first "500") was a fine gentleman, a champion driver and a very great development engineer, and I wouldn't want him to suffer any embarrassment, " and adds,

"nor the Indianapolis Motor Speedway. They have publicly credited me with leading the race and each year send me something to let me know I have not been forgotten." [42]

Ralph Mulford began his career with the Lozier company in 1901 when it was a boat building concern and found himself named competition driver as the firm entered the automobile industry. Its product was one of the most esteemed in automotive circles and competed with the Mercedes, Locomobile and Pierce-Arrow. Mulford became one of the most proficient racers of the day, especially in those 24-hour events mentioned. He did have some solace in 1911 as he gained enough points to be named AAA National Champion and went on to lead a successful life. He stated as an 85 year old: " Believe me, we didn't make many mistakes (in the Initial 500) I guess it's sufficient to say I still think there was a default (sic) in the scoring and that we-Billy Chandler was riding with me-won the race, instead of getting second as the record books say." [43]

Scoring problems aside, the reported 80,000 spectators who attended the first Indianapolis 500 proved the format was desirable enough that one day the race would earn the title of The World's Largest Single Day Sporting Event. Carl Fisher's footprint in the sands of automobile racing time would be permanent.

Such prestige was given to the event one manufacturer, talented Harry Stutz was able to call his creation "The Car That Made Good In A Day" after it finished eleventh. The vehicle became the basis for his next model, the desirable Stutz Bearcat that would define a generation of auto enthusiasts as being dashing young masters of the road. Stutz's non top-ten finish generated more publicity than Ralph Mulford's second place while winner Harroun announced his retirement from driving.

Mulford was right about Ray Harroun. He was

Harroun was also heralded for his drawing board accomplishments in the field of engine design. Indianapolis based Nordyke & Marmon were able to advertise Harroun drove one of their vehicles 500 miles at an average of 74.61 MPH. [1,2]

a great development engineer. As early as 1905 he had constructed his own racer and two years later introduced what is probably the lightest land speed record vehicles ever made when he debuted his eight cylinder, air-cooled, bicycle tired, 468 pound racer for a record attempt at Ormond Beach, Florida. The versatile Harroun originally built the unique V-8 engine for an airship and said: "In experimenting with my kite I fastened the air machine to my motor car and pulled it through the air. Several times I rode high in the air on this kite and stayed up ten or fifteen minutes." [44]

Harroun had been a mechanic on the Buick factory team in 1906 and went on to become chief engineer at Marmon where he designed the Marmon Wasp that would carry him to the first Indianapolis 500 victory. It was a unique vehicle in itself as it was the only single seat machine in the field. He overcame protests from fellow competitors who whined he would not be able to tell who was behind him by installing what is commonly referred to as the first rear view mirror. He further proved his technical prowess by designing, and later opening his own carburetor company in 1913-14. He worked for Maxwell Auto Company in 1914 to design their 1915 race engines and when the firm left racing, soon to be WWI ace Eddie Rickenbacker recognized just how good the cars were and persuaded Fisher and Allison to provide the money to buy them from Maxwell and use Prest-O-Lite as the sponsor. Rickenbacker had become a top flight race car driver who would have future dealings with Fisher and Allison.

Harroun created a masterful piece of engineering in 1915. He incorporated a two-piece crankshaft assembly that utilized its own counterbalances in place of a flywheel. His dual overhead camshaft arrangement featured a unique valve treatment that aided the vehicles to become among America's fastest track racers of the era.[45] His name had not only become known as the "500" winner, but his engineering achievements were recognized throughout the automotive press and when he decided to design an entire automobile carrying his name, the Harroun Motor Corporation was capitalized at ten million dollars.

A plant was erected at Wayne, Michigan and the first vehicle appeared in 1917, just prior to the start of WWI. The plant received a large contract for government munitions and spent the war years fulfilling it. Problems collecting on the government contract plagued the firm and it was doomed because of the post war recession. The Harroun car "gave every indication of being a sterling success", but unfortunately total production was approximately 1,105 from 1917-1922 and Harroun Motors passed into history.[46] A versatile man, Ray Harroun would cross tracks with Carl Fisher when he was middle-aged to help construct yet another Fisher dream, a beautiful board speedway called Fulford By The Sea we will detail in a later chapter.

While Ray Harroun's name would forever be remembered as the winner of the first Indianapolis 500 and Eddie Rickenbacker would become known to the USA population as an extraordinary flying ace, Carl Fisher could see that his newly crowned Brickyard was about as complete as it was going to be. "The Greatest Race Course In The World" was standing on its own and did not require any more creativity from its builders.

"They sure as hell can't complain about the track surface now," Fisher said. From now on, racers from around the world knew that The Brickyard was not a place where masons went to ply their trade.

Carl's attention would now turn toward a road not designed for race cars and bricks would not be used for its construction.

Program covers from the early Speedway events are sought after by collectors. This one is from the Labor Day events in 1910. [11]

Chapter 4
The Coast to Coast Highway

"It doesn't make any sense to buy a car capable of going from here to California if there aren't any roads good enough to take you there. Let's build a highway that goes from New York to California."

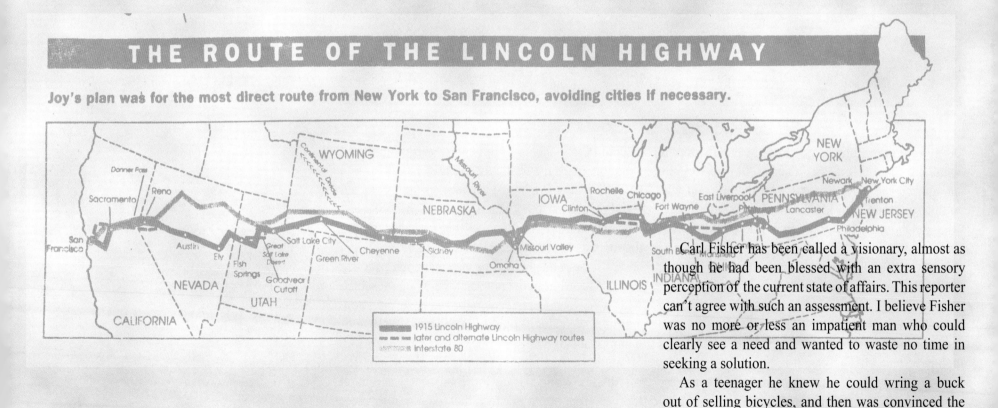

THE ROUTE OF THE LINCOLN HIGHWAY

Joy's plan was for the most direct route from New York to San Francisco, avoiding cities if necessary.

▬▬▬	1915 Lincoln Highway
▬ ▬ ▬	later and alternate Lincoln Highway routes
▬▬▬	Interstate 80

Carl Fisher has been called a visionary, almost as though he had been blessed with an extra sensory perception of the current state of affairs. This reporter can't agree with such an assessment. I believe Fisher was no more or less an impatient man who could clearly see a need and wanted to waste no time in seeking a solution.

As a teenager he knew he could wring a buck out of selling bicycles, and then was convinced the public was going to purchase automobiles, so they needed a dealership in his town. It did not take divine intervention to know the automobile manufacturers needed a place to test and race their products so he

Model T in the mud: Man with a pole works to free the car which has sunk into the "road".

tracks that led mostly from farm to market. Only the railroad barons understood the need to move product and people from one point to another. Our horse-drawn vehicles were reduced to nearly a crawl when going from town to town. Today's bumper sticker that banners "If You Got It A Truck Brought It" could have been used at the turn of the century by inserting the word Wagon.

Although we Americans hailed the Romans for their engineering exploits we didn't copy all their examples. Our city buildings displayed Romanesque craftsmanship, concentrated design and state of the art construction techniques but the long-forgotten chariots of the ancients had better roadways than what we had in our grand new world in the United States of America. The Romans built thousands of miles of adequate roads, many of whose remnants exist today.

built the Indianapolis Motor Speedway. His investment in Prest-O-Lite is also proof positive he recognized the need for better headlamps and was willing to gamble on his intuition. It is unfortunate we could not locate additional information about the man who sold Fisher the Prest-O-Lite concept, Fred Avery, for we know he approached one or more automobile manufacturers with the idea before Fisher took the bait and it would have been interesting to see who turned him down. Later in life Carl said the Prest-O-Lite idea had been shopped around for years before he and Allison bought it.

As a bicycle rider he would have been very familiar with the condition of the roads bordering Indianapolis and it was easy to assume that if the automobile was going to prosper, its occupants would require a system of adequate byways. Because his automobile dealership was the finest in the city, he had

to continually encounter travelers who commented about the roads they had recently traversed.

Thus it didn't take a visionary to yell from the rooftops, "What this country needs is a good road from one coast to the other." Fisher's strong suit was that he was no Armchair Archie. He didn't look at a circumstance and provide the instantaneous criticism so often heard from the rank and file when presented with a new concept. Fisher looked at a situation, surmised the natural conclusion and said, "Well god-damnit, let's fix it."

While our nation had progressed along with the rest of the world during the Industrial Revolution to turn iron ore into steel that would ultimately change the face of the earth and the daily lives of its inhabitants, we did not do much to move people from one city to the next. Our system of roads at the dawn of 1900 was abominable. We had a collection of mud

Graphic proof of why Henry Ford's Model "T" gained favor with the populace before the U.S. invested in reasonable roads. [9]

Another example of America's rural roads that were a challenge to man and machine. [1]

The mood that seemed to run throughout the country during the first decade of the 1900's was the horseless carriage which was a rich man's toy, naturally piloted by city slickers who had never loaded a bale of hay or plowed a furrow in their lives. Consequently, local governments were loath to invest in smooth thoroughfares to accommodate these noisy, nose-in-the-air interlopers who wanted to wave at the field hands as they sailed by. Nevertheless, the self-powered carriages grew in numbers and had to evoke envy by those still looking at the south end of a horse on their way to town.

Carl Fisher contained the enviable trait of passion for a project. Of course it was in his interest to see improved roads especially in his hometown, but once

again he believed the natural conclusion of good roads was to have one, just-as-soon-as-we-can-build-it, that crossed the entire nation. Initially, he became so focused on road improvement he ran for and was elected to the post of Marion County Commissioner on the Progressive Party ticket in 1912.

In a story titled "Fisher's Salary To Go To Roads" [1] Carl promised he would not only donate his $2,500 stipend to the cause of better roads, but would match the sum from his own pocket.

Jane tells us Carl continued his use of the publicized word when he wrote to famed author of the day Elbert Hubbard in 1912 and said:

"As you know, Mr. Hubbard, the highways of America are built chiefly of American agriculture

and politics, whereas the proper material is crushed rock or concrete. We believe one magnificent highway of this kind, in actual existence, will stimulate as nothing else could the building of enduring highways everywhere that will not only be a credit to the American people but that will also mean much to American commerce. Will you pitch in and help?" [2]

Hubbard did in fact come to the Fisher home, (named Blossom Heath) and discussed Carl's plan to build this new coast-to-coast highway and gave his full support to the project.

Fisher's plan was to enlist the automobile manufacturers in an industry wide campaign to raise the funds for construction of the road. Carl had estimated it would take ten million dollars to build the highway and in a long, mellifluous letter to the most famed man in the automobile industry, Henry Ford, he outlined his proposal.

To paraphrase, Carl asked for 1/3 of 1% of each (of their gross profits) for three years or 1/5 of 1% for five years. Carl proposed cooperation of all automobile owners by offering two classes of memberships at $5.00 and $10.00. He wanted to steer clear of politics in the endeavor when he said:

"I am of the opinion that the automobile people can build and present to the automobile users of the United States this road without any outside assistance, and can be handled by the large automobile men in the same way they handle their business affairs, and the road will be finished and pushed thru without delay and deliver on time; where if we attempt to mix up with government appropriations or if politics is allowed in any way to creep into the proposition, there will be numerous delays and wrangles and possibly graft." [3]

Carl provided Ford with a detailed accounting of material pricing and covered every imaginable objection in his solicitation.

A decade before Carl Fisher solicited Henry Ford for funds to build the Lincoln Highway, the budding auto manufacturer had been introduced to Fisher's old pal, Berna Eli (Barney) Oldfield who poses with Ford prior to their victory over Alexander Winton in 1902 at Grosse Point, Michigan.[1]

Canvas rooftops may have offered the participants of Fisher's "Hoosier Tour" some protection from the sun but the road they were following insured all other elements would be experienced.[1]

Henry Ford's company by 1912 had become the premier automobile-producing firm in the world. He had been through three incarnations of trying to manufacture an automobile since he made his first spindly vehicle in 1896. In 1899 he attracted investors to form the Detroit Automobile Company which lasted all of nine months. It was followed by The Henry Ford Company in 1901 but Henry resigned in little over a year. The Ford Motor Company made its debut in 1903 with the Model A Ford. For the next five years subsequent models were produced until finally the Model T Ford became its mainstay. The vehicle would stay in production through 1927 until it was replaced by the new Model A Ford that would be produced from 1928-1931. The world would see some 15 million Model "T"'s produced to make Henry Ford the world's richest man. In 1912, he was already enjoying phenomenal success.[4]

Less than a week after Carl wrote to Henry Ford, he and Jim Allison were to stage a dinner at the Indianapolis Deutches Haus (German House) on September 10, 1912. He would solicit members of the fledgling automobile industry to back his plan for what was termed the "Coast-To-Coast Rock Highway".[5]

Undoubtedly attendees for the dinner witnessed a transformation of transportation as they stepped off a water driven train and were taken to their Michigan Avenue destination via horse drawn carriage, electric or gasoline-powered vehicle. The streets had to be adventuresome as the spector of a bolting horse couldn't have been out of the ordinary. There were more carriages than cars. To be sure, the nation was on its way to being motorized, but now in the fall of 1912, a man was about to feed them, cajole them and ask the assemblage for ten million dollars to build a trans-continental highway when more than the vestiges of the horse-drawn vehicle were clip-clopping their way down Michigan Avenue outside the building where they were enjoying their dinner.

Our dinner attendees would not take a second look at a man standing in front of his Model "T" Ford, bending over and reaching for the crank on the front that required a healthy tug in order to start the vehicle. These men, Fisher believed, would have vision enough to realize the automobile would soon be crossing the entire continent, if they had a road to do it on.

He was right. More than $3,000,000 was pledged at the dinner and Carl's publicity machine was set in motion. Publicity of the day had to be obtained mostly through the nation's newspapers and magazines. Communication from just one part of town to another was a challenge as telephones had not been universally installed when Fisher was promoting his plan for a cross-continent highway. Consequently, spreading the word and gaining publicity nation-wide was a monumental task.

Samuel Morse had obtained a patent on a device in 1837 to transmit electrical currents in long and short intervals, thereby inventing the Morse code telegraph system making telegrams possible. Then Italian Gugliemo Marconi studied Nikola Tesla's inventions and transmitted a wireless signal in 1895 when he was but 21 years old to set the stage for the invention of radio.[6] But in 1912 the radio had not come into wide usage and the printed word was the only real means of obtaining publicity.

The first public radio broadcast in the US was heard in 1910 in a demonstration by inventor Lee DeForest. Previously two men named Dunwoody and Pickard had perfected their experiments with lead crystals that ultimately led to the production of radios by countless amateurs. DeForest's work resulted in high quality radio broadcasts.[7] Fisher's world was nearly as primitive in terms of communication in

1912 as it was three quarters of a century earlier but radio broadcasts would soon filter into every home equipped with electricity.

In 1912 the 38 year-old Fisher had gained so much respectability he could solicit, and expect not only replies, but cooperation from some of the most famed names in the country. His solicitation of Henry Ford brought a response from Ford's trusted secretary/treasurer James Couzens that said in part:

"Pending our having a Director's meeting at which time we will be very glad to take up the matter of the contents of your letter.

"Frankly however, the writer is not very favorably disposed to the plan, because as long as private interests are willing to build good roads for the general public, the general pubic will not be very interesting in building good roads for itself. I believe in spending money to educate the public to the necessity of building good roads, and let everybody contribute their share in proper taxes. Most people will not work if they can get a living without it, and I believe the same can be said in respect to most any public undertaking that is done by private interests.

"However I will put the matter up, as stated, to our Board of Directors as soon as we have had a meeting, which will possibly be some time next month, however we will let you know the attitude of the Directors."[8]

When we see cars of yesteryear restored and displayed in museums, we don't usually conjure up images of what their early life was like. This is a participant of Fisher's "Hoosier Tour".[1]

Carl takes a break for a cigar during his "Hoosier Tour". [1]

Historians have agreed Couzens had more influence over Ford's decisions than any other employee of the burgeoning firm. Ultimately, even though Fisher had managed to convince Vice President Charles Warren Fairbanks, Senator Albert J. Beveridge, Thomas A. Edison and others to write to Ford in support of the program, Ford ultimately turned down the proposal. [9]

Fisher's plan to involve Ford in his fund raising would undoubtedly have had a snowball effect on the rest of the industry. Even without Ford's support money came in from many others. The Hudson Motor Car Company promised $100,000 in early 1913. Automobile businessmen in Salt Lake said they would raise a million and a half dollars if Colorado would do the same and the move prompted the Colorado legislature to enact a bond issue for the cause. Seventy five miles from Carl's home, businessmen in Terre Haute, Indiana raised $5,750. [10] Driving across the nation was appealing to more every day.

Cross-country automobile trips had entertained American newspaper readership and brought the disdainful expected comments because the task seemed so foolhardy during the first decade of the new century.

Probably the most documented early excursion was enacted in 1903 by Horatio Nelson Jackson and Sewall K. Crocker a twenty-two year old (former bicycle racer of course) who had been working in a gasoline-engine factory in California. [11]

Previously the husband and wife team of John D. and Louise Davis attempted a continent crossing. Louise was a journalist who convinced two newspapers to sponsor their 1899 attempt that would begin in New York City and end in San Francisco. They were aboard a seven horsepower Duryea whose mission it was to prove American cars were at least equal to the English and French machines of the day. They made it as far as Chicago before giving up. [12]

Triumphant, flag waving drivers were often greeted at a particular terminus for having conquered Mother Earth. [1]

Mascot Bud the Bulldog was "the only member of our trio who used no prafanity on the entire trip." reported cross-country Winton driver Horatio Nelson. [10]

Then in 1901 Alexander Winton himself, the extremely talented engineer and designer we wrote of earlier attempted the crossing from San Francisco to New York.

"If success in this endeavor is possible," the Motor Vehicle Review noted, "Mr. Winton will surely achieve it."

Only 530 miles from his starting point Winton was forced to state, "This automobile has taken more abuse and hard service than any machine ever stood, but with all her power it is utterly impossible to drive through this sand. A Winton motor carriage cannot be expected to work a miracle." Winton and his publicity agent Charles B. Shanks went no further.[13]

The aforementioned Crocker convinced Horatio Nelson the only vehicle sturdy enough for the trip was in fact a Winton. Unable to find a new car, they found a used 1903 model with about a thousand miles on it and reportedly paid more than the new price for the unit.

Nelson was prompted to attempt the trip after making a fifty- dollar wager to a fellow upscale citizen over drinks at the University Club in San Francisco. His slightly used Winton was equipped with a twin cylinder 20 horsepower engine and by the time it was loaded with enough gear for a long safari it weighed a ton and a half.

Their trials and tribulations are carefully documented in a wonderfully illustrated book titled *Horatio's Drive: America's First Road Trip* by Dayton Duncan and film-maker Ken Burns. Burns made a documentary of the historic continent crossing as well. Horatio Jackson documented the journey with his trusty Kodak camera. Along the route they purchased a young, light-colored bulldog named Bud to serve as mascot. The pup held his position admirably, especially after being fitted with a pair of goggles to keep the dust from his eyes and was, as Jackson noted, "the one member of our trio who used no profanity on the entire trip."[14]

The Winton carried its passengers into New York City 63 days, 12 hours, and 30 minutes after leaving San Francisco, thereby winning Jackson fifty dollars for the wager he placed that was based on completing the trip in less than 90 days. Jackson estimated he had spent eight thousand dollars on the venture and later commented to his grand-daughters he never did collect on the bet.[15]

Fisher's plan of a coast-to-coast highway was probably looked upon as a nutso idea after city dwellers read of Nelson and Crocker's exploits through what they would have termed to be the wilderness.

By 1910 there were 180,000 motor vehicles registered in the United States but twenty states had no road department and federal funds had not become available.[16] Carl's plans were distributed through his Ocean-to-Ocean Highway Bulletin that first saw publication in 1912 and while the campaign was receiving considerable publicity through the nation's press, Henry Ford's reluctance would, as Fisher knew, hinder progress.

Fisher received a letter from another captain of the automobile industry although his name wasn't as

This Packard driver, believed to be Henry Joy is assured the road ahead to Laramie is passable. [1]

well known as Ford's. Henry B. Joy, the president of the Packard Motor Car Company, pledged to fund $150,000. Joy wrote:

"I think your Good Roads Committee, who is working up the ten million dollar fund, ought to get up a protest to Congress on the expenditure of $1,700,000 in a monument in Washington to Abraham Lincoln."

Joy wanted to see the money allocated for the Lincoln Memorial go to road building, "for the good of all the people in good roads. Let good roads be built in the name of Lincoln." Joy's father had been a

supporter of Lincoln's campaign and Joy, while only a year old when the famed President was elected, had great admiration for the fallen hero. [17]

Henry B. Joy became the recipient, through his own vision it should be added, of the pioneering efforts of the Packard family of Warren, Ohio in the nascent automobile industry. The Packard clan had been successful merchants in a diversity of products ranging from hardware and all manner of building materials to "high-grade incandescent lamps". James Ward Packard became fascinated by the horseless carriage in the 1890's. He, like Fisher obtained a DeDion gas-powered tricycle and soon had an employee working on a design to further its development. [18]

In August of 1898 Packard took delivery of a new Winton automobile that would ultimately lead him to manufacture a vehicle under his own name. [19]. Packard historians love to recite the statement reportedly made by Winton to Packard after the latter repeatedly complained about the negative aspects of the machine. One Hugh Dolnar, who is considered the pre-eminent automotive journalist of the pre WWI era reported in the Dec. 28, 1901 edition of *The Autocar*:

"Mr. Winton, who is English born, replied with all the suave consideration of a true British manufacturer to the effect that the Winton waggon (sic) as it stood was the ripened and perfected product of many years of lofty thought, aided by mechanical skill of the highest grade, and could not be improved in any detail, and that if Mr. Packard wanted any of his own cats and dogs worked into a waggon, he had better build it himself, as he, Winton, would not stultify himself by any departure whatever from his own contestably superior productions." [20]

The manufacturing oriented James Ward Packard had obviously contemplated such a venture

Henry Joy, President of the Packard Motor Car Company.

previously and sallied forth to create what was to become one of the world's most prestigious automobiles. By November of 1900 a full page ad could be seen in *The Horseless Age* bantering the new vehicle with impressive statistics that told of driving from Cleveland to Buffalo, a 225 mile trek in 13 ½ hours and "Our Special has been driven 95 miles on average country roads in four hours." At least two generations of automobile buyers would become familiar with the company's slogan that first appeared in the October 3, 1901 edition of *Motor Age* that said, "Ask The Man Who Owns One". [21]

As is so often the case with product names that

Henry Joy was extremely proud of the work he and his associates accomplished building the Lincoln Highway. Joy was a hearty soul who made several cross-country trips. [1]

have become commonplace, the creators of the Packard motor car would only remain in control of their own destiny for a couple of years. Even though the Packard family had long ago proven their business acumen, their fate and that of Carl Fisher's highway would ultimately be led by Henry B. Joy.

By the turn of the century Joy was in his own right a wealthy man. His father James had made a fortune with the Michigan Central and Chicago, Burlington and Quincy railroads. Never having hawked a newspaper or magazine to the line's customers, James' son Henry was accorded an education at Phillips Academy in Andover, Massachusetts and the

Sheffield Scientific Institute at Yale University. He rose to become President of the Fort Street Union Depot in 1900 and had interests in Utah mining and was an official of the Peninslar Sugar Refining Company of Caro, Michigan. He became a Packard car owner in 1900 and soon owned 100 shares of the firm that produced it. Another 150 shares were purchased soon thereafter to up his investment to $25,000. A reporter asked him to explain his enthusiasm for the firm and he was said to have replied that it "got so that if I were given my choice of losing either my legs or my Packard, I didn't know which I would rather have kept." [22]

Once again as we have seen throughout history, the tinkerer and promoter type of individual such as Fisher needed the highly accountable Joy for the highway project. James Allison provided the constant hand-on-the rudder in Fisher's Prest-O-Lite venture. Henry Joy was the perfect compliment for what became known as the Lincoln Highway. While Fisher was business-oriented enough to track activities of his own enterprises the board-meeting oriented Joy probably wasn't capable of "giving them a good cussing" as Fisher had been known to do when dealing with recalcitrant supporters.

Another road group had proposed a Lincoln

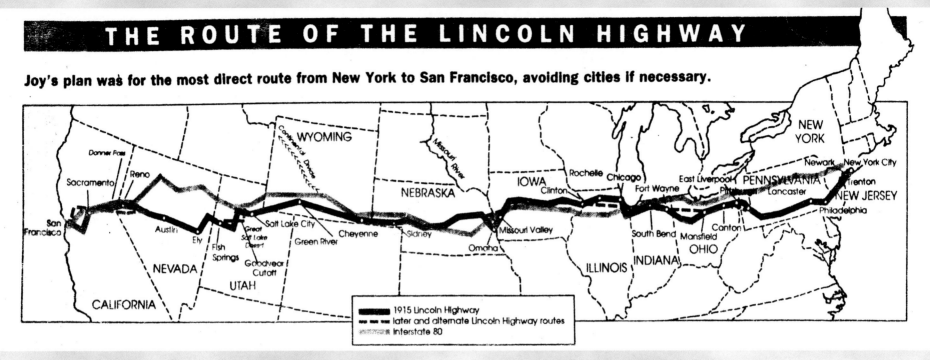

THE ROUTE OF THE LINCOLN HIGHWAY

Joy's plan was for the most direct route from New York to San Francisco, avoiding cities if necessary.

Legend:
- 1915 Lincoln Highway
- later and alternate Lincoln Highway routes
- Interstate 80

The original Lincoln Highway route parallels what is now Interstate 80.[2]

Memorial Highway to run from Gettysburg to Washington but the aforementioned Lincoln Memorial garnered the funds the group had hoped to tap and their plan failed. Later, they relinquished the name to the Fisher group.[23]

Fisher had not revealed a precise route for the highway in early 1913, but significant interest had been shown and many states were pledging money and full support. In July a meeting was held in Detroit and the Lincoln Highway Association was formed with Joy being named president and Fisher and Arthur Pardington as vice-presidents. Carl himself was not present for the meeting as the official announcement came of the group's purpose: "To procure the establishment of a continuous improved highway from the Atlantic to the Pacific, open to lawful traffic of all description without toll charges;

such highway to be known, in memory of Abraham Lincoln, as "The Lincoln Highway".[24]

True to form, Fisher did not attend the meeting and we can imagine him saying, "Ok, you fellows have the idea of what we want to do, work out the details, I have to get busy drumming up some more money."

Fisher was leaving Indianapolis at this time on what became known as the "Hoosier Tour". It was comprised of members of the Indiana Automobile Manufacturers, most of whom who would blaze a trail to San Francisco while some split off and went to Los Angeles.

The Lincoln Highway author Drake Hokanson tells us Joy and Fisher disagreed vehemently about the usage of the Lincoln name. We can well imagine the off-the-cuff Fisher would have inherent

differences with the by-the-book Joy. Fisher's methodology is revealed in his wife's biography when he is quoted as saying, "It is perfectly easy to get assistance for the Lincoln Highway Association, if your directors only go after it. I think you're too easy on them . You should first give them a good dinner, then a good cussing, whenever you want money." [25]

Carl received a letter from A.G. Batchelder, Chairman of the American Automobile Association Good Roads Committee telling him that some day a fine statue would be erected that honors him as the first man give American a transcontinental highway. Carl replied:

"I am not much on statuary—and right now I think it is a good time to pull out personally and take away from our possible subscribers the idea that this road plan is mine. If any particular noise is made for

any particular person or small clique of persons, this plan is going to suffer."[26]

Seventy odd Hoosiers set out with Fisher on the Hoosier Tour and Indianapolis 500 winner Ray Harroun was chosen as a driver of one of the vehicles. Carl's wife wasn't allowed to accompany her man as he claimed the journey would be too tough on her. She said the vehicles reminded her of those that would be leaving for an African Safari they were so loaded with supplies.

From the starting point in New York City the original Lincoln Highway went across Pennsylvania to upper Ohio and through the tip of Indiana and Illinois. It dropped down to cross central Iowa and Nebraska then touched the bottom of Wyoming and went back up to cross Utah and the lower part of Nevada before entering California.

The all important press coverage was assured when a member of the *Hearst Syndicate* joined as well as reps from *The Indianapolis Star, News* and an observer from the **Royal Automobile Club of England** signed on. W.S Gilbreath, secretry of the Hoosier Motor Club had also been retained to insure publicity along the route. *The Chicago Tribune* thought enough of the venture to send a reporter.[27]

While the group set a goal of 150 miles per day they were delayed by the endless greetings of those wishing to curry favor in hopes of being the towns included on the final route.

"Every night there was a banquet, a supper or some other celebration with more speech-making, and as the local newspaper reporters and the newsmen in the party vied in sending out stories about each meeting, the tour evoked tremendous publicity and interest," Fisher wrote.[28]

Overall the tour was a tremendous success. Governors and Mayors along the way promised everything from cooperation to cash for the project.

Ma and Pa settle in for dinner at a roadside camp. This is a 1923 photo, taken after the Lincoln Highway became a reality.[1]

A.Y. Gowan, president of the Lehigh Portland Cement Company, pledged a minimum of 1,500,000 barrels of cement to the project and said a committee had been formed to study and assist the plan.[29] Gowan would remain a close friend of Carl's for life.

While the publicity generated was satisfying, Carl's goal of ten million dollars proved to be unattainable within the foreseeable future. Henry Joy proposed that Illinois, Iowa, Nebraska, Wyoming, Utah and Nevada all invest in what he called "seedling miles." He wanted them to produce a mile of finished road so citizens could actually see what they were going to drive on. But concrete was not in wide usage and the public did not trust the new material.

One report noted:

"They knew it couldn't last. It didn't show signs of wear, but moisture and Michigan winters were sure to be its undoing. How could this stuff pour like liquid one day, then, a few days later be rock hard, impervious to pounding wheels, horses hooves, freezing and thawing? No doubt many pocket knives came out to scratch at the hard surface, as people shook their heads and looked closely for the first signs of failure." [30]

Fisher's idea was finally set in stone as depicted by this craftsman-like bridge along his beloved highway. [1]

"The seedling mile was a turning point in road travel," says Ruth Franz, national secretary and Illinois State Director for the Franklin Grove based Lincoln Highway Association. In her state a 10-foot wide strip of concrete, a mile long had been built in the town of Malta, about five miles west of DeKalb in 1914.

"Few people know about the seedling mile, but it was a very significant event in the history of transportation," notes Terry Martin a biology instructor who convinced Kishwaukee College's Phi Theta Kappa organization to research the test road in Malta.

"Malta became a primary place for the donation (2,000 barrels of cement) because it's very muddy," Malta historian Ivan Prall reports: "A couple of years ago I interviewed a lady who was 95 and recalled the early days of the test strip." She said, ' They would get up to 30 miles per hour and then reach the end and fall in the mud and the car would be buried up to the frame. They'd have to go get a team of horses to pull them out."[31]

The width of the seedling miles was later widened to 18 feet and the final route was presented in 1913.[32] In 1914 the production of motor vehicles exceeded that of wagons and carriages for the first time in the U.S.[33] The decision was made to educate the public, as Ford's Couzens had originally suggested. Consequently, the seedling miles themselves served as the best sales tool thus far conceived. By 1915 Carl Fisher's interests lay in Florida and he effectively

Frank Seiberling, founder of the Goodyear and Seiberling Tire Companies was an early supporter of the Lincoln Highway and later headed the effort.[1]

left the management and promotion of the Lincoln Highway to others.

Ultimately the federal government appropriated a 75 million dollar fund that would be distributed over a five-year period and required all states to establish highway departments. The Lincoln Highway Association wasn't pleased with the guidelines however, as the Fed had no set precise

priorities that would in fact aid the Fisher dream. Then in 1918 another bill was passed by Congress that did in fact have a direct effect on the Lincoln Highway. Frank Seiberling, the man who succeeded Henry Joy said, "Upon passage of such a bill, the Lincoln Highway Association could feel that its work was accomplished and that it had successfully achieved the ends for which the organization was incorporated." [34]

Seiberling as you will recall was the founder of what would become the world/s largest tire producer, Goodyear Tire & Rubber Co. He was heralded for his inventiveness in developing the straight-sided and corded tires along with the detachable rim. After Goodyear faltered in 1921 he stepped down from the presidency, but rebounded to start Seiberling Tire at age 61. Henry Joy's services had been transferred to the war efforts in 1917 and he later remarked in 1939," I consider the Lincoln Highway the greatest thing I ever did in my life." [35]

The money raised by the Lincoln Highway Association was spent mostly on educating the public and erecting road markers along the route that became friendly, familiar signposts to all who traveled the trail-blazing effort. Nevertheless, the name Lincoln Highway slowly disappeared and was replaced by a cacophony of numbers. The New York Times displayed their objections to the removal of the revered name when they stated:

"The traveler may shed tears as he drives the Lincoln Highway or dream dreams as he speeds over the Jefferson Highway, but how can he get a 'kick' out of 46 or 55 or 33 or 21? The roads of America would still be on paper if the pleas that were made ten years or more ago had been made on behalf of a numerical code." [36]

History would prove a numerical road could gain public sentiment as we recall the song "Get Your Kicks On Route 66" by the time the 1960's rolled in as the fabled westerly route made its own memories.

Records show Fisher himself had donated $25,000 (over half a million in 2010 dollars) in trust to the project that today is buried under wider, faster by-ways that traverse the land. It is estimated that about a dozen of the original 3,000 markers set by the Boy Scouts still exist. Carl Fisher, Henry Joy and Frank Seiberling are names that are familiar, gentle reader, to historians.

Drake Hokanson said it well when he commented:

"The United States would have eventually gotten paved highways even without the example set by the Lincoln Highway. The democratization of the road came with cheaper cars and the working person's desire to own one. The country simply could not go long with millions of cars and dirt roads: the change was inevitable. What the Lincoln Highway Association did was speed up the process: it made the public accept the idea of long roads built not for local convenience but for the benefit of everyone-roads for the nation, not just the county. This was the Fisher idea, a road for the whole nation as an example to all and a path for all-a democratic ideal that lived on in the words of songs, the names of little hotels and streets, a chain of concrete markers, and the restless psyche of America." [37]

For his next project, Fisher would have to create some of the land itself to build upon and once again they'd call him "Crazy Carl".

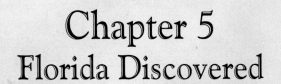

Chapter 5
Florida Discovered

"What is that guy doing, trying to clear all that jungle out of there?"
"He says he going to build one of the most beautiful cities you've ever seen."
"I think he's nuts. That place was meant to be a jungle and he ought to leave it alone."

Every salesman looks for a self seller. You show the item to the prospective buyer, and the product is so desirable it sells itself. Scotch tape is a perfect example. Carl would find that his next self-seller didn't have any recognizable attributes the first time he saw it. He would become a Florida land salesman. Selling Florida land became so important to him he would earn the title of Land Developer by creating land where it wasn't.

Soon after he married Jane Watts in 1909 the couple took a boat trip to Florida. Carl's natural bent to look at a situation and become bestowed with its positive possibilities would never leave him until his dying day and his achievements in Florida would affect generations for all time.

In 1821 Florida land was purchased from Spain by the United States and by the time Carl and Jane landed they were relegated to a place called Navy Cove after being forced ashore because of a hurricane. Navy Cove is in the Pensacola area near Gulf Breeze and known for its beautiful beaches. Jane reports she and her new husband left their ship, Eph, beached on the sand and lived like beachcombers for days, setting up housekeeping on a deserted quarantine station.[1]

After oyster fishermen helped them winch their craft back to navigation status, Carl made arrangements to ship it north on a flatcar, but was soon notified it was too large to pass under a bridge en route. Carl's new friend John Levi offered to sail the vessel around the Gulf of Mexico to Jacksonville. He later wired Carl:

"Arrived safely. Miami pretty little town. Why not meet me here instead of Jacksonville?"[2]

Jane recalls the area instantly smote her and her man and Carl made a deal to buy a couple of lots ostensibly to build a semi-retirement home. When apprised the seller was raising the agreed upon price, Jane tells us Fisher yelled out, "Tell her to go to hell!"

While back in Indianapolis Fisher received a postcard heralding the qualities of a lovely home owned by Alonzo Q. Bliss, a maker of herb medicines. Without consulting Jane, Fisher bought the property, which was promptly named The Shadows.[3]

The Miami Carl and Jane encountered was, by and large, the result of another dreamer's resourcefulness, Henry Flagler.

Henry Flagler rose from an itinerant preacher-farmer's son to garner massive wealth along with his more famed partner, John D. Rockefeller, motive force of the monolithic Standard Oil Company. Rockefeller continually credited Flagler as being the real brains behind their massive oil enterprise.

The Rockefeller-Flagler combination formed

Henry Flagler's investment in bringing rail service to South Florida was a major reason for the success of the area. [2]

the Standard Oil Company on January 11, 1870 with full paid in capital of $1,000,000.[4] By 1882 the Standard Oil Trust had capitol of $55,000,000 and properties valued at $75,000,000 making it the largest business concern in America. The partners in the organization were summoned to appear before a United States Senate Committee "Which was inquiring into certain business practices of the new business."[5] Public sentiment concerning the

organization reached such a fever pitch that one day in the future, the government would in fact break up the monopolistic firm, but that's another story for other books. Suffice to say Henry Flagler became wealthy beyond compare from his activities in Standard Oil. His biographer estimates his wealth at between ten and twenty millions by the time he was 53 years old.

He spent 2.5 million dollars in the city of St.

Augustine to build the luxurious Ponce de Leon Hotel, opened in 1888. Simultaneously he constructed a smaller hotel close by named the Alcazar and soon had a third property named the Cordova. He would build a residence in the city by 1893 and the town became a wintertime resort for other wealthy Easterners.[6] The Flaglers became the city's most prized residents. His fame and penchant for development in South Florida grew steadily. Flagler's efforts throughout his real estate developing career spared no expense and set astonishing examples.

Flagler continued his developments and pushed south as he bought up and built railroads and land. By 1894 he had opened one of the largest wooden structures in the world, The Royal Poinciana Hotel in West Palm Beach. It is said that through the efforts of one persistent female named Julia Tuttle, Henry Flagler decided to extend his railroad, and investments 70 miles south of Palm Beach toward a settlement known as Fort Dallas at the mouth of the Miami River.

Ms. Tuttle had decided to make the area her home and by 1891 she owned 640 acres of land. With an eye toward development, she tried to convince Flagler to extend his rail line through the wilderness to reach her tropical holdings and to invest in the area. Initially Flagler wasn't impressed but when Florida experienced her coldest winter in 1894-95, a pair of freezes in December and February ruined the citrus crop as far south as Palm Beach. A Flagler representative visited Tuttle's Biscayne Bay region and reported the freeze had not affected the area at all. Suitably impressed, Flagler took up Julia's offer of free land as enticement, and decided to extend his rail line. Ms. Tuttle had also extracted a promise from the oil baron to construct a Flagler quality

hotel. He did so and took up 15 acres to construct the beautiful Royal Palm.

With the attendant development the city of Miami began its transformation from wild to cosmopolitan. Miami was incorporated in 1896 with 502 voters.[7] Soon Flagler built an electric light plant and the expected other improvements followed suit.

Consequently when Carl and Jane visited the city in 1910 population had grown to 10,000. Jane loved the tropical climate and hoped her husband would

scale back on his frenetic activities, especially now that he had reported the sale of Prest-O-Lite had netted him the sum of $5. 6 million dollars mostly in Union Carbide stock.[8]

However, once Carl started poking around his new neighborhood he came across what was known as "Collins Folly". This object of derision was a half-finished wooden bridge in-between the waters of Miami and the peninsula that lay two and a half miles away. The peninsula contained a beautiful beach that extended for miles on the Atlantic and

Patriarch John Collins, center was a horticulturalist who had dreams of growing saleable produce on what was to become Miami Beach. His plan for a bridge to his property ultimately sparked Carl Fisher to invest in the barren land. [2]

The Collins bridge became the longest wooden span in the world and sparked the development of Miami Beach.[2]

Fisher, like everyone else, had to wonder just what it was Mr. John Collins had in mind with this bridge.

Collins had retained the same attorney Henry Flagler did, one Frank Shutts. Coincidentally, Shutts hailed from Indiana and had performed services for Carl. By being anointed by Flagler, Shutts' reputation in Miami couldn't have been better. Shutts told Carl:

"You know Carl, you've got plenty of money and you're too young to retire. Why don't you lend that old man some money and let him finish his bridge? It would give you something to do and give you an interest down here."[9]

John Collins had to be a man in tune with Carl Fisher's heartstrings. Fisher was a few weeks shy of his 39th birthday and by the standards of the day John Collins at 74 was living on borrowed time. Carl had to meet this old codger who must have had a hell of a dream. It was evident his half-built bridge had already devoured significant cash.

And thus Carl Fisher was introduced to an oceanfront like he'd never seen before shortly after taking a few steps from Collins Canal. I for one believe the tale that says Fisher looked left, right, straight ahead and literally proclaimed that there has to be a new city built right here, and right now. Old-timer, you are going to get your bridge done and we're going to do some business.

Fisher wound up with a lien on the bridge plus a couple of hundred acres of Collins' land. Soon, Carl was dealing with the successful Lummus brothers, John and James. John (J.N.) had been a dispatcher for the Atlantic Coast railroad line and James (J.E.) could tie his success back to Henry Flagler who had used him as a commissary contractor. By the time the brothers met Carl they were both bank presidents and had invested in Collins, and land for themselves. Carl loaned the duo $150,000 and garnered 210 more acres for himself plus mortgages on additional

property. The trio partnered to fill in land occupied by mangroves and jungle in order to create salable property.

The writer believes Fisher took one look at the phenomenal beachfront and literally made up his mind, on the spot, that he had stepped upon some of the most desirable land he had ever seen. It didn't matter the land behind the beachfront was about as inhospitable as can be imagined. It was marshy swamp, gnarly mangroves, tropical, which meant mosquitoes and all manner of bothersome insects called it home. Fisher could see the finished product straightaway. Any beach this great, he had to think, is a magnet for human beings. They would need everything you could imagine, from streets to houses to hotels and gardens. He probably asked himself why no one had begun to build a town here already. This place needed a town, a city.

Previously some investment in the peninsula had

Fisher was probably around forty years old when this photo was taken. [2]

been made as Richard M. Smith, who also began a ferry service from the mainland, built a bathhouse. Later another Smith, Avery and a partner named James C. Warr saw an "opportunity to establish a pleasure resort and transportation proposition" invested in a pair of 60 foot double decker boats to service their investment and named their dream "Fairy Land". [10]

A man named Henry B. Lum foresaw the land as being perfect for installing a coconut grove and went through all manner of machinations to bring his idea to fruition. He ultimately met a fellow man-of-the-land at a meeting where like-minded farmers shared growing information, John Collins the farmer bridge builder Fisher had helped. Lum convinced Collins to invest in the coconut grove. After three years and the planting of 334,000 plants the land won the battle as few coconuts were produced.

Collins never lost faith that he could ultimately make the land pay and continued his quest. He was a Quaker born in 1837 and had success in the north extracting edibles out of Mother Earth. He forged ahead and planted 2,945 avocado trees with some success. Eventually his sons and son-in-law joined the venture, to insure the old man didn't squander the family fortune. They had to agree, however, the produce that was finally raised on the land was first class, and yes, they all believed the land was ripe for real estate development, so they agreed to build the bridge. [11]

Collins discovered he had to utilize concrete to surround the wood pilings for his bridge because the marine borers found the virgin wood to be tasty. The entire operation proved too costly and was halted when the structure, the longest wooden bridge in the world at the time, was past half-completion. [12]

With Carl's infusion of money new interest was generated for the land. The bridge was opened on

Carl trails behind the team of driver Ralph DePalma and Rupert Jeffkins after the pair pushed their dominating Mercedes over the finish line at the 1912 Indianapolis 500. [4]

June 12, 1913. It had required 2,100 pilings to sustain its 18' usable roadbed. Fisher was somewhere in the hinterlands of the Midwest on his Lincoln Highway promoting his "Hoosier Tour" at the time the bridge opened to give you some idea of our subject's penchant for keeping as many balls in the air at once as he could.

Just prior to Carl and Jane's trip to Miami, Fisher and his associates were staging their second Indianapolis 500 in May of 1912. The AAA had not been amused with inaugural winner Ray Harroun's single passenger racer equipped with a rear view mirror. They mandated each car should carry a riding mechanic for the 1912 event. The sanctioning body also voted to limit the number of cars starting a race. The rule limited entries to one car for every 400' of track; 13 on a mile and multiples of that number for tracks of greater length. Thus the two and a half mile Indy oval was limited to 33 cars. [13]

As it turned out 24 cars started the second 500 due simply to a lack of entries. The handsome Ralph DePalma aboard his huge chain-driven Mercedes dominated the field. He had a two-lap lead at the halfway mark and was five laps ahead with 100 miles

Carl congratulates a surprised Joe Dawson who believed the best he could do was a second place finish before the DePalma entry gave out. (4)

to go. He and his riding mechanic Rupert Jeffkins completed 198 laps of the 200-lap grind and came to a stop in the Northwest turn, victims of a broken connecting rod.(14) A reinvigorated Joe Dawson who had earlier turned his mount over to relief driver Don Herr was plugging along in second place when his crew gave him the "GO" sign.

DePalma and Jeffkins had no choice but to walk back to the pit area, and decided to take their vehicle with them, pushing and pulling along the way. With Ralph alongside manning the steering wheel and a panting Jeffkins pushing from behind they became the darlings of the crowd. Carl trailed the duo by a

few yards as they inched their mount the last 600 yards toward the finish line. Dawson of course was lapping them all the while and was declared the winner. The largest ovation of the day went to the DePalma entry and he redeemed himself three years later by crossing the finish line first in the 1915 event. The pushing-the-car-scene became one of auto racing's most publicized photos and remained so for decades to come. Your reporter created a quarter scale bronze sculpture of the scene.

The second Indianapolis 500 was a tremendous success and the race was now cemented as being the premier long distance event in the world.

Once back in Florida Carl found the Lummus brothers to be enthusiastic partners. They had pre-dated Fisher in their investment of developing the beach and their Ocean Beach Realty Company had sold over $40,000 in lot sales during 1912.(15) Credibility for the development was received when the Miami Metropolis reported: "It took faith to undertake the job of making the waste of sand and the mangrove swamp into an attractive and habitable place, but faith marches at the head of progress, and there are now few doubters as to the ultimate outcome." (16)

Consequently the beach now had three developers in Collins, the Lummus brothers and Carl. J.N. Lummus' own words are our best source for the events that were taking place in what surely looked like a warm wilderness:

"Early in 1913 Carl G. Fisher came into my office and introduced himself…Fisher said to me, 'I see you are clearing a great deal of land on the peninsula. What are you going to do?' I told him we were going to build a city fronting on the ocean. He wanted to know the amount of land which we owned and I told him. 'Well,' Fisher said,' why don't you do it all at one time?' I told him we had a very good reason and that was the lack of funds. This conversation must have started something, for within six weeks after my brother and I met Fisher, we had arranged to borrow one hundred and fifty thousand dollars from him at eight percent interest. But we also gave him one hundred and five acres of land off the north end of our property as a bonus for the land. We had paid one hundred and fifty dollars per acre for the land we gave Fisher. This deal, and this deal alone, started the big development in Miami Beach. It could not have been done otherwise."(17)

Land was sold via public auctions for the incubating city, and while not generating prices the de-

Auctioneer Doc Dammers looks out over a sea of straw kadys and cloche hats as he describes the once-in-a-lifetime opportunities to buy Florida land. [2]

working only a couple of hours in the killing heat.

"The pigmy high palmetto had slender roots that reached out like tentacles from the thick tap root, and these deceitfully delicate-looking roots turned the steel blades of the machetes. The palmettos were almost impossible even for mules to uproot with chains and grappling hooks. I have seen Carl with his hands at a smaller palmetto trying to break it free from the sand, cursing until I stopped my ears.

"I know Carl began to suspect he was licked. The jungle was stronger than any man. Great as was his personal fortune, the building of this kingdom in the sand was making terrible inroads on it. And there was no let-up in sight." [20]

Further insight into Carl's boyish personality can be gained from re-reading the oft-repeated quote he

velopers wanted, did enhance the project. Auctioneer E.E. "Doc" Dammers was enlisted and he must have delivered a carnival atmosphere as attendees were enticed with china, crockery, leather, vases, dinnerware, Oriental rugs, etc. sold in between-lot sales. Carl's land was much more inhospitable than that of his partners, but Miami Beach historian Howard Kelinberg said of him, "He had a genius for marketing that eclipsed his colleagues in land sales and development." [18] Fisher said he would plot 77 city blocks and build streets that were as wide as boulevards. As we might

expect, Carl's original plans to develop 1,000 acres eventually reached 2,600. [19]

We know some of Jane Fisher's recollections about her husband's career may have been seen through the proverbial rose-colored glasses, but there is no mistaking her description of the task of clearing, filling and actually building the land he was to develop.

"Carl sent in hundreds of Negroes with machetes to clear the jungle. Foot by foot, their backs dripping with sweat and covered with mosquitoes, they hacked away through the palmetto and mangrove,

As proud as any big-game hunter, Carl poses with one of the prizes of the day, an uprooted tree that stood in the way of his dream. [2]

Chapter5

Preceeding page, upper and lower: The transformation from swamp to land was enacted by these dredges that droned on for many years. [2]

yelled when his friend Al Webb designed a triangular shaped plow blade to unearth the palmettos. Webb was an auto-racing pal who had a shop in Indianapolis. The story goes Webb warned Fisher it would be extremely expensive to ship the plow to Florida: "Why Carl, it'll cost a thousand dollars just to ship this plow."

"Ship it," demanded Fisher.

"Well we need a Caterpillar tractor to pull the plow after we get it to Florida. That will cost five thousand dollars more."

"Then goddammit, buy a tractor and ship it off tonight."

The machinery was too heavy for the Collins Bridge, so a barge was rented to move it across Biscayne Bay.

With Carl sitting on the back of the tractor, Webb allowed the three-cornered blade to slip into the land

Chapter 5

and meet its foe. The palmettos snapped like ferns.

"Look at 'em boil Al. Look at 'em boil. Boil you goddam roots," Fisher exclaimed.

Jane adds, "The tired Negroes resting on the mattocks joined in the jubilant chorus: 'Boil old roots, white man say boil!"

Carl took a turn aboard the tractor and was soon hollering, "Gee-sus, look at 'em boil. Kee-rist-on-a-bicycle, look at 'em boil."[21]

Carl and his partners were on their way toward changing the landscape of the earth that would ultimately bring instantaneous smiles and looks of wonderment. However, he had to fill in marshes and actually dredge up material to build land where there wasn't any before his stage would be set for the public to act upon.

Dealing with a machine known as a dredge was an entirely different matter than pulling up trees. Fisher would buy himself an education in the art of dredging. Fisher hired three dredges to fill the land. The largest was named the Norman H. Davis, a huge floating piece of earth moving equipment. It had a 1,000 horsepower engine that powered pumps enabling it to throw a twenty-inch stream of bay bottom a mile through piping. Aided by two smaller units called the Florida and the Biscayne that pumped twelve-inch streams of buried sand, silt, muck and marl, the landscape was painstakingly transformed. [22] *Billion Dollar Sandbar* author Polly Redford was probably not the first to call the dredged up muck sloppy Cream of Wheat.[23]

The Cream of Wheat mixture had to settle, drain and harden for about six months before it could be disturbed. Carl initially cleared 32 acres on what was known as Bull Isle, the place where the Collins Bridge ended, and created a road to the peninsula itself. The tract was later named Belle Isle in 1914. [24]

"After the dredge work was done, " J.N. Lummus

Examples of some of the first homes built in Miami Beach. [2]

wrote, *"we looked over a wide area of sand and muck and thought that after the silt settled, all we would have to do would be to survey our properties, and sell more lots to build the city by the ocean. This was not the case. The filled-in land became dry, and the gentle breezes were no longer zephyrs. The wind actually blew up sandstorms, so we had to plant grass on our man-made ground."*[25]

Initially Carl had named his section of the beach, Alton Beach, as the name seemed to strike a chord in him when he saw it on a freight train that said, "Chicago, Northwestern & Alton R.R.".

He built a miniature rail system about a mile long to carry supplies while crews re-carved the land

This 1915 photo gives us a nice over-view of what was to become Miami Beach. As we can see, landscaping and trees made even the bare land look desirable. [2]

Shown here standing alone, Carl Fisher's Lincoln Building would soon be accompanied by some of the nation's most prestigious retail outlets. [2]

that would later become the famed Lincoln Road. He had passes printed up and mailed them to his fellow railroad presidents across the country, some of whom returned the favor with like chits for their own systems.[26]

Development continued, albeit slowly and by 1914 the Lummus brothers had sold 178 lots. They went so far as to offer free lots on the new Collins Avenue to the first 25 people who would build homes to the Lummus specs. Over 30 lots were given away and J.N. noted that the homes were typical beach houses and fairly inexpensive to construct.

For the season of 1913-1914 the beautiful Royal Palm Hotel opened in Miami to a New Year's ball.[27] The Fishers were never considered socialites although they often entertained at home, especially when Carl had located a potential land buyer. Jane and Carl's long-tenured servant Galloway had to be ready to serve lunch or dinner to varying audiences

depending upon Carl's whim.

The previously mentioned Frank Shutts became the publisher of the *Miami Herald* and he along with his afternoon rival, the *Miami Metropolis* were enjoying Miami's current growth. The city had experienced a 44 percent rise in population over the past twelve months and had 18,240 residents.[28]

The papers were mellifluous in their description of the new development on the beach and *The Herald* reported:

"Transformed from a wilderness in to a park, almost in an instant as though by the waving of a magic wand, Alton Beach today seems a fairy land, and the story of its development during the past twelve months reads like a romance, to which, however, "finis" has by no means been written, for each day sees some new beauty added to it.

"Today this entire track has been cleared of jungle-like growth, millions of cubic yards of sand

These photos depict what the land looked like before this area became the classy Lincoln Road. We are surprised to see the lack of power driven machinery.[2]

have been pumped in: more than a hundred acres is covered with a velvety carpet of fine grass, homes are in the course of construction, streets and boulevards made, shrubbery and trees planted, a golf course laid out and according to Mr. Fisher "work has only begun."[29]

Although the newspaper ran two columns of type listing Carl's improvements, Fisher bought a two-page ad to further elucidate on the project. Electricity and phone services were ready by January 1914; city water and sewage the following December. Now Carl was busy outfitting his new lady with all the trimmings. She would definitely be gussied up. Still called Alton Beach, rock roads were being laid; a 300' ocean pier was underway in addition to "the finest in Florida" golf course.-[30]

Carl's first building, appropriately named The Lincoln joined a pair of eight story office buildings he erected. Jane recalls Carl and John Levi argued over the width of the new Lincoln Road and Fisher said:

"Then make it twice as wide-make the godamn thing a hundred feet wide. I tell you that Lincoln Road is going to be the American Rue de la Paix." [31]

Grandstands were being erected to accommodate Carl's latest promotion, professional motorboat races. Carl had previously raced his 66-foot Shadow against his Lincoln Highway supporter A.Y. Gowan's Speedjacks, a 77-footer. The wily Fisher bet Gowan and the loser had to pay to bring the winning craft to Miami for the season. Fisher lost and gained his usual amount of publicity for the event that was heralded by the respected Motor Boating magazine.[32]

Carl put together a small fleet of motorboats and enlisted the services of some of his Indy 500 driver friends. Through his interest in boats Carl would soon become good friends with Gar Wood, a name

From bicycles to race cars to speedboats, Carl Fisher's competitive spirit found an outlet that captured his enthusiasm. He maintained a life-long love of things mechanical, especially if they could carry a human being at speed. (2)

Fisher's idea for a regatta once again proved he was able to deliver entertainment the public loved. (2)

that became legendary in the world of motor boating. Wood's initial fortune was made by inventing a mechanical device to assist in the unloading of coal trucks. Soon, the self-taught mechanic found himself the owner of a boat yard in partners with Chris Smith, who would go on to greater things with the manufacture of his own Chris-Craft boats.(33)

Fisher's regatta attracted not only a competitive field that pleased the onlookers but produced two buyers for land, Charles Kotcher and Robert Henkel who were to build homes on Belle Isle.(34) Carl entered four boats and won with his Shadow (35) Carl liked to use the same name for his craft over and over. Thus there was a Shadow J (for

Jane), a Shadow II, etc. To remind him of his own vulnerability he christened one of his boats Zolene.

The Zolene episode is one that Carl and partner Jim Allison would probably have preferred to forget. A man named John Andrus "who was recently paid $30,000 by the Government for a discovery he made in toughening armor plate" claimed he had unearthed a way of "breaking down water without the use of great heat." Andrus method allowed him to use a little naphtha plus two secret ingredients to transform water into a substitute for gasoline.(36) So complete was Andrus' ruse a two-day test at the Indianapolis Motor Speedway had Fisher saying, " The only question remaining is that of injurious

effects upon the engine, and we do not apprehend any. Tomorrow the engine will be taken apart and examined thoroughly. We will then know if the new fuel is the complete success we now think it is."(37)

A Marmon was run for 1,000 miles at the Indy track at an average of fifty miles per hour while knowledgeable onlookers "conceded Zolene was the coming fuel" if no ill effects were to be seen in the engine.(38)

Carl loved inventions and this would not be the last one that sparked his soul. As it turned out of course, the only memory Carl had of Zolene was the name written on the side of one of his boats. Carl had exclaimed to John Levi and friends, "Boys, do you know what this means? Why it's the biggest discovery since the telephone." Andrus claimed his chemistry would even work with salt water, so Carl had a Prest-O-Lite manager ship a container from New Jersey. Jane tells us Carl lost about $30,000 on the scheme.[39]

Carl did come home one time with an invention that would at least prove one day to be universal. It was a huge wooden box that Jane believed had an "ice-making motor" designed to keep ice, and the contents of the box cold. Carl called it an iceless icebox.[40]

The version Fisher invested in didn't pan out and later one Alfred Mellows approached General Motors founder Billy Durant with a device he called a "Frigerator". Durant invested in the device, gave it to General Motors and they turned it into the Frigidaire. [41] Carl must have derived some satisfaction from knowing the refrigerator concept was successful.

While contemplating the building of what would become Miami Beach, Fisher knew the area could become a desirable wintertime resort for the snow-bitten Northerners. He also knew there wasn't a good way for them to travel from the Snow Belt to Florida's sun. The country needed another road, he mused, from the North to the South.

The plan he hatched would ultimately be known as the Dixie Highway. By late December of 1914 he was writing to Indiana Governor Samuel Ralston asking for support, which ultimately brought results.

Roads in the South were neglected after the Civil War. Southern legislators opposed Federal spending on roads, "because of higher taxes and fears that the Federal government was usurping state rights and violating the Constitution."[42]

Nevertheless, the increasing number of automobiles in the U.S. would command the expansion of the highway system itself, and Carl's latest

From Montreal to Miami, the Dixie highway promised Southerners their country would be visited by sun-seekers.[2]

suggestion can be viewed as common sense.

The crucible for the formation of what was initially called "the Cotton-belt Route" was held in a meeting of Governors in Chattanooga, Tennessee. Sponsored by the Chattanooga Automobile Club, Governors from Indiana, Illinois, Florida, Kentucky and Ohio in addition to 5,000 Dixie Highway Boosters (as the road was now being called) attended on April 3, 1915. Over 200 counties from ten states were asking to be included on the route. Carl was one of the delegates from Indiana. [43]

The best laid plans of the men in attendance supports the old saw that says a camel is a horse designed by committee. Lexington, Knoxville and Ashville wanted an Easterly route while Indianapolis, Louisville and Chattanooga chose a more Westerly road. The contentious meeting in Chattanooga was the first of many that resulted in the inclusion of parallel routes which in total would make the highway the longest in the nation at 3,984 miles.[44]

By October of 1915 the Dixie Highway Pathfinders Tour would arrive in Miami, with Carl in the lead vehicle. The procession came from Chicago to Indianapolis where Carl Fisher had to be thinking, "Follow me fellas. I've got some really great beachfront property to show you. "

Earlier in the year, on March 26, 1915 Carl and his fellow developers pooled their efforts and incorporated the town of Miami Beach, Florida. There were 150 souls living on the beach at the time and 33 of them were registered voters. Fisher partner J.N. Lummus was elected Mayor.[45]

Lummus had been the main motivator behind incorporation and fathered a plan to provide a park. "We graded the park, planted Bermuda grass and coconut palms, built a ten-foot concrete walk the full length and paid for the upkeep of the park until 1917," he wrote.[46]

While the developers were in the midst of planting hundreds of thousands of trees, one commanded attention. The beloved Hoosier poet James Whitcomb Riley, a frequent visitor to the Fisher's home, assisted in the celebration of the new town by composing a poem to commemorate the planting. He said:

We plant this tree
Beside the sea
In trust, that it yet may wave
Through shower and shade
In sunny hours
For other eyes as glad as ours[47]

James Whitcomb Riley had been born in the same town, Greenfield, Indiana as Carl. Riley wandered into the journalism business and began adding his poetry to his writings. His simple and jaunty style found acceptance among the readership and he ultimately profited greatly, leading him to leisure in Florida. Here's an example of one of his popular tomes:

"Little Orphant Annie's come to our house to stay, An' wash the cups an' saucers, an' brush the crumbs away, An' shoo the chickens off the porch, an' dust the hearth, an'sweep, An' make the fire, an' bake the bread, an' earn her board-an-keep..."

Carl had commented to his wife, "For two cents I'd go to Europe," earlier in the year, and knowing her husband's penchant for making and then undoing plans, she immediately booked passage on the Imperator to cross the Atlantic. No sooner had they arrived and been greeted by race driver friend Johnny Aitken that Carl told Jane, "Pack up, we're leaving in the morning. Johnny says there's going to be a war. There's going to be a hell of a show over here. I don't see how America can keep out of it."[48] Jane describes a frantic trek to London, (after a quick visit to the LeMans track) in their efforts to gain passage back to America, her hopes of a leisurely European vacation dashed. The war situation was so tense a British cruiser accompanied their ship, the Laurentic for about a hundred and fifty miles out into the Atlantic. She notes Carl said, "This time it will

Carl's Roman Pools promised patrons tranquil waters and continuing entertainment. [2]

Carl and Charles Kotcher in front of the exclusive Cocolobo Cay Club, a facility designed for the wealthy fishermen. [2]

be the airplane. Men will develop wings in war."[49]

News of the hostilities affected the U.S. economy, and of course development at the beach. But investment continued and Carl purchased what was the Collins Pavillion and added a second swimming pool, restaurant, stage, ballroom, and shopping plaza. He had a Dutch windmill constructed and renamed the complex the Roman Pools. It quickly became a popular spot for everything from swimming lessons to concerts, parties, lectures, dinner and dancing. [50]

In a continuing effort to attract the wealthy, Carl

and partners Charles Kotcher and James Snowden bought two small islands in the Florida Keys in 1916. There amidst some of the best fishing in the U.S. they constructed the exclusive Cocolobo Club. A day's trip from Miami Beach, the crystal clear waters became a favorite spot and magnificent enticement for Carl's new wonderland. [51]

Soon Carl would proclaim, "I expect to see Miami in a very few years as prosperous as Los Angeles.

We have everything they have and much they can never have."[52]

Chapter 6
"Citizen Soldier"

"We'll get all the farmers to paint gigantic numbers and letters on their barn roofs.
The pilots will be able to see them from the air and they can find their way at night."

Carl Fisher's creativity led him to author a lengthy article titled "A Proposal For National Defense" in 1915, soon after World War I had begun and America had not yet entered what would become known as "The Great War".

His continuing interest in aviation has already been established, even though he never became a pilot of fixed wing aircraft.

Carl wanted to see production of ten thousand aircraft, "If built on a standardized plan and by a manufacturer of pleasure cars whose annual output is in the hundreds of thousands, would not require an outlay in dollars much if any greater than is represented by the cost of a single super dreadnaught of the latest class now being laid down." [1]

Fisher called for the building of training fields from Portland, Maine to Jacksonville, Florida on the Atlantic and from Seattle, Washington to San Diego, California on the Pacific. He advocated specific aircraft, a bi-plane with a multi-cylinder water cooled engine and went on to say it should be a two-man plane. Fisher did observe that at present the dropping of explosives from aircraft was not yet as successful as hoped, but that efficiency could be developed.

Our sixth grade-educated subject was by now displaying a level of articulation and journalistic ability generally thought to be reserved by one of much higher education. Carl's continual reading surely assisted him in becoming not only a very readable writer, but also a man who displayed serious study of the subject matter of which he was writing. He closed his article thus:

"To blindly hold invasion impossible, or if attempted that the invaders could be driven back into the sea between 'sunrise and sunset' is to be indifferent to all the experience of war as it is being conducted on the greatest scale in history from 1775 to 1898, all of which is calculated to make an American grieve that so much blood and money had to be wasted in each of our wars, solely because in not one instance have we ever been prepared, though lack of preparation has not kept us out of war." [2]

Meanwhile, the war was affecting not only his Miami Beach development, but activity at the Indianapolis Motor Speedway as well. While 24 cars had competed in the 1915 race, with Ralph DePalma winning the event after finishing 23rd in the 1913 race and not running in 1914. DePalma once again had engine trouble with only a couple of laps to go but was able to nurse his mount home for the victory.

For the 1916 race only 21 vehicles took the starter's flag, and DePalma was not among them. Reportedly there was friction between he and the Speedway operators over appearance money. Fisher's group was forced to bankroll a third of the field either through outright ownership of the cars or financial assistance. Pete Henderson, Howdy Wilcox, Gil Anderson, Johnny Aitken, Tom Rooney, Charles Merz and soon to be WWI ace Eddie Rickenbacker all drove

cars that were entered by the Indianapolis Motor Speedway Team Co. or Prest-O-Lite. In addition, the race had been cut to 300 miles for two reasons. Some fans had complained of the length of the race and the promoters were skeptical of the quality of the race cars available. They didn't know if a credible number were capable of actually running for 500 miles.

Fisher and his partners had obtained a pair of cars previously run by the Maxwell car company that were excellent. Carl made a deal with driver Eddie Rickenbacker to maintain the team and the future fighter pilot brought a sense of true management and organization to the operation. He would later prove his business prowess by purchasing the Speedway and becoming a successful airline executive. We'll learn more about him later. [3]

Al Bloemker, the author of the oft-quoted *500 Miles To Go*, was an Indianapolis newspaperman who ultimately became a vice-president of the Speedway and its public relations man, reported that Fisher balked when notified DePalma demanded appearance money saying:

"Do you have any idea of what will happen if we pay him as much as one nickel? We'll wind up paying through the nose from now on-not only to DePalma, but to every other prominent driver. It would wreck the Speedway and every track in the country. I'd rather lock the gates right now and call off the race. We don't need DePalma or anyone else that much." [4]

Carl then directed his efforts to the war and proved his patriotism in a letter to old pal Colonel Bumbaugh when he wrote:

"I am making an application to get an Aviation School in Indianapolis and I think I am going to succeed, and if so, I will have a job for you in both divisions, the balloon corps and the flying squad. Say nothing about this until I hear from

the Government." [5]

Fisher later related to Bumbaugh:

"I haven't any companies to promote and nothing to sell, and I want you to keep your mouth absolutely closed regarding any plans that I may have mentioned to you. My principal effort will be to tend such services as I can to the Government, without charge: of course I realize that I will have to make arrangements to pay men of your caliber for your work, but don't get mixed up on the idea that this is a promoting scheme." [6]

Through his efforts the Speedway was utilized for aviation work and Carl was placed on the National Advisory Committee in Aeronautics where he was appointed chairman of the Landing Fields and Flying Routes Sub-Committee of the Civil Aerial Transport Committee. His territory became the Midwest. [7]

The Speedway races were canceled for 1917-18 and partner Frank Wheeler dropped out of ownership by selling his stock to Jim Allison. Minor income was derived from the track by utilizing it as a test bed for the locally produced Marmon cars. Some 2,998 vehicles were tested prior to delivery and each was charged $1.25. Unused land was also used to grow 48 acres of oats, 40 acres of wheat and 28 acres of timothy. [8]

With the addition of the Chenowith Farm the Speedway property had expanded to 529 acres. Thus it made a perfect location for a landing field and repair depot for the aviation efforts that were now being enacted by the government. Planes were to fly between Dayton, Ohio and Rantoul, Illinois. Night flying became a priority and Carl's efforts were lauded in the process. *The Public Ledger* of Philadelphia said:

"The originator of America's first cross-country night-flying course is Carl G. Fisher, a young millionaire business man and philanthropist of

PUBLIC ✦ LEDGER
THE MAGAZINE SECTION
Philadelphia, Sunday Morning, September 8, 1918

AMERICAN NIGHT-FLIERS PREPARE TO BOMB THE HUN
First Fly-by-Night Course in the U. S. Affords Our Aviators Training for Flights Over Germany

Indianapolis, the man who conceived and built that city's famous Speedway, where before the war the classic 500-mile automobile races were held on the finest race course in the world.

"The idea of night flying and the necessity for training young Americans how to operate their planes in the dark has been a hobby of Mr. Fisher's since America entered the war. He was convinced that the time would come when the signal corps and the aviation service would recognize the necessity for giving our cadets a preliminary course in night flying before they were sent to England and France to take their post-graduate work behind the firing lines.

"In order to fill a need before it was felt, Mr. Fisher, a chairman of the mapping committee appointed by the national advisory committee on aeronautics, began nearly a year ago to establish a well-marked air route from Dayton, Ohio to Rantoul, Illinois as an aid to the training of our aviators." [9]

Philadelphia's Public Ledger devoted their Magazine Section to the efforts of Fisher and his Midwestern team to mark night routes for aviators. Some of the specialized markings are shown. [2]

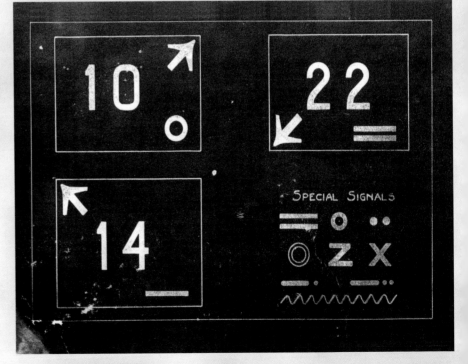

Carl had arranged for barns to be painted with numbers and arrows with "gargantuan proportions- from six to ten feet long and from twenty-four to thirty six inches wide" to guide the pilots along the route along with beacon lights.[10]

Between the Speedway and Dayton and Rantoul barn roofs were painted at an average of about two miles apart. The system also used red and green lights to direct the airmen as drifting off course to left and right was a major consideration. The system was proclaimed a complete success.[11]

The 276 miles between McCook Field in Dayton and Chanute Field in Rantoul became the first regular airplane route in the US and other than the odd newspaper mention, Carl's efforts and undoubtedly cash investment went largely unheralded. [12]

Carl continued his quest to aid his country, and aviation in general with a telegram to Brig. General George O. Squiers, the Chief Signal Officer of the Army that read:

"I am offering free of charge to Colonel Clark my polo field and waterfront for a temporary flying place for the Engineering Department this winter. All that I ask is that the property is maintained and returned to me in the condition in which it was taken. As I understand from Colonel Clark the regulations do not permit the Government to spend any money on borrowed property, all maintenance, runways, et cetera will have to appear as rental for the property. Can't you arrange to handle this differently as I do not wish to be on record as charging the Government rental for this property?" [13]

Carl had invested $40,000 to bring clay from the Everglades to construct the polo field in Miami Beach in hopes of attracting the wealthy who participated in the sport. He was offering it to the government.[14]

The 1916-1917 season in Miami had been the most successful to date and Carl wanted to insure his investment would at least be protected while the Government utilized his Florida property. He and his fellow developers had every reason to believe their dream city would become a boom town. Permission had been granted to build a street-car line in Miami Beach, which Carl funded, and work had begun on the Tamiami Trail, the road that crossed the Everglades. A bond issue had been passed in 1916 for the road.[15]

Carl's involvement in the war effort directly affected his Miami Beach development in some very positive ways. We located a letter he wrote to H.E. Talbott, Jr. of the Dayton-Wright Airplane Company that said in part:

"I understand from very reliable authority that the Italians are about to a point where they want to build a large plane, equipped with not less than five motors and with pontoons, which will be capable of going across—and I believe that at a considerable expense one plane of this kind can be made.

The Pomilio brothers of Turin, Italy, as you probably know, are all located here at the Speedway and are working on some new fast and large bombing models. Three of the brothers are experienced pilots and operate the second largest factory in Italy.

For a long time I have been very anxious to be a passenger on the first plane to go across—and while I feel that I could not afford to pay the Pomilio brothers for the design and preliminary expense of making a plane of this kind, I am willing to donate $50,000." [16]

Fisher's comment of "going across" referred to the Atlantic Ocean.

Talbott, Jr. was an ardent polo player and convinced Carl to invest in a first-class polo facility that included stables, blacksmith shop and clubhouse. Talbot also bought property and built a home called "Fieldstone House", one of the most palatial on the beach. His father Harold, Sr. made a few eyebrows rise in an "oh well" expression when he died on the third tee of the Miami Beach Golf Course in 1921. [17]

Harold Talbott, Jr. had a long and continuing interest in aviation and automobiles. Along with his successful father he was instrumental in helping the Wright brothers in building their first wind tunnel and later invested in the Wright's aircraft venture by forming the Dayton-Wright Airplane Company. It went on to employ over 12,000 workers who churned out 38 planes per day for the WWI effort and became the nation's largest producer. He was also one of the original investors in locomotive mechanic Walter P. Chrysler's efforts to manufacture a vehicle under his own name. Talbott became the third Secretary of the Air Force in 1953.[18]

It has been said the letters he has written can often determine a man's true personality. The following letters show our subject venting his feelings to James Deering, the founder of the successful International Harvester Company, and the man who built Villa Viscaya, a multi-million dollar castle estate in Miami. Carl's year of 1919 began with a snub he found extremely bothersome.

January 24, 1919
"Dear Mr. Deering,
Frankness between men is always best, and that is the spirit in which I am writing.

Not long ago, one Sunday morning, I rode over to your place with a friend to let him see your gardens. The pass you sent me had been left at my office, and your guard stopped me at the gate. I explained that the card had been forgotten. He was courteous enough, saying he knew I was Mr. Fisher, but he had to obey his positive orders to admit no one without the pass, no matter who it was. He agreed to telephone up to you, which he did; but after keeping my guest and myself waiting half an hour the report came back that you were not at home.

I happen to know that you were at home, and resent very much the treatment I received, not that you couldn't see me if you were engaged, but that I was refused admission to the home of a man whom I considered a friend, at any time I wished to come.

Such being the case, I cannot accept any future invitations from you. For while I may have no right to give orders to your servants, or countermand instructions you give them, I can at least save myself future annoyance by not opening myself to a re-occurrence of such a miserably unpleasant thing.

Yours very sincerely,"
Carl Fisher

Less than a week later Carl wrote again:

January 30, 1919
"Dear Mr. Deering,
After receiving your very frank letter, I can better understand the mental attitude of the chap who said, 'God save me from my servants, and I'll look after my own soul.'

I am perfectly willing to consider the incident as not only entirely closed but as non-existent. If you will agree to have a cocktail chirping on the ice and ready for me whenever I turn my infuriated Ford loose in the direction of your gatehouse.

With all good wishes I am
Yours sincerely," [19]
Carl Fisher

Carl penned a letter to Ralph DePalma on July 22, 1919 that not only showed his concern for war veterans, but also may have been somewhat of an olive branch offering to the driver who was denied (late) entry to the 1916 event after Carl had refused to pay appearance money.

"Dear Ralph:
The hospital here at Fort Benj. Harrison has about 750 badly shot up young men from this last war. There is one thing that these young fellows want to see more than anything else in the world-at least they say they do: they want to see a match race at the Speedway and they want to see Ralph DePalma, Barney Oldfield and Wilcox together.

I told the Colonel in charge of the fort the other day that the Speedway would donate the Track and the Officials, and that we would get the Motor Corps to donate the automobiles to haul these poor devils out to the Speedway. I also told him that I would try and get you fellows down here to drive an exhibition for these boys.

We have a couple of Peugeots and one Premier that are in good shape-and we would like to have you come down with your Packard. Wilcox can drive one of the Peugeots and if you can't bring your Packard along, you and Barney can drive the other two cars of ours.

I (think) that for a program, if we could get your consent and Oldfield's, we would have a ten (10), twenty (20), and thirty (30) mile race for a Gold Medal. In the twenty-mile race we would have a stop on the fifth lap for a tire change. This is about the only program I could think of that would not run into considerable expense for tires, mechanics, etc.

I feel that we can't do too much for these poor devils who are all shot up. There will be about seven hundred of them in the Grand Stand and it will take

about four hundred automobiles to haul this number, as in some cases it takes an entire automobile to haul one cripple. There will also be a large number of officers, nurses, etc.

On receipt of this letter won't you please wire me if you will come. The tentative date is August 12th.

I would like to get Joe Boyer to come with a Frontenac if I could or Louis Chevrolet, and make it a four-cornered affair. But we can't give them, a real thriller unless we can get you and Oldfield to come down.

Let me hear from you."
Sincerely,
Carl Fisher [20]

The Indianapolis Star reported on the upcoming speed event at the track and gave all concerned due credit for their involvement. The August 20, 1919 edition of The Indianapolis News carried a report of the activities after completion.

"About 1,600 soldiers from Ft. Benjamin Harrison witnessed exhibition automobile races at the Indianapolis motor speedway yesterday afternoon. Many of the men were wounded soldiers in convalescence at Ft. Harrison Hospital.

T.E. Myers, general manager of the speedway, acted as starter. The events were put on in true championship racing style.

The drivers were paced in the famous white speedway by N. H. Gilman, treasurer of the Allison experimental company. With Gilman rode Colonial Robert Tyndall, commander of the field artillery, Rainbow division.

Joe Dawson in a Peugeot won the first race, a five-mile event. It marked the reappearance of Dawson on the speedway track after a number of years in which he had been out of the racing game. Howdy Wilcox, who won the 150-mile Liberty Sweepstakes here in

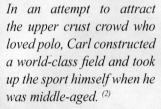

In an attempt to attract the upper crust crowd who loved polo, Carl constructed a world-class field and took up the sport himself when he was middle-aged. [2]

May, finished second. He also drove an Indianapolis owned Peugeot. Tommy Milton, in a Premier, was third. The time was 3:33, an average of 84.5 miles an hour.

In the ten-mile race, Milton had engine trouble and did not finish. Wilcox crossed the tape first and Dawson finished second. The time was 7:19, or an average of 83.53 miles an hour." [21]

We did not find any mention of the vanquished DePalma taking part in the event who may have remained recalcitrant due to his previous money grievence with Fisher. Possibly he was still peeved Fisher had refused his late entry for the 1916 race when Carl refused to pay appearance money.

Fisher was busy juggling the Florida and Indiana activities during the war, and saw both prosper soon after the Armistice was signed on November 11, 1918.

His new Flamingo Polo Field opened in February of 1919 and proved to be one of Fisher's wisest investments. He had built three golf courses, the Flamingo, the Alton Beach and the Bay Shore, "the only golf courses in the world constructed from nothingness" that would also gain their own respectability. Within a few years the LaGorce Championship on a course of the same name, offered the sport's largest prize, a $10,000 purse. [22]

Although starting to display middle aged paunch, Carl took up polo himself and became a formidable competitor. He surely wasn't society oriented as most of the participants and spectators were, but he had no trouble mingling with the competitors. He attracted the world's best. One was Tom Dryborough, a seventy-two year old who wrote praises about Fisher's facility that led to international credibility.

Carl footed the bill to bring over the entire English polo team at a reported cost of $50,000. Among the team were Lord Cromwell, the Marquis of Waterford

*Preceding page and above: Carl and Jane's Shadows home became a proper setting to
entertain the wealthy Carl was attracting to the Miami Beach development.* [2]

and a Captain Rex Stewart. This pair responded to the area by purchasing $73,000 in land and presumably built suitable abodes.

The United States Army polo team trained at Carl's facility giving it an air of officialdom.[23]

Jane became enamored with the social side of the game and waxes on contentedly in her memoirs. She tells of the gala dinners she hosted at the couple's palatial "Shadows" home.

"Three hundred and fifty guests sat down to supper in the dining room opening on the sea, palms and stars, while the native music throbbed on through the night. At intervals, Reinald Werrenrath sang arias that

had thrilled Metropolitan listeners in New York, and Sybil Cromer, a lovely figure in Spanish costume, crooned Cuban songs from the balcony.

"At the height of the evening, Carl disappeared and I later found him in bed, asleep under his pictures of Lincoln and Napoleon. The next morning he insisted that it had been one of the best of parties and he'd had a wonderful time. 'Only I know when to go to bed,' he commented amiably." [24]

Jane relates Carl's personal servant Galloway had a clicker to count the number of guests who attended a polo ball that featured a field in miniature so the participants could replay the game on paper-

mache' horses. Galloway informed Jane she had just shaken the hand of the four hundred and fiftieth guest at one point.[25]

If Carl Fisher was in his element at a dusty race track, his need for speed was easily transferred to the water. He was deeply involved in the building of speedboats throughout the years when he was a wealthy man and financed the Purdy Boat Works for construction. He along with Jim Allison had the Allison Engineering craftsmen supply adaptations of the famed Liberty aircraft engine for their yachts.[26]

Partner Allison had formally formed the Allison Engineering Company on September 14, 1915. His partners in the Speedway knew they had to financially back cars for their 1916 event, and three teams were ultimately formed. Driver Johnny Aitken was central to Allison's involvement and served as the team's manager, chief engineer and driver. [27]

Jim Allison ultimately built a shop a couple of blocks west of the Indianapolis Motor Speedway on Main Street in the town of Speedway, just across the street from their sprawling Prest-O-Lite factory. In April of 1917 when America declared war on Germany, Allison shut down the racing operation and turned the shop's attention toward obtaining war related work. [28]

What started out as a race car maintenance facility must have had a very impressive machine shop, and the talent to run it. We know one Norman H. Gilman became superintendent and chief engineer in 1917 and served a highly distinguished career that culminated in 1936. He was awarded the United States Navy's prestigious E Award for exceptional loyalty, service and dedication. [29] He invented the Gilman bearing; a steel-shelled bearing that replaced troublesome bronze. His final incarnation of the bearing was a magnificent success and "extended the Liberty's (engine) service life from tens to hundreds of hours."

Allison had Gilman direct his efforts toward a marine engine and the result was a 12 cylinder 425 hp, 1,500 rpm power plant that was smooth and quiet. It was based on the aircraft Liberty engine the firm would produce. A dozen of the units were produced; four for Allison, two each for Art Newby and Carl, and four to sell at $25,000. Carl's 80-ft. Sea Horse fitted with his pair of engines could crack off 26 knots en route from Long Island to Manhattan. Carl would come to know Long Island intimately, as we shall see later.

Just as Carl had assisted in transforming the Florida landscape, Jim Allison's machine shop was expanded to first 50 employees, then 100 plus 150 temporary draftsmen for the war effort. The firm produced "high-speed crawler like tractors for hauling artillery

Although raised on different sides of the tracks, Carl and Jim Allison remained life-long friends and business partners. [2]

The Liberty V-12 engine as manufactured by Allison Engineering and several other firms as well. A much modified version was used by Allison, Fisher and friends in their yachts. [2]

Carl's Sea Horse yacht which featured a pair of the Allison V-12 engines. It could run 30 MPH. [2]

to this day. Aitken also managed the teams of Joe Dawson in 1912 and Jules Goux in 1913 when each won the "500". [32]

Significant changes had come to the world during the war years. Predictions of exhaustion of oil through massive war consumption would prove to be erroneous. Wireless communication in the form of ground to aircraft was a quantum leap for the aircraft industry. Radio beams along coastline towers guided ship's navigation better than ever before. Agitator washing machines became the standard of the world. A man named Clarence Birdseye started freezing fish and found a massive market for his product. Dial telephones came into existence and the machine age marched on. From 1859-1919 our output increased 33 times but it took only a seven-fold worker increase to accomplish the task. Just before the Roaring Twenties

and battlefield equipment. Whippet like tanks, tank tracks and production superchargers." [30]

The most significant, and interesting to Jim and Carl, was the engine that "had automobile stamped all over it—eight cylinders, water cooled, a Delco battery instead of magnetos," commented automotive historian Carl Solberg. It was the Liberty aircraft engine that would insure Allied supremacy in WWI.

The engine became an integral part of Jim Allison's life throughout the war and his firm's capabilities in producing it further cemented the Allison name in high quality US manufacturing. Eventually General Motors would inhale the Speedway, Indiana firm that had yet another direct link to Carl Fisher.

The production version had 12 cylinders and was

based on the beautiful British Rolls-Royce design. Allison Engineering was responsible for building the precise master models with a set of tools, jigs, fixtures and gauges so other manufacturers could hold the unit to necessary tolerances. Ultimately 20,748 engines were produced and Allison built several hundred of them. [31]

One of the men who assisted in the formation of Allison's race team and shop didn't live to see the firm realize its full potential, was Johnny Aitken. He competed in virtually every Speedway event since its opening then died of bronchial pneumonia caused by the influenza pandemic that swept 21 million to their death. Aitken started 41 races at the Speedway and won 15 events, a statistic that stands

Carl and one of the most famed boat designers of the 20th century, Gar Wood. [2]

Program covers for the 1919 and 1920 500 Mile races. [11]

and attempted to set about enlarging the island and making a deep water seaport. He was opposed by E.G. Sewell and the Miami Chamber of Commerce in what would turn out to be a long running dispute that lasted for decades. [35]

For Carl's activities at the Speedway immediately following the war, it was business as usual and the 1919 Indianapolis 500 would have a full field of 33 cars. To start the year off, Carl was again nudged by a race car driver for financial assistance. His Speedway manager, T.E. "Pop" Myers wrote to Carl on January 16, 1919:

"Dear Mr. Fisher:

A day or so ago Louis Chevrolet stopped in Indianapolis and made quite an extended call at this office to talk over the racing situation of 1919. It seems that the principal thing that influenced Chevrolet to come to Indianapolis was to learn if it would be possible for him to get any sort of a guarantee as to the matter of expenses.

Chevrolet explains that he is very short of money and he would like very much to enter three of his cars for our event but unless he can get some assurance of some help on his expense account in the event of none of his cars winning any prizes, he will be able to come with only one car. He states emphatically that he will be here with one car, guarantee or no guarantee, but if we could see our way clear to help him out, he would like to come with three cars as stated above.

The writer explained to him that this was entirely foreign to the policy of this company and that he felt quite sure that none of the owners of this track would approve of such a proposition and for that reason could offer him no encouragement.

I am advising you of this situation that in the event you think it desirable to have all three

were to be ushered in America produced two-thirds of the world's oil. Trustworthy flight has been accomplished along with the modern day red, green, amber traffic light. Automobile manufacturers produced 1,745,792 cars of which 42% are Model "T" Fords in 1917 alone. Two years earlier Ford had produced their millionth vehicle. One, a truck, was modified in 1915 to tow a trailer, becoming the first-tractor trailer outfit. Invented by a blacksmith, wagon-maker named August Fruehauf, his firm went on to become the largest maker of tractor-trailers in the world. [33]

While fabricators of steel structures were finding

their work made easier through the use of electric arc welding as opposed to riveting in 1920, Carl was happily making the dirt fly in Miami Beach. He had sold $132,000 worth of lots in 1918 and more than doubled the amount to $300,000 in 1919. He had deliberately raised prices by 10% over the previous year and announced, "We will continue to raise prices at least 10% each year as we try to give our customers an investment that substantially and steadily grows in value." [34] He had also set up the Miami Beach Bay Shore Co. with the Collins family and had controlling interest. It was at this time he bought a 30-acre island south of Government Cut

Howdy Wilcox in a Speedway owned car, a Peugeot that he drove to a win in the 1919 Indianapolis 500. [4]

of his cars and would therefore want to advise Chevrolet differently from the information the writer gave him.

Very truly yours,"
T.E. Myers [36]

Louis brought three Frontenac Motors entries to the track in 1919 and drove one of them to a seventh place finish after looking like he had the car to win

earlier. Chevrolet experienced an aberration late in the event when he lost a wheel on the front stretch and his hub cut a timing wire. The wire caught driver Elmer Shannon across the throat and the man nearly bled to death before reaching the pits.

On the 45th lap Arthur Thurman died in his Duesenberg when it overturned in the northeast turn. His riding mechanic Nicholas Molinero was critically injured.

In front of Grandstand G on the 97th lap, the gas tank on Louis LeCocq's Roamer exploded killing him and riding mechanic Robert Bandini.

The tragic event was won by Howdy Wilcox in a car owned by the Speedway. [37]

Fisher was running on all cylinders during this period of his life. Even with the occasional hiccup of investing in a Zolene or iceless icebox, he was making commerce happen and having a great time doing it.

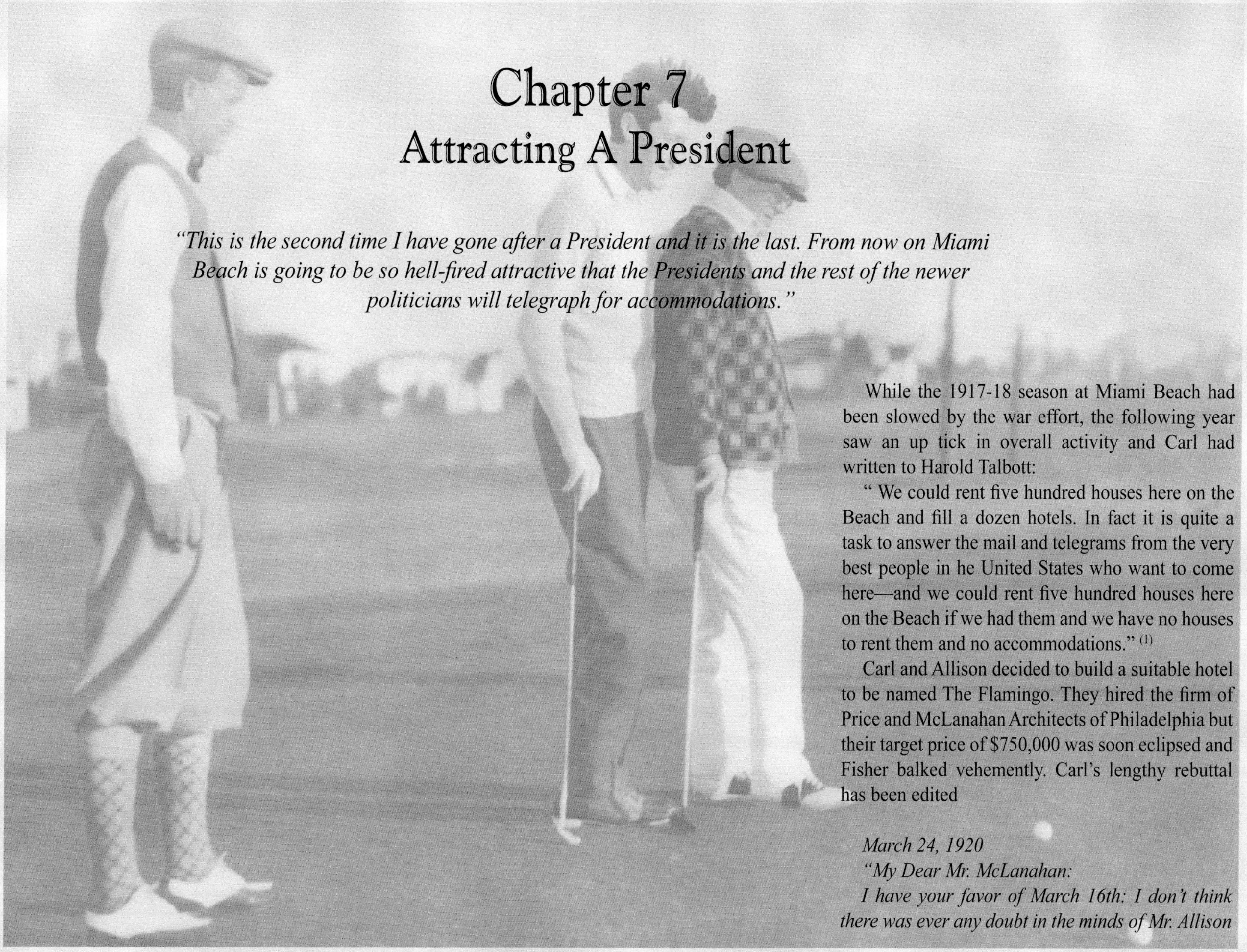

Chapter 7
Attracting A President

"This is the second time I have gone after a President and it is the last. From now on Miami Beach is going to be so hell-fired attractive that the Presidents and the rest of the newer politicians will telegraph for accommodations."

While the 1917-18 season at Miami Beach had been slowed by the war effort, the following year saw an up tick in overall activity and Carl had written to Harold Talbott:

" We could rent five hundred houses here on the Beach and fill a dozen hotels. In fact it is quite a task to answer the mail and telegrams from the very best people in he United States who want to come here—and we could rent five hundred houses here on the Beach if we had them and we have no houses to rent them and no accommodations." [1]

Carl and Allison decided to build a suitable hotel to be named The Flamingo. They hired the firm of Price and McLanahan Architects of Philadelphia but their target price of $750,000 was soon eclipsed and Fisher balked vehemently. Carl's lengthy rebuttal has been edited

March 24, 1920
"My Dear Mr. McLanahan:
I have your favor of March 16th: I don't think there was ever any doubt in the minds of Mr. Allison

and myself, or in your mind until you opened the bids, that at least we commissioned your Company to design for us a hotel that would not cost over a million dollars-and at any time while you were drawing these designs for us, if you had ever hinted to us that a building such as you were designing was going to cost us two million or even a million and a half dollars, we would have told you at that time to quit.

I think if we could have had bids of $1,200,000 on your hotel, we might have stretched the extra $200,000 and gone ahead. In fact, I remember quite distinctly when we started on these plans with you that we tried to have you design for us a hotel that would cost about $750,000—and then after a great deal of talk you finally got us into the mind to consider a million dollars as the limit-but I certainly considered this the limit and I am sure Mr. Allison did too.

We are now building a hotel of 200 rooms that will, in our estimation be suitable for this work. It will answer the same purpose and be of the construction and type, which we expected you to design-and this building is going to cost us within 5 to 10% of our estimate. I am going ahead with this hotel myself and I am building this hotel, which I consider suitable for considerably less per square foot than the design you submitted.

I feel, honestly, Mr. McLanahan, that you really paid no attention whatever to our requests for a simple, practical hotel, but that you did try to design a very

Upper left and above: The standard beach outfit left precious little room for sunburn or hormone excitement until Jane Fisher bared her knees with this breakthrough suit. [2]

fine and complete hotel regardless of what it might cost Mr. Allison and myself. This was not what we wanted: it was not what we asked you to design-and in sending you $15,000 on the drawings that you did make before the bids were opened and before our eyes were opened to what we were into, I have felt that the error was entirely yours, and so does Jim, and this it is up to you to carry the burden which you should carry in making this error.

Rather than have any great arguments about the matter, and knowing that you did spend considerable money in getting out these drawings, I have felt inclined to just forget the $7,500 and chalk it up to experience-but when you undertake to tell either Jim or myself that you were not to blame for the bids on this hotel and that your design was as simple and not more expensive per cubic foot than the design we have adopted, and that you had no definite instructions that the hotel was to cost no more than a million dollars-then we have arrived at the parting of the ways, as far as you are concerned as an architect and our company as a builder is concerned-and needless to say we would rather strongly object to paying any more on this contract than has been paid; and as stated, "the writer" at least feels that you have been overpaid and that you owe us at least $15,000 on the Flamingo Hotel drawings as a result of your not following instructions and not paying any attention to the wishes in the matter of costs.

I regret, of course, that this has ended as it has, but I am absolutely satisfied in my own mind of the course we have taken and of the statements made in this letter—and I am a little disappointed that you do not acknowledge your error in the matter without argument.

Yours very truly, (2)
Carl Fisher

Carl's friends John Oliver LaGorce , John Levi,

Carl spared no expense in outfitting the Flamingo Hotel (2)

and Jim Allison had been extremely impressed with a "cloud of flame" they took to be a sunset when they visited Andros Island in the Bahamas. As the cloud lifted they realized it was in the wrong direction for a sunset and discovered it to be a flock of Flamingos. Thus Carl wanted his new hotel to be not only named after the beautiful birds, but to utilize their form and image in its appointments. (3)

Fisher commissioned the famed wildlife painter Louis Agassiz Fuertes to create murals in the new hotel to memorialize the leggy birds. Unfortunately Fuertes' paintings of the birds were the only ones that would survive. We imagine Fisher envisioned stately looking Flamingos strutting around the lawn of his

new hotel attracting finger pointing and comments from the suitably impressed guests. John LaGorce described the birds:

"A flaming mass of brilliant scarlet bodies, jet black beneath the huge wings, with their long, slender necks gracefully lowering and raising their Roman-nosed heads as they sought beneath the water for the tiny spiral shell, known to scientists as 'cerithium', upon which the Flamingo lives exclusively in its native habitat."(4)

Fisher had no luck keeping the birds alive and it wasn't until a dozen years later that Joseph Widener's colony of Flamingos at his Hialeah racecourse would survive to become a tourist attraction.(5)

Carl didn't need the birds in order to have his hotel gain prominence. It had 200 rooms that faced the ocean or Biscayne Bay, an eleven story tower, private docks, boathouse, laundry, men's club, broker's office, shops and was surrounded, with a cornucopia of plant life.

Carl had hired a pair of Japanese gardeners named Shigezo Tashiro and Kotaro Suto who planted Australian pine, Arabian jasmine, Brazilian pepper, Chinese holly, Canary Island date palms, Hong Kong orchids, Mexican flame vine, Rangoon creeper and Surinam cherry to transform the Beach into a lush garden. Eventually the pair set up a nursery business and prospered.(6)

Jim Allison had dropped out of the Flamingo development and Jane reminds us Carl's attitude was: "There are only two times in a man's life when he is justified to take a chance-when he can afford to, and when he can't."(7)

At Jane's urging Carl commissioned gondolas to be built to add to the flavor of the Flamingo. In the voluminous file of letters he wrote to his friend John LaGorce of the National Geographic he said:

"I wish I could tell you in time about the gondolas we are building. I had Purdy come down on a rush

With the new Flamingo Hotel in the background, gondolas glide serenely to create a peaceful atmosphere. [2]

order and we are going to build six of them in twenty days. I have some of the most wonderful Bahama Negroes you ever saw to push these gondolas around. They are all going to be stripped to the waist and wear big brass earrings. And possibly necklaces of live crabs or crawfish. Too bad you can't say something about this on the front page of the Saturday Evening Post, but I really believe it will be alright."[8]

LaGorce didn't have anything to do with the Saturday Evening Post, the nation's most popular magazine at the time, and Carl was just being a bit flippant in his request.

The negro in the south was surely not treated like an American citizen during this era. Nevertheless, Fisher seems to have displayed a sensibility for the blacks that was in advance of his fellow citizens. Early on Jane tells us of the incident whereupon a black worker fell into a vat of tar while working at the Speedway, Carl took the man to a hospital where service was denied and Fisher became livid and swore he'd put the facility out of business. Jane claims both Carl and Jim Allison withdrew their support for the hospital. She also notes the time a train conductor told Carl's servant Galloway to move to the Jim Crow section of a train they were traveling on and Carl said, "I'll bet you any money you like that if you take off your shoes and Galloway takes off his, he'll have the cleanest feet."[9]

Carl's letter to Frank D. Stalnaker of the Indiana National Bank gives us an example of Carl's concern for the blacks as he said:

"I had a talk today with Mrs. Ellinwood and I am very anxious to help, in some manner, provide a place for colored women and colored children of this town to be properly taken care of. It is a job that the city and citizens together could combine on and make a thoroughly first-class place that would be properly

managed, and be large enough to furnish several branches of assistance.

" I have noticed recently that the old workhouse is vacant. This is a very large and substantial building that could be really turned into a wonderful Community Welfare House and particularly for the colored people as it is in about the proper location. Do you happen to know whether this building could be secured for this purpose, and do you think it would be possible to get the cooperation of the city and a substantial number of business men to complete the job?

Very truly yours,"(10)

Carl Fisher

Carl's partner Thomas J. Pancoast outlined the problem he believed the city faced regarding blacks in a letter to Carl that said in part:

"We have a problem on our hands here that is going to be a little difficult. I am afraid to handle, and the longer it goes the more difficult it is going to be. About two years ago the Negro in Miami had very few liberties, and as you know, they were not allowed to drive an automobile. The tourists who came to Miami with their Negro drivers resented this very much, and as we didn't want to keep the tourists away we finally opened the door to the Negro driver. Then the Negroes of the town commenced to buy cars and now on Thursdays and Sundays especially, the Negroes come over to the Beach car load after car load. Just this afternoon inside of an hour there have been perhaps twenty-five cars go by our office, everyone loaded to full capacity with Negroes."(11)

Pancoast waxed on for five more paragraphs describing the problem and suggested a man be

appointed as a Deputy Sheriff to "handle the Negroes."

We could not locate a Fisher reply to the letter. Carl was actually scrambling to raise cash to finish his Flamingo project in 1920 as a sharp economic downturn gripped the country in 1920-21. In reality, Carl's land sales had been going extremely well and by the end of 1920 he had tallied $1,966,000 in lot sales.(12)

John Collins' bridge was sold to a group who ultimately turned it into the Venetian Causeway and Islands, so the stage that had been set was now hosting a continuing line of performers.

Carl's Flamingo did reach completion and he wrote:

"I fully realize that all people are not going to be able to pay the rates we will charge. The Flamingo is an extravagant hotel-it just has to be. It has probably cost more money for the number of rooms than any other hotel in the United States. We had to build it in spite of hell, high water and the Union-and she is built!" (13)

The Flamingo was built in the area south of Indiana Creek that comprises the southernmost 23 blocks of the

Previous and above: Soon after Jane bared her knees, the Miami Beach bathing beauty was promoted by Carl and his press agents.[2]

main barrier island that separates the Atlantic Ocean and Biscayne Bay. It was the first section of the city to be developed and became known as South Beach. Today it still features many Art Deco, Streamline Moderne and Nautical Moderne buildings that were erected in the 1930's.

While Carl threw a New Year's eve party in December 1920 to open the Flamingo, Jim Allison had plunked down a couple of hundred thousand dollars to build what was possibly America's finest aquarium that opened the next day. Carl's pal LaGorce had scheduled a *National Geographic* story on Allison's new creation along with a general story on Miami Beach in the January 1921 edition. It helped that Carl had purchased advertising in the journal as well. [14]

Ever the promoter, Carl had begun a campaign before the hotel was officially opened to attract President Elect Warren G. Harding to Miami Beach as the attendant publicity would carry around the entire U.S. and naturally readers would say, 'If it's good enough for the President, then it's good enough for me.'

Fisher had written to then Senator Harding, "Miami Beach has become the real garden spot of the sub-tropics and is especially attractive to lovers of outdoors because the bathing in the surf or in the great Roman Pools nearby, the eighteen and nine-hole golf courses, the polo, tennis and last, but not least, the splendid sport fishing, all make for health and a thorough enjoyment of every hour." [15]

Carl had the unsolicited help of Ohio State Senator William M. Miller who had also suggested a vacation in Miami Beach to the President-Elect as Miller lobbied Harding's campaign manager Harry Daugherty for the trip. Harding penned a note to Fisher saying:

"I wish I could come and make a long stay. The simple truth about the matter is, however, that my plans will not admit of such an enticing program. We are coming south soon and I am expecting to get a rather hurried glimpse of Miami and the Beach. We shall not be able to stay, and the nature of my travels is such that I will not be in a position to accept any courtesies of public nature. I very deeply appreciate your interest in extending your tender of courtesy

and hospitality. If the circumstances were different I should certainly rejoice to accept." [16]

Fisher sent his slender secretary Ann Rossiter to Ohio in an attempt to see the new President and she wrote:

"We arrived at Mr. Harding's at eleven thirty and found a dozen or so committees, individuals numbering about eight or ten on missions of all kinds waiting to see Mr. Harding. I was much surprised to be taken in away ahead of everyone else. He gave us a full half hour in the midst of his rush, was most courteous, asked me all about the Beach. He leaves for the South within the next ten days and will be in Miami probably two days on Senator Freylinghuysen's house boat-but in that time will surely visit the beach, play golf and make your acquaintance.

"Personally, I feel that it is something to have him promise to come over to the Beach and play golf-and feel, further, that this personal call, personal touch, or whatever you want to call it may not be without results."[17]

Carl had previously lost patience when he heard from Harding and wrote to John LaGorce:

One of the manicured Spanish oriented estates that dot Miami Beach's landscape.[2]

"This is the second time I have gone after a President and it is the last. From now on Miami Beach is going to be so hell-fired attractive that the Presidents and the rest of the newer politicians will telegraph for accommodations. We certainly will never make another effort to get them here.

"I feel like a "Nut" and I certainly don't think a hell of a lot of Harding because he has not answered either one of my letters and telegrams so between you and me and the gate post Harding and the whole outfit can go to Hell as far as I am concerned." [18]

LaGorce wrote back to Fisher and explained "There is no hotel in the country that wouldn't break its neck to offer Harding accommodation and entertainment gratis for the publicity and advertising value of such a thing is well known....Now if they do show up down there and want to be friends with you, for Heaven's sakes don't go hide in the corner and get mad." [19] LaGorce explained that Harding understood the Washington hotels were refusing to rent a room for less than a week with a minimum of $300 a room and Harding wouldn't stand for it.

Naturally the City of Miami planned to welcome the new President but when Senator Freylinghuysen's houseboat arrived it continued to the Flamingo Hotel. Jane tells us that Carl, "shanghaied the President right out from under the pipsqueak Miami reception committee and took him up to the Flamingo Hotel penthouse where a poker game and plenty of Scotch were waiting.[19]

Carl's comportment was disciplined for the new Commander in Chief. The President-elect spent the next two days playing golf (with an elephant as his caddie), swimming and fishing off Carl's Shadow VI while squeezing in the obligatory photo opportunities along the way. Harding said, "Because

Outdoor dancing added to the luxuriousness of the Fisher properties.[2]

of the attractiveness of Miami and Miami Beach, I hope to come here again. The beach is wonderful. It is developing like magic." [20]

We'll learn more about Fisher's use of elephants to gain publicity a bit later.

Fisher would long remember that January 31, 1921 when Harding arrived as the event created the anticipated press reviews. Carl's old friend A. Batchelder, chairman of the executive board of the AAA in Washington, D.C. wrote to Carl: *"The dispatchers up here didn't leave out anything: Fisher, Allison, Flamingo, Lincoln, Shadow, L'Apache, Cocolobo and of course Thompson, besides, etc. etc.*

"You certainly handled the job in great shape, and I again take my hat off to the firm of Fisher

and Allison." [21]

By this time in his life Carl was used to dealing with the captains of industry on a first-name basis and he was able to approach them as a peer. Jane says the popular tune of the day when she and Carl were courting, "In My Merry Oldsmobile" became their song and, "We sang it harmoniously, riding over the dusty, rutted dirt roads around Indianapolis".[22]

Through his involvement selling new cars Carl became acquainted with many manufacturers and R.E. Olds was one of them. Olds had assisted his father in the production of stationary gasoline engines as a young man and was central to the production of a vehicle under their name. Their car became the first to employ what we now call

Croquet and tennis were never considerations for Carl until he built facilities for others on the Beach. (2)

and reassemble the car-but it isn't so much of a job for the factory to do this work before it is assembled. Personally I think that the manufacturer who pays a little more attention to the spring equipment will reap some benefit, as the majority of coupes ride hard, especially after the springs get rusty.

If you have never tried this out on your own I would like to have you do it and you will see what a wonderful difference it makes, to take down your front and rear springs, therely (sic) polish them, then reassemble with graphite and wrapped with tape-you will find a velvety sensation in the riding of the car that is entirely absent without this treatment.

If not too much trouble, would like to have the springs on these two coupes polished before they leave the factory. We have altogether here and at Miami, six Reo Coupes, and I am going to get new ones as these are getting pretty old.

Yours very truly," (23)

Carl Fisher

Carl had previously written to Olds granting him free passes and seating to the Indianapolis 500 and included a paragraph outlining, "We are making a new three million yard fill at Miami Beach and building several more islands. I hope you will be able to come down and look the place over." (24)

Consequently, although Carl was used to dealing with noted names in industry, his coup of attracting the President of the United States to Miami Beach has to be one of the highlights of his life. He had prior correspondence with W.C. (Billy) Durant, President of General Motors first thanking him for his $100,000 donation to the Lincoln Highway project, and later notifying him that a representative would be dropping off some brochures about Miami Beach. In one letter Carl noted: "We have at Miami Beach every season several hundred of the kind of men you like to know,

assembly line techniques but circumstances proved the son would leave the company and start another using his initials R.E.O. as its brand name. Fisher evidently liked the vehicle but had his own ideas for improvement. He wrote to Olds:

"Dear Mr. Olds:

I would appreciate it very much if you would interest yourself in a couple of Reo Coupes that are coming thru for me at the Factory some time in the next month.

About five years ago you made up a Reo Coupe for

Mrs. Fisher and I explained to you at the time that I would appreciate it very much if you would have the springs polished before the job was assembled as it made a much easier job. This order was put thru the factory and this particular Coupe is the easiest riding Coupe we have ever had in this district. I think a big part of the success of the riding qualities of this car was due to the fact that the springs were thoroughly polished and they were just a little bit lighter than the usual equipment

After receiving the Coupe here, it is quite a big job to tear it down, take the springs off, polish them

President-Elect Harding gave the Fisher properties a publicity boost when the developer convinced him to relax on the Beach for a few days. [2]

who have been everywhere in the world and who can afford to live any place or spend their vacations in any spot on earth-and they unhesitatingly say that there is no place in existence that equals Miami for all-round Winter amusement." [25]

By the time Carl's Flamingo Hotel opened in January of 1921 the law of the land said making a bottle of Scotch available to, of all people, the President-elect of the United States, was forbidden. A year previously on January 16, 1920 the 18th

Amendment to the Constitution had been passed over the veto of President Woodrow Wilson. The Volsted Act that prohibited the sale of alcoholic beverages was passed and would be in effect until December 5, 1933. In-between times neither Miami Beach, nor virtually any other city in the United States would be bereft of alcoholic beverage. Carl and his cohorts would not allow something like a little federal law inhibit the party atmosphere that was part and parcel of Miami Beach, Florida.

Continuing his correspondence with captains of industry we note many were of a like mind. A letter from his good friend Albert Champion from the A.C. Spark Plug Company, (Champion had sold the rights to his name but was back in business with General Motors using his initials for his spark plugs) said:

"My Dear Carl:
Regarding the beer you wanted, I was in Detroit yesterday and got into that proposition. The following

Taking a client for a cruise set the stage for selling property.[2]

Boy" and "Humdinger" at $5,000. The facility would ultimately be joined by other Fisher hotels named The Boulevard, The Nautilus and The King Cole.[27] America was about to discover Florida and create one of the nation's greatest land booms. Carl had prepared well and his fortunes would skyrocket, but personal tragedy would accompany as well.

is what may be done.

Arrangement can be made to ship a carload of 500 cases which would be packed in vinegar barrels at $8 a case. They will guarantee to deliver to any siding that you name. That would come from Canada, go right through Buffalo, and they are all set along the line.

The other proposition which costs more per case would be a truck load of 100 cases that would be delivered to your place at approximately between $12 and $13 per case.

Of course with the latter proposition you would not have to worry about handling anything from the siding to wherever you want the beer. Let me know whatever you decide. You can wire me simply stating "Ship a carload or truck load." and I will see that the

matter is taken care of. It would take about three days for a truck, and somebody should be on the job when it arrives. I will try to be posted when they start so I can advise you.

With very best regards to you and Margaret,
I am, Sincerely,
A. Champion[26]

Although supposedly bereft of alcohol, Carl and The Flamingo were ready to meet the decade of The Roaring Twenties. A cost sheet uncovered in his Florida files shows his letter to the McLanahan architectural firm seeking a facility that would cost right at a million dollars was far off the mark. The grand total for The Flamingo was $1,731,652 which included over $4,000 for his beloved gondolas and two other boats "Sunny

It was a long way from selling magazines on the railroad to having his hair cut on a warm veranda and Carl appears to be enjoying every moment.[2]

Chapter 8
Dreams & Nightmares

"An elephant? Someone sent me an elephant? What am I going to do with it?
Wait a minute....she will get us a million dollars in publicity."

Carl Fisher's prior performance record has shown us he is one who tries to wring every ounce of goodness out of an idea. He can see what he believes to be, and can convince you, the natural conclusion of things. He learned early on the adage that nothing happens until something is sold.

In correspondence with W.W. Atterbury, President of The Pennsylvania Railroad we are given a first-hand example of Fisher's adolescent determination as he wrote:

"I started quite early with the Pennsylvania. I was news butcher on the Pennsylvania railroad when I was 15 years old, running out of Indianapolis to Chicago to Vincennes and to Louisville and to Pittsburgh for the Union News Company and I am going to tell you how I had to put it over the Pennsylvania in order to stay on the road.

"In those days we had books that had more or less nude pictures in them that we sold to the farmers and someone in authority issued an order that we should not sell those books on the trains. I was fired by the Union News company office in Louisville division, under my own name. I was the best salesman out of the Union News Company office at that time and the manager was compelled to turn in so much money every day or he would lose his job, so I went out two hours after I had been fired from the Louisville Division, on the Vincennes division under my name backwards using my middle name, Graham. They caught me after a time on the Pittsburgh Division and I was fired again from the Pittsburgh end but hired again under the name Graham Carl for the Chicago Division the first week so I went to Cincinnati and worked......" etc* [1]

Fisher's determination coupled with his inherent natural sales ability proved to be hallmarks that would be displayed throughout his lifetime. While he considered himself to be the master of his own fate he never would achieve the harmonious relationship he hoped for between his parents. His continuing

Right: Wearing a familiar floppy hat, Carl stands next to the score board of one of his popular polo matches. He is accompanied by one of his canine best friends. [2]

Below: Carl and his father Albert pose in this photo that had to be taken not too long before the elder's death. The elder Fisher was an alcohol oriented man who was never able to provide the stability and the encouragement Carl craved throughout his life. [2]

correspondence with his mother and father validates his sincere interest. Here is an excerpt from a 1919 letter to his mother.

"Dear Mother:

I had Van make out a lease to you, during your lifetime of the new house which has just been finished. We had it painted a light yellow and it is a beauty. It is light and airy, has a big living room and the prettiest fireplace you ever saw. It has a fine yard and Tashiro (one of Fisher's Japanese gardeners) is putting all sorts of flowers around the place. We are going to have Bougainvillea over the gate and up the side of the porch. It is an old fashioned English house, and I am sending you a booklet with a marked picture of it and the plans. It has a dandy garage and two automobiles and a laundry. It has a big, light airy bathroom; and a side porch that you can sit on. I think we will put yellow awnings on it and finish it in light wicker.

Now all you have to do is pick out who you are going to have live with you next Winter." [2]

Letters to his father lacked the loving tone found in writings to his mother as evidenced by the following.

"Dear Father:

On June 2nd, 1917 I gave you $600.00 for a Ford, which you decided not to purchase. You advised me that this money was in the bank

I am willing to give you annually, sufficient funds for you to live on without booze-but I have to know that the money I give to you is properly used.

Regarding the Florida land I have decided that I am not going to bother with it. I already have enough troubles without having a farmer on my hands in northern Florida who is more or less green with the conditions there.

In your letter of the 20th you state that you are making expenses. Am I to presume by this statement that the $600 I advanced you on June 2nd, just a year ago, has been expended?

Let me hear from you.
Yours very truly, " [3]

Carl must have been lobbying for his parents to re-unite and the couple did get back together again for a time in 1919 but Jane tells us Carl's father "drifted away" from the relationship and "Carl never mentioned him again." [4]

The single greatest thrill and ultimately disappointment of Carl's life arrived on October 13, 1921 when after a grueling four days of labor and a Caesarian operation, Carl, Jr. was born. Jane and Carl's friends noted the baby was definitely a chip off the old block.

Carl was beside himself for the grief he saw Jane endure and said, "Never again, Jane honey. I'll never let you go through this again." [5] Jane notes she and Carl were happier than ever before during 1921 as she recounts the time she spent hand-making clothes for their long-awaited child to appear. She speaks lovingly of the nursery she created at their Indianapolis Home, Blossom Heath. Jane perceived she herself at least accepted the agony of the childbearing and eventual loss, but it became part and parcel of Carl's existence.

Their child lived 26 days and went cold in Jane's arms. A home nurse tried to reassure the new mother that little babies get cold quickly but an emergency operation failed to save the child. Jane said, "It was pyloric stenosis-our baby had literally starved to death and we had not known." [6] There had been an obstruction at the base of the infant's stomach and he starved to death.

Jane lamented Carl, Jr.'s dying signaled the real ending to their marriage and they would never be complete again. Carl did not want his lady to go thru childbirth and backed away from the "customary caresses and kept him from my room at The Shadows" [7] The couple had been married for 13 years when their son was born.

They left their Indianapolis home forever. They would never again live in Blossom Heath and in 1928 it became the Boys Preparatory School of Indianapolis. The facility is 4,380 square feet and was renamed the Park School for Boys in 1949 and has since been blended into the Marian University complex. [8]

Carl's father died in June of 1921 which must have added to Carl's emotional woes as he had also lost his good friend Frank Wheeler in May of the same year. Wheeler had been plagued by advanced diabetes and gangrene in one of his feet. He committed suicide by shooting himself with a shotgun. [9]

Carl's younger brothers had also passed from this vale as Earle fell victim to diabetes in 1910 at age 34 and Rollo was a cancer victim in 1912 when he was 32. [10]

Adding to Carl's stress in 1921 was a severe economic downturn that saw Fisher strapped for cash. He sold his auto dealership interests in Indianapolis and was forced to borrow money.

Fisher was forced to cancel plans for a new hotel due to his financial status but had enough other business interests to keep him occupied. He had a long, arduous circumstance concerning the Dixie Highway project which had been dragging on for years. The highway linked ten states and the miasma of political intervention frustrated the even-tempered Michael M. Allison, president of the association, who said in part in a letter to Fisher:

"Dear Carl:

I am straddling the fence with conflicting emotions. I do not know whether to give up in disgust, and wash my hands of the whole damn business, or try to put on an educational campaign of two years, and try to elect representatives in the Legislature who have some sense and are substantially honest, and a governor of like proportions." [11]

Fisher's correspondence on the Dixie Highway project runs to several thousand words and it is easy to understand his frustration as continuing squabbles from the various agencies introduced him to the bureaucracy of road building.

"But I'm dammed if I am going to give up five thousand dollars to a bunch of people who won't help themselves," [12] Fisher wrote to Allison regarding the inhabitants of Tennessee with whom he was particularly annoyed.

At one point Fisher planned to give the Dixie

Highway Association one third of his wealth but changed his mind and in another letter to Allison promised to provide $2,500 annually for ten years if Miami Beach prospered. Overall, the idea of the north-south roads proved to be one that drew its own natural conclusion, the building of the roads themselves. The project was finally completed in the late 1920's, yet another monumental task Fisher saw as reality a long time before it was done.

Fisher must have felt significant frustration over his financial problems in 1921 to have divested himself of his automobile sales and repair interests as these were the original flagships of his career. Nevertheless, the next few years would see his fortunes skyrocket with a real estate boom in Florida, the type of which the nation, and probably the world, had never seen before.

We have not been able to locate an appropriate photograph of the illuminated sign that was erected in 1922 for winter-time display on the corner of New York's Fifth Avenue and Forty-Second Street that bantered "It's Always June In Miami Beach".[13]

Fisher had already proven he was not one to sit around and wait for business to come to him, he had to put forth a concentrated effort to draw people to his beloved beach. He decided to sell sun and fun. After Jane's wholesale remodeling of the current bathing suit of the day, Fisher decided that pretty girls brought pretty attentive smiles, from potential beachcombers. Miami Beach, Florida would become known as the place to see bathing beauties. The frost hardened public would have to be envious of seeing a leggy lass feeling the sand twixt her toes, while a driveway full of snow beckoned.

Everett Sewell (known as Ev), Miami's head of the Chamber of Commerce, and ultimately a public foe of Fisher's, was responsible for staging the first bathing beauty parade and contest in 1920.[14] Fisher,

along with one Steve Hannagan (a fellow enthusiastic Hoosier who served an apprenticeship on two Indiana dailies which led him to become publicity man at the Indianapolis Motor Speedway, and then to Carl's Miami Beach operation)[15] launched a publicity campaign centered around beauties and Miami Beach.

Hannagan would remain a staple in the Fisher organization for many years to come and he is generally credited with being a creative and effective force in his field. It was Hannagan who made sure the dateline said "Miami Beach" when it was reported that Fisher friend Julius Fleischmann, the yeast magnate got off his horse at a polo match and died of a heart attack. Nevertheless, the beauty and the beach idea didn't produce considerable results and Fisher himself realized he had made a mistake. He told a reporter: "I was on the wrong track. I had been trying to reach the dead ones. I had been going after the old folks. I saw that what I needed to do was go after the live wires. And the live wires don't want to rest." [16]

Fisher had literally one-upped the city of Miami when he lured President Harding to stay at Miami Beach and Carl did make a serious attempt to soothe any ill feelings. He offered to pool advertising resources with Miami and initially wanted his New York City sign to read, "It Is June In Miami and Miami Beach". [17] The offer was rejected.

As though the spirit were on his side willing to assist him in publicizing his development, Carl was presented with a perfect object to do so. One Ed Ballard, a Fisher friend who once had an interest in the Ringling Brothers Circus sent Carl a baby elephant named Carl II. Fisher was elated at the gift and wrote:

"I never saw so many possibilities for advertising and I am certain I am going to get a million dollars worth of publicity out of this elephant. One of the

Preceeding page and right: Carl gained an immense amount of publicity from the two elephants, Carl, Jr. and Rosie he maintained as shown by these photos depicting their activities from posing as a golf tee, to hauling concrete block, and acting as photographer for a bevy of beach beauties. (2)

One of Carl's elephants gleefully toting area kids on a cart. (2)

and spooked by the surroundings "eased her anxieties with a long loud-defecation that drove customers helter-skelter from the bank. It was, say all the old-timers, the biggest deposit that Miami Beach First National ever had." (20)

Rosie's legend was cemented when she was standing next to a parked trolley that had its windows open and began snooting her way into passenger seats looking for food. She startled an inebriated soul who awoke and screamed, "Snakes! Snakes!" and jumped from the car, breaking his ankle. The incident cost Fisher $5,000 to settle.(21) Fisher didn't need more trolley expenses as he had invested heavily in building the Miami Beach line to aid land sales, but the venture lost money as did his foray into supplying electric power for the city.

The Florida Fisher files contain several letters from Carl to his friend Jack LaGorce concerning the elephant and the problems Carl went through in order to obtain U.S entry papers for a trainer. The man was ultimately brought to Florida but the elephant had already bonded with one Aaron Yarnell, a gardener who had success with Carl's first elephant, and rejected the specialist Carl had worked so diligently to obtain.

Fisher was ready for the real estate boom of the 1920's judging by the upscale salesroom he built in downtown Miami. It contained Spanish -style décor complete with a 6' x 35' mural of Miami Beach. Resident author Polly Redford tells us the sales office lasted only two seasons: "After that, it was no longer necessary: there were more customers than lots."(22)

The years 1922-25 proved beyond doubt believers in Miami Beach, (and one could say all of Florida) were right all along. Florida was the undiscovered heaven of the United States and multitudes would head south to create a land boom of monumental proportion.

particular things we are going to do with him is to make him tamp down the polo fields between games, also carry trees, haul ice and work in the garden. I have sent to India for a special Mahut, red cap, brass collar, camel smell and all. We are going to teach him to swim in the sea and pull gondolas, etc. " (18)

Carl received another elephant, "Rosie" in 1923 and was ecstatic about her as he wrote:

"She is kind and gentle as a Newfoundland dog. She hauls her own food in a cart. She gives herself a bath from a hose, and she can do the Black Bottom better than most Harlemite entertainers. She has been photographed in possibly millions of films; rotogravure pictures by the thousands of feet have been run by all the newspapers in the country." (19)

Author Howard Kleinberg commented the publicity Rosie brought to Miami Beach for about a decade was invaluable.

The inevitable added to Rosie's legend when she was led into the Miami Beach First National Bank holding a passbook in her trunk to make a deposit,

Although Fisher changed his tactics and honed in on sports as Miami Beach's most desirable attraction, other developers succeeded by delivering everything from planned communities to swamp land. The Florida land boom attracted the riverboat gambler personalities as well as the respected celebrities.

By 1928 land sales and concurrent money flow had slowed. As a promotional tool Fisher hatched a plan to name each of the eighteen holes of the LaGorce Golf Course (named for his close pal, John LaGorce) after a celebrity who had visited Miami Beach.

The honorees are a who's who of the day and while author Polly Redford (*Billion Dollar Sandbar*) has already printed the list it is worth repeating:

1. Gene Tunney-world heavyweight boxing champion, soon to retire, marry an heiress, and disappear forever into High Society.
2. Grantland Rice-dean of American sportswriters
3. Harvey Firestone-President, Firestone Tire & Rubber Company, whose estate later became the Fountainbleau Hotel
4. Tommy Meighan-Paramount Studios, Hollywood, California
5. William Kissam Vanderbilt-"Willie" one of the few Vanderbilts to grace Miami Beach, was an auto racer, amateur explorer, big game fisherman, and holder of a merchant marine Master's Ticket (all oceans, unlimited tonnage).
6. Tex Rickard-fight promoter and owner of Madison Square Garden.
7. Edgar A. Guest-newspaper and greeting card poet made forever famous by Dorothy Parker's critique, "I'd rather flunk my Wasserman Test than read the poems of Eddie Guest." (Note: A test for detection of syphilitic infection)
8. Will Rogers-cowboy, vaudeville comedian, movie star, and syndicated columnist, generally loved by American audiences.
9. Reinald Werrenrath-popular concert baritone, a long time friend and drinking companion of Carl's.
10. Gar Wood-millionaire inventor and speedboat champion.
11. Eddie Rickenbacker-race car driver, World War I flying ace, owner of Indianapolis Motor Speedway, later president of Eastern Air Lines.
12. Ring Lardner-sports writer, raconteur, short-story artist whose baseball stories captured the American vernacular as no others have ever done, before or since.
13. Walter Trumbull-sportswriter for the *New York Evening Post*
14. John Golden-Broadway playwright and producer of many hits; Seventh Heaven, Susan and God, Skylark.
15. Glenn Curtiss-aircraft pioneer, owner of large tracts of land north of Miami.
16. Arthur Brisbane-leading news columnist of the day, and a great booster of Carl's Montauk development. His articles appeared daily on the front page of the New York Evening Journal.
17. George Ade-Indiana humorist, author of *Fables in Slang*.
18. Arthur Champion-developer of Champion Spark Plugs and a great friend of Carl's, his was the only posthumous name at LaGorce. He had died the summer before on a trip to Europe.

The highly respected Aladdin construction firm took advantage of the Florida construction boom of the Twenties and invited the public to view their construction techniques in person. Aladdin had previously accomplished massive building efforts during WW I to aid American troops. [2]

Carl Fisher's Miami Beach had risen from swampland and dubious head-shaking critics to become one of America's most famed cities. Fisher found himself once again attracting the right people to carry out his visions. When he looked at the tan sand he must have continually seen green surrounded by an eruption of color in every form imaginable. The landscaping of Miami Beach became the dress that would be husbanded by its proud population. Growing natural beauty in lawns, gardens, flowers and trees gave even the depressed a wink of beauty. Soon, any viewer of Miami Beach, either in person or looking at photographs came to expect a mushrooming of colors and green tranquility that said, "We grow beauty here."

William Kissam Vanderbilt, known as Willie, the auto racing oriented multi-millionaire who was heir to the New York Central Railroad and a close Fisher associate. A very accomplished mariner, he traded one of his yachts to Carl for Fisher Island, another creation of Carl's that added to the glamor of Miami Beach.[2]

The previously mentioned gardners Kotano Suto and Shige Tashiro were joined by Fred Hoger an Indianapolis employee of Fisher's who would become the landscape engineer charged with designing and nurturing the cornucopia of plant life. Fisher's idea was seemingly to create a botanical garden that masqueraded as a city and continually give its occupants the feeling that attention to detail was paramount. [23]

Carl's personality forced him to follow the adage of "if it's almost right, it's wrong," and propelled him to keep spending as profits began pouring in. His Alton Beach Realty Company recorded $1,966,000 in sales during 1920, yet as noted, Carl himself had to scramble to make ends meet. His new luxury hotel, The Flamingo, proved Fisher was a man who definitely put his own money into his dream and the hotel was an immediate success.

He subsequently attracted the upper class (whom author Polly Redford has accurately called the "gasoline aristocracy") to build in Miami Beach including old friend Frank Seiberling, President of Goodyear Tire & Rubber and his rival Harvey Firestone, Alfred J. DuPont, Gar Wood, Albert Champion, Harry Stutz (Indianapolis manufacturer of the famed Stutz Bearcat automobile mentioned previously) Roy Chapin of Hudson Motors and C.F. "Boss" Kettering, the man who perfected electric starters for automobiles and who went on to an illustrious career with General Motors. Boss Ket and Fisher became life-long friends as Carl continued his interest in things mechanical and later invested heavily, with Kettering, in the development of diesel engines. The Sloan-Kettering Foundation familiar to Americans today is the result of Kettering's labors as well as those of another famed General Motors executive, Al Sloan.

Department store magnate J.C. (Cash) Penny built a home as did his rival Kresge along with Colonel Stanley Rockwell. Rockwell's name is still known to metallurgists today as being the founder of the Rockwell Hardness test, a process that allows rapid non-destructive determination of the hardness of heat-treated steel by measuring depth of a diamond-tipped probe.

Fellow racing enthusiast Willie Vanderbilt (whom we read of earlier as being founder of the Vanderbilt

Cup) races constructed an estate.

George S. Parker of Parker Pens became a resident. He gained fame and phenomenal fortune after receiving a patent in 1894 for his "Lucky Curve" ink feed which was claimed to draw excess ink back into the body of the pen when not in use. He later developed "Quink" a quick drying ink that did not require blotting. Between 1920 and 1960 Parker Pens were either the number one or two best sellers in the world.

Another home builder was tobacco man R.J. Reynolds, whose firm could lay claim to supplying America with twenty-five percent of its chewing

Photo on preceeding page and above: Fisher's Nautilus Hotel project added more credibility to his vision of creating islands in the sun where the public would become enamored with the Miami Beach lifestyle. So important were the leisure activities of playing with balls that Carl had statues erected paying homage to sports. [2]

tobacco. He also supplied the nation's most popular cigarette and pipe brands, (Camel and Prince Albert).

W.L. McKnight of 3M (Scotch tape) built a mansion and shared Carl's love of luxurious, fast boats.

Lindsey Hopkins, whose Coca-Cola interests were monumental also became a resident. Your reporter knew Hopkins well as this Southern Gentleman maintained his interest in automobile racing for decades and became a car owner at the Indianapolis Motor Speedway long after Fisher sold it. Hopkins

told me Fisher was "one of a kind, a man dedicated to his own ideas."

Possibly because Fisher had not been a land developer previously, (or maybe it was the promoter spirit in him), he took the extraordinary act of buying a full page newspaper ad to inform the buying public that Fisher property would increase in price ten percent annually. It was a daring strategy he enacted in 1919 when land sales were slow. The ad read in part: "If you wish to purchase property from us this season you may do so knowing the price will

be advanced next year at least ten percent over the season. We try to give our customers an investment in a home site or business site that substantially and steadily grows in value." [24]

Carl considered the money he generated to be a tool to use for building more, to enhance the community. By 1923 he commissioned the 189 room Nautilus Hotel, then the King Cole a year later and The Boulevard in 1925 when the Florida boom was in full swing. By 1925 there were 56 hotels and 4,000 rooms available in Miami Beach. He had constructed the Beach's first hotel, the Lincoln, a small 35 room facility just before America entered the first World War.[25] Carl's fortune by 1925 was far in excess of the millions he and partner Jim Allison had extracted from the Union Carbide Co. after selling their Prest-O-Lite firm. Figures of his net worth from fifty to a hundred million dollars have been bandied about.

Fisher's name became known throughout the nation. One of the most popular humorists of the day, Will Rogers, wrote one of his widely-read weekly columns about Carl.

"America has about a hundred and ten million people. Now out of all this herd there are about 99 9/10 percent of us that just drag along and what we do or say don't have much effect on any of the rest of the mob. But, scattered among these 1/10 percent, every once in a while you run into some odd individual, some queer Bird, that is out of the natural beaten path of human beings. We all go up the main road, while they take the trails.

I fell afoul of just such a duck. Henry Ford? No. He is not the one I am talking about.

But this other one that I want to tell you about has, next to Mr. Ford, been responsible for causing more dissatisfaction and unrest among contented people than anybody I know of. He is Carl G. Fisher, the man who took Miami away from the alligators and turned it over to the Indianians.

Had there been no Carl Fisher, Florida would be known today as just the turpentine state...he rehearsed the mosquitoes till they wouldn't bite you until after you bought.

He was the first man smart enough to discover that there was sand under the water. So he put in a kind of a dredge, "all day Sucker" arrangement, and he brought the sand up and let the water go to the bottom instead of the top. Up to then, sand had been used to build with, but never upon.

Carl discovered that sand would hold up a Real Estate sign and that was all he wanted it for. Carl rowed the customers out in the ocean and let them pick out some nice smooth water where they would like to build, and then he would replace the water with an island, and you would be a little Robinson Crusoe of your own. And today the dredge is the national emblem of Florida.

A generation of Americans knew the comedic Will Rogers as an engaging writer/entertainer who was remembered for his oft-repeated phrase of, "I never met a man I didn't like." Rogers was a frequent Beach visitor and house-guest of Fisher's.[2]

This guy has done more unique things, even before he ever heard of Florida, than any man I ever met, and I met Al Smith, Al Jennings, Calvin Coolidge, Rudolph Valentino, Senator Borah, Ben Turpin and the Prince of Wales." [26]

For decades Will Rogers name was known to Americans for his statement of, "I never met a man I didn't like." Rogers was a down-home country gentleman whose (successful) mission it was to make people smile. As we write this tome three quarters of a century later I think it is reasonable to say Will Rogers was at least as popular as our talk show hosts Johnny Carson (deceased), David Letterman, Jay Leno and as respected as much as icon Andy Rooney, known to mix humor into his serious journalistic endeavors, on the popular 60 Minutes television show.

While Fisher was building Miami Beach others were not deaf to the sound of land titles being exchanged and South Florida became a developer's dream. George Merrick created the still phenomenal Coral Gables community on the Miami side of Biscayne Bay and Addison Mizner was the guiding light responsible for the upscale Boca Raton development. A successful real estate developer by the name of J. Perry Stoltz built a structure that made Carl's eyes shine with pride when the Fleetwood Hotel was built during 1924-25. N.B.T. Roney put two million dollars into the Roney plaza located at Collins Avenue and 3rd Street. It opened just in time for the opposite end of the land boom in all of Florida.

We came across an illustrated sheet in the Florida Fisher files detailing Miami Beach's growth from 1921-1928 and present it here to depict the transformation: [27]

The positive and humorous adjectives used to describe the U.S.A. in what has become known as The Roaring Twenties give us a picture of the

	1920	1928
Population	650	Over 10,000
Assessed Valuation	$5,540,112	$44,087,050
Bank Deposits	$336,703	$4,224,617
Public School Enrollment	157	1,850
Postal Receipts	No record	$60,580
Number of telephones	551	5,371
Number of Electric Meters	300	4,413
Gals Water Consumed	30 Million	706 Million
Hard Surface Streets	30 Miles	90 Miles
Miles of Concrete Sidewalks	15 Miles	86 Miles
Number of Hotels	5	61
Number of Apartment Houses	9	196
Public Library Circulation	None	39,610

boundless enthusiasm Americans had for every facet of life. It had to be one of those ages where the collective spirit of the population commanded we see and experience both the highs and lows of all our social endeavors. America had left behind the stodgy Victorian era of the late 1800's and proved we could arm ourselves with enough home grown ammunition to make us a powerhouse of the world. We were bringing ourselves up to sky level in sleek airplanes while gliding over the landscape in ever increasingly reliable transportation, and of course doing it faster. By the time the 1920's arrived the corsets and puffed sleeves your mother wore were history.

While Jane Fisher raised her hemline on the beach, her sisters did the same on Main Street U.S.A. as daring young ladies became known as "flappers" who performed on a dance floor and any other floor such as we had never seen before. They wore short skirts and short cropped hairstyle called a "bob" which meant hair was cut off straight from the shoulder up. The cut was used for convenience and sanitation by those highly functional women who served in World War I . The 1920's flapper ladies made the bob the in-style do of the day. Then again, paintings of Roman ladies of the second

century show they too preferred the bob, presumably modeled on their leader's own preference.

The flippant attitude of the flapper resulted in a dance craze that swept not only the nation, but the world. First introduced by famed dance producer Florenz Ziegfeld (featuring a cast of Afro-Americans) in 1923 during a musical named "Running Wild" the Charleston dance was introduced.

The participants performed outward heel kicks combined with an up and down movement achieved by bending and straightening the knees in time to the music." [28] The Black Bottom dance seen in a 1926 Broadway production is said to have become popular the world over. We recall Fisher's letter where he described his elephant as being able to do the Black Bottom dance.

While the flappers X'd their hands and knees in a stationary wobble, the up and coming young man might well have been seen in a raccoon coat, bell-bottomed trousers and strumming a ukelele. If so, he was anointed as being a "shiek". As F. Scott Fitzgerald's valuable *"The Great Gatsby"* tells us, our shiek probably drove a brightly colored roadster. They didn't call them convertibles back then.

We recall one of Henry Ford's most enduring statements was, "You can have any color you want as long as it is black," in referring to the paint selection available for his Model "T" Ford. Henry did go on to sell 15 million "T's" from 1908-1927, but the old girl brought him to his knees. Son Edsel had long tried to convince his puritanical old man the car was out-dated and nearly bankrupted the firm. Then, the largest attended, most anticipated, successful introduction of an automobile in history took place when, guided by Edsel, Ford went back to its roots and introduced the Model "A" in 1928. Never before or since has the introduction of an automobile caused such commotion as throngs paced Ford showrooms world-wide.

Consequently our shiek could have been picking up his flapper in a brightly colored Model "A" roadster on their way to dancing the Charleston and the Black Bottom. The excitement generated by Ford's latest had been mirrored in Florida for the prior few years creating the explosion of land sales.

The unprecedented prosperity America experienced in the 1920's fed an economy destined on self-destruction as we later learned from the legendary stock market crash of 1929.

Florida land was being sold and re-sold for so much profit a virtual frenzy was created for ownership. Spread of the word is necessary to create a collective thought and without television we still relied heavily on the printed word. We were dedicated readers of *"The Saturday Evening Post"* the famed publication founded by Benjamin Franklin. One journalist for the storied publication is credited with fueling the Florida boom more than any other. Kenneth Lewis Roberts was a historical novelist who penned eleven articles for the "*Post*" between 1922 and 1926.

"Roberts, better than any of his contemporaries, sold twentieth-century Americans on the belief that no matter what their profession, assets or status in life, Florida was for them." [29]

Just prior to the land sale boom that began in 1922 Jane was making a heroic attempt to save her marriage and entered into adoption proceedings with one Mazie Rattay of Indianapolis. [30] Mazie had a three-year old son and a precise account of why she wanted to relieve herself of the child does not exist. Carl wrote to her and stated he and Jane would take the child on a 30-60 day trial basis and Carl said, "if I decide to keep the little boy then you and I can talk about some arrangements to pay your way out west." [31]

At the end of the negotiations it was Jane's name and not both that appeared on the adoption papers. Carl initially consented his half of the adoption but changed his mind and said, "After talking the matter over, we thought best to let this adoption go through as it is by Jane, for a year or so; after that time, if no complications arise, we can change it to a mutual adoption." [32]

Fisher paid Mazie five-hundred dollars annually for son Jackie, and also corresponded with the boy's birth-mother for a time thereafter, advising her on a

Jane Fisher did her best to replace the son she and Carl had lost soon after birth by adopting a youngster and this photo seemingly depicts a contented couple. Nevertheless, Carl did not bond with the lad and began his downward spiral into the world of alcohol. [2]

minor real estate transaction. [33] Fisher was not able to bond with the boy as Jane had hoped. Since the death of their own son, Carl had been consuming more alcohol and strayed to other bedrooms. Jane knew of Carl's infidelities [34] and the couple agreed to a separation agreement in November of 1924 [35].

Carl and Jane's parting was as harmonious as may ever be imagined. Carl would continue his financial and emotional support for his Jane for the rest of his life.

Carl's success at the time of his divorce was considerable, and growing. He had opened his Nautilus Hotel in January of 1924, sold $6,000,000 in land sales the previous year, then took in $8,000,000 in '24 and rode the wave of 1925 dollars that saw $23,419,782 roll into the Carl Fisher container. [36]

It was believed Carl Fisher was so strong financially, it would take a hurricane force to make him wobble.

Chapter 9
The Tide Changes

"I'm going to build another race track."

The decade between 1920-1930 was pivotal in Carl Fisher's career as his fortune, like many others of the era soared gloriously and ultimately went into a tailspin. Fisher watched his seemingly insane investment in Miami Beach paying off financially and therefore socially as the influx of money and the people who brought it transformed the new city into a place of unequaled desirability.

Fisher and partners were still the proprietors of the most famous automobile race in the world, the Indianapolis 500. The Indianapolis Motor Speedway (IMS) was being ably run by T.E. "Pop" Myers and a small staff as the over 500 plus acre facility ran only one event per year, so Fisher did not have to concern himself with day-to-day operation.

As noted, the "500" had been canceled for the war years of 1917-18, was reduced to a 300 miler for 1916 and had returned to normalcy by 1919. [1]

Post-war activity at IMS was encouraged by Carl's acquiescence to adopt the new International

Formula for grand prix cars limiting displacement to 183 cubic inches.

"We must go along with the French if we expect to keep the Indianapolis race on an international basis" Fisher said.[2]

The race itself had changed dramatically since its inaugural in 1911. Custom built racing machinery replaced passenger car manufacturers and the latter had no reason to financially support the event. Subsequently, a Lap Prize Fund was instituted at the urging of George M. Dickinson of the Indianapolis based National Motor Car Company that would add an additional $20,000 to the $50,000 purse. The leader of each of the race's 200 laps would receive $100. Then Delco offered to actually match the Speedway's prize fund if every starter in the race utilized their ignition systems, but the plan was vetoed by Carl who said:

"Everyone connected with racing is happy to have such strong support. But as long as I have a voice in the matter, the Speedway will never permit one company to offer cash inducements for the use of its products which other companies in the same field may not be able to meet. The Speedway is the best proving ground for the automotive industry, and it must be kept open to everyone with a new product or new idea." [3]

Although in 1920 the event did pay $93,550 in total purse, Fisher was looking for ways to increase revenue and wrote a detailed one-page letter to partner Jim Allison .

We present the letter to our readership here to not only show Carl's penchant for patience in recouping an investment, but the next to the last sentence is surprising to those who believed Carl wanted to preserve his creation at any cost. He was seemingly ready to cut the track up into a subdivision.

"Dear Jim:

I have been thinking a lot lately of the Speedway possibilities for the year after next and they don't look at all bright, unless we decide to do something. If we decide to spend as much as five or seven thousand dollars in foliage, we won't have very much showing next season.

I have thought considerable about the possibilities of a fine golf club together with a club house and a swimming pool. I believe that swimming pools could be made to pay handsomely for ten days in May, twenty days in June and sixty days in July and August, and ten days in September. In other words, if we make a big golf course, play grounds, swimming pools and polo fields out of the Speedway, it will be, at least, a very good looking plant to inspect for next year and the following year.

We can get a barrel of publicity on the fact that we decide to make this change and I believe that thousands of people who have not been to the Speedway for two years will come to see the races and incidentally to see the Speedway decked up in its new garb.

It is going to take two years to work up polo to a point where we can enter some big games that will pay but if the Speedway has a golf course and is made the center of athletic diversions, I believe that it might carry allong (sic) its overhead with some small profit and be interesting enough to inspect, and in the next two years pay for the improvements I refer to.

The swimming pools and bath house would cost $40,000-$50,000. We could build a good golf course with our present layout, costing $30,000 to $35,000. We might make a large club of the place at a membership of $30.00 a year and have the golf members pay extra for whatever they get except

polo. The golf course at Miami Beach makes about $20,000 per year, net.

We may get through all right next year, but we must do something and do it economically. The time to start is now. I think we could get enough publicity to draw at least ten thousand people next year and the following year who would not otherwise attend.

It will be probably four or five years before it will pay us to cut up the Speedway.

Program Cover for the track's only race. [16]

Construction of a board speedway was accomplished in only a few weeks time. [15]

Racing Car (and as fine a racing book that has ever been written on the subject was published under that very title by Griffith Borgeson). Pete DePaolo averaged 129.295 for the facility's only race.[5]

The Golden Age was represented by first, Fisher's own building of the Indianapolis Motor Speedway but is best remembered by historians as the era of the board tracks.

For the reader to fully understand the significance of Fisher's investment of over a million board feet of lumber it took to build one of these wooden bowls of speed, we need to digress momentarily and provide some history. The times themselves were memorable in the annals of sports history as fans of baseball, golf, tennis and horse racing can attest and the (main) era of the board speedway from 1915-1925 drew crowds that rivaled all other sports.

The Twenties are remembered for such sports greats as Babe Ruth, Lou Gehrig and the 1927 Yankees; Man O' War became the most famous horse; Jack Dempsey and Gene Tunney drew 100,000 fans to watch their boxing match in Chicago's Soldier's Field; The Four Horsemen of Notre Dame delighted football fans so much that their coach Knute Rockne had an automobile named after him; Red Grange's five touchdowns in one game made him a household name while tennis ace Bill Tilden set a lofty standard. Automobile racing on the board tracks brought capacity crowds to the sport that just a few years' prior had utilized horse racing tracks for most of the premier events. No roar of the 1920's was greater than that heard echoing off the wooden board speedways. The cloth and leather helmeted race car drivers of the era gained notoriety and respectability heretofore unknown.

The era officially began on June 26, 1915 with the opening of a race track at 9th Avenue and 12th

Think it over and I will talk to you about it the next time I see you,
Yours,"
Carl G.. Fisher [4]

One might surmise Fisher thought of utilizing the Speedway property for another purpose entirely. He had to have been keeping an eye peeled toward other successful tracks and he was fortunate enough to have lived in one of the most romantic and harrowing periods in the annals of professional automobile racing: He not only witnessed the narrow-tired, watchmaker-perfect, wheeled-instruments of the day careen around gigantic wooden saucers of a half to two miles in diameter, he built the track that held the fastest race ever held when he constructed Fulford ByThe Sea, a mile and a quarter oval, just a few miles from Miami Beach. Carl Fisher lived in the era that has been called *The Golden Age of The American*

Street in the Chicago suburb of Maywood. Only weeks before, the Indianapolis Motor Speedway had completed its fifth running of the Indianapolis "500" with fan favorite Ralph DePalma limping his Mercedes home to victory during a soggy weekend. The new Chicago Speedway Park Association literally upstaged the solid Brickyard by drawing in over 85,000 spectators to its wooden track and staged an event that saw the winner average 97.59 mph, eight miles per hour faster than DePalma had gone at Indy.[6]

As has been the case with so many other men mentioned in this book who were to have a significant effect on the times, roots of the board track racing era can be traced once again to the bicycle. John Shillington "Jack" Prince said of himself at the end of the 19th century, "I was considered to be the champion bicycle racer of the world." Prince, an Englishman was contracted to construct a wooden velodrome on the site where a few years hence Carl Fisher would attend the nation's first automobile show, Madison Square Garden. Soon Prince was building similar tracks around the country and by 1910 he and one of the most unheralded engineers in the early history of the automobile, Fred Moskovics, would construct a full size speedway that was unique in the world.

Moskovics commented, "I had made a wager with Howard Marmon (founder of the automobile of the same name) that a car could hold a speed of 100 miles an hour on a closed course. Howard was thinking in the more conventional terms of the driver having to slow down for the turns, but I had something else in mind." Moskovics laid out a circle 45 feet wide and banked at an angle of 20 degrees 25 feet above ground at its perimeter. Fisher's old bicycle and auto racing pal Barney Oldfield came as close as you can get to winning

Barney Oldfield poses with a roadster complete with Oldfield Tires in this publicity photo showing the viewer the severity of a board track's banking. [16]

A six pack of skinny-tired racers at Sheepshead Bay. [1]

the bet for Moskovics when he turned a lap at 99.39 mph around the Venice, California track named Playa Del-Rey, but the Hungarian born engineer ultimately lost his bet as no one ever exceeded that speed during the track's three year lifespan.[7]

Today we see the snake-like appearance of NASCAR cars roping their way around high banked paved super-speedways in a maneuver called "drafting". Yesteryear's dean of auto racing writers Russ Cartlin, recalls the execution of this movement most likely was discovered at another board track (in which Fisher spearheaded the initial effort and had stock in the facility) Sheepshead Bay in 1915. The slipstream created by a moving vehicle allowed a trailing driver to tuck in close behind the car ahead and literally be towed at the same speed. Staying too close resulted in an overheated engine so drivers would veer right and left to capture cool air, but straying too long would result in losing the tow. Thus, there was a rhythm of cars swaying back and forth that was ballet like in performance. Remember, the cars that raced on the boards at Sheepshead Bay and other wooden speedways did not have fenders. Touching another car's spinning wheel with one of your own could result in disaster.

When the Prince/Moskovics track at Playa Del Ray proved successful the dapper looking Prince (always photographed in bow tie and derby hat) utilized his charm to convince others to construct similar facilities. When he hooked up with civil engineer Art Pillsbury to construct the most beautiful of all board tracks in Beverly Hills, a partnership had been forged that would see the pair go on to build tracks at Culver City, San Carlos, Kansas City, Charlotte, Rockingham and Laurel.

Prince was no engineer and Pillsbury was an excellent one. Pillsbury later said, "One of the

Board Speedways were built througout the country:

Track Name	Location	Length (miles)	Years
Playa-Del-Rey	Venice, CA	1*	1910-13
Oakland	Elmhurst, CA	1/2*	1911-12
Chicago	Maywood, IL	2	1915-18
Tacoma1	Tacoma, WA	2	1915-21
Omaha	Omaha, NE	1.1/4	1915-17
Des Moines	Des Moines, IA	1	1915-17
Sheepshead Bay	Brooklyn, NY	2	1915-19
Cincinnati	Cincinnati, OH	2	1916-19
Uniontown	Uniontown, PA	1.1/8	1916-22
Beverly Hills	Beverly Hills,	1.1/8	1920-24
Fresno	Fresno, CA	1	1920-27
Cotati	Cotati, CA	1.1/4	1921-22
San Carlos	San Carlos, CA	1.1/4	1921-22
Kansas City	Kansas City, MO	1.1/4	1922-24
Altoona	Tipton, PA	1.1/4	1923-31
Charlotte	Pineville, NC	1.1/4	1924-27
Culver City	Culver City, CA	1.1/4	1924-27
Rockingham	Salem, NH	1.1/4	1925-28
Laurel	Laurel, MD	1.1/8	1925-26
Fulford	Miami, FL	1.1/4	1926
Atlantic City	Amatol, NJ	1.1/2	1926-28
Akron	Akron, OH	1/2	1926-30
Bridgeville	Bridgeville, PA	1/2	1927-30
Woodbridge	Woodbridge, NJ	1/2	1928-31

*Circular track, all others were ovals. The circular track offered the driver no let-up of constant g-forces.

notorious defects of the earlier banked ovals had been the difficulty of getting on and off the curves. The transitions were abrupt, tricky and dangerous. So I used a Searles Spiral Easement Curve. This is a formula widely used in railroad engineering whereby a train is led into a central curve through a series of small curves of ever decreasing radius. The formula includes the elevation of the outer rail to a calculated degree and the purpose of all this is to

Cars preparing for the start at Fulton. [2]

achieve a smooth ride around curves at speed." [8]

Three time Indianapolis 500 winner Louis Meyer said in his Forward to Dick Wallen's fine book, *Board Tracks, Gold, Guts & Glory*:

"It seemed to me that the boards were pretty easy to drive, and I personally don't think it required any special talent to race on them. Of course, I had to refrain from slipping and sliding on board tracks, just as I did at Indianapolis. The straighter I went, the faster I went. It was always necessary to hold the car up

Barney Oldfield, standing, was in attendance for opening of the Fulton track. [2]

Large crowds like this one seen at Culver City were normal for the board speedway races. [15]

Overhead view of the Culver City track. [15]

until the apex of the turn before I could relax. I recall no problem with neck strain because the banking and the speed kept me upright in the cockpit at about 128 mph, which was fast at the time. Obviously I had to watch myself. The wood sometimes absorbed oil, making it slippery. I remember also that if I turned left in the corners, the car had a tendency to dive, and that's the reason why several dirt track specialists lost their lives on the board tracks: they were used to over-steering in the turns." [9]

Fisher knew Prince had been building two board speedways per year since WWI with each one being just a little faster than its predecessor. The "Championship" cars as they became known were kept busy from March through November running for significant purses and by 1925 the board tracks were the expected venue. Once again Jack Prince's hand was called upon to assist in building Carl's new track Fulford-By-The-Sea near Miami. He was aided by a man we've already met, Ray Harroun. Harroun was named construction supervisor and as one of the most talented self-taught automotive engineers of the day, the position most likely didn't stir his senses. After all, Art Pillsbury had previously built entire board speedways in just a few weeks time utilizing massive numbers of nail-pounders who simply followed plans.

Bob McDonough toured the new facility that featured you-can't-walk-up-them 50 degree turns and blistered around the wooden bowl at an average speed of 142.902 mph, a new mile and a quarter speed record. He was driving a Miller entered by Fisher pal Tommy Milton. The retired Barney Oldfield served as honorary flagman for the event that saw Florida's largest ever paying crowd to date. Over 20,000, watched the 18 entrants race their finely crafted Miller and Duesenberg built

Automotive genius Harry Miller was responsible for many of the most respected race cars and engines of the 1920's so we present a few examples of his work. [13]

Fred Comer poses in his rear-drive Miller at the 1925 "500". [4]

machines. Pete DePaolo eclipsed the average for a 250 mile race by more than 20 miles per hour when he averaged 129.25 and collected $12,000 on Feb. 22, 1926, George Washington's birthday.

The race cars of the era have endured as being the most perfectly ever constructed for usage, overall appearance and functionality. Today many of the vehicles are preserved and faithful replicas have also been constructed.

Carl anticipated his new race track would open the racing season in the future. Fisher had invented the Biscayne Bay Regatta prior to the auto race that featured aptly named "Biscayne Babies" speedboats commissioned by Fisher and built by the man he could call his personal boat-builder, Ned Purdy. Ten identical eighteen-footers were supplied to Indy 500 drivers Ray Harroun, Louis Chevrolet, Tommy Milton, Harry Hartz, Pete DePaolo, L.L. Corum, Wade Morton, Jerry Wonderlich, Phil Shafer, Ira Vail and William Knipper. Chevrolet won over the popular Milton

Leon Duray in a low-slung front-wheel drive Miller, 1927. [4]

Fisher's board speedway lumber poses in its unintended position after the hurricane. [2]

Fisher's employees surveyed the Miami Beach hurricane damage to determine how much of their boss' investment had been swept away by the violent storm. Carl himself was ensconced in yet another massive development when the storm hit as he had discovered Montauk, the outer-most tip of New York's Long Island and had plans to build the "Miami Beach of The North.". When notified of the storm Carl's typical attitude was displayed once again as he said, "Hell, if it's going to cost me anything I'm sorry I didn't see the show." [15]

When his Fulford-by-the Sea speedway ran its race in 1926, Carl had just turned fifty-two years old. While his financial house was seemingly in order, his own home life had changed significantly since the death of his infant son. He could not have been in the best emotional spirit when the Miami hurricane hit. His mother had died in August of 1925; his wife said she felt deserted and had gone to Paris with her adopted son Jackie and noted in her biography:

"Sometimes there were gay jaunts to Paris, cocktails at the Ritz, shopping, theaters, the galleries. There were entertaining men in Paris ready to kiss the hand, dance and sympathize with the neglected wife of an American millionaire." [16]

who would go on to become one of Carl's closest associates. The rapid McDonough was not among the boat pilots. [10]

Fisher gave us some insight about his attitude when after a yacht club celebration a speaker praised his accomplishments and said Miami Beach had been "Fisher's dream."

Wife Jane tells us Carl muttered, "Wasn't any goddamn dream at all. I could just as easily have started a cattle ranch." [11]

Then came the fateful day some seven months after the inaugural race at Fulford when Hurricane Andrew blew into town on September 17, 1926 and turned the Miami-Fulford Speedway, and much of Miami Beach into hulking piles of scrap. The track became the shortest-lived of all that were built. It was wiped out and there was no possibility of rebuilding . The 1.5 mile track

at Atlantic City was the only large facility built after Fisher's track and by 1927 only eight races were held on the boards. In 1928 the schedule was down to half a dozen events and although ten events were held in 1929, the era was effectively over. [12]. Deterioration of the wood itself had long been a problem and there are many accounts of repairs being made while races were underway that un-nerved some of the participants as their trust in the surface had evaporated. It has been reported little flags were installed on the racing surface noting "Board Out Here" and driver Eddie Hearne believed a dead man was having his head pummeled as it bobbed up and down through a hole in the track. The problem was linked to youngsters who had found a parting of the boards and curiously popped up to look through. [13] The last board track race for Championship cars

Miami Beach had seen the old Collins wooden bridge turned into the Venetian Causeway that carried droves of speculators into the Fisher Promised Land, and Carl warned those who would listen that the profiteers landing in south Florida would ultimately cause massive problems. To recap briefly, the landscape of Miami Beach and surrounding communities had changed so drastically in such a short period speculation was running rampant. The sky-scraping buildings that had gone up not only in Miami Beach by 1925, but in George Merrick's "Master Suburb" in Coral Gables just a few miles away were being publicized as no other development had ever been in the history of the U.S. Merrick spent three million dollars in advertising in one year to lure

Considering Mr. E. A. Perry's office shingle appears to be a moving target, we surmise he may be tabbed as being one of the Binder Boys trading in Florida land. [2]

Fisher is credited with building the Community Church on Lincoln road. He continually assisted St. Patrick's church with land donations, funds and use of his yacht for nuns' recreation. [2]

customers to his dream city. His ten million dollar Coral Gables Biltmore Hotel and attendant country club glistened in the Florida sunshine and were proof positive that massive sums of money was being spent on the land near Fisher's development. [17]

However, the arrival of what has been called the Binder Boys (rhymes with cinder) threatened the economic balance in Florida. Speculators were shuffling land sales with as little as a ten percent deposit and mortgages were tacked on as the "binders" on the properties were sold time and again with each transaction bringing profit to the seller. These land options were hawked and traded in the streets, hotel lobbies and virtually

wherever seller could attract another speculative buyer. Often times lot sales were advertised to attract buyers in an auction style atmosphere and prospects would buy from blueprints depicting what the proposed subdivision was supposed to look like. The Arch Creek section of Miami Shores land sale was held in late 1925 and after only two and a half hours of selling, thirty-three million dollars in sales had been generated. [18]

We present here a letter written by Fisher to his good friend James M. Cox, publisher of the *Miami Daily News* to display Carl's attitude toward fairness in the marketplace. Remember, Fisher demanded buyers of his property put down a twenty-five percent payment with the remainder of the purchase price to be paid in three years.

"My Dear Jim:

If you are keeping in touch with the buying of Florida property you must know that literally millions upon millions of dollars is being shipped into Florida for the purchase of land, lots, apartment houses, etc. Some of the property now being sold in Florida will not bring as much money in thirty years as it is selling for now. An enormous amount of money is coming from small speculators who invest nearly all they have. There is a tremendous amount of misrepresentation. There are an enormous amount of statements made that "sharks" never expect to keep and also a great many statements that are made by people who think they are going to do certain things but who fail to come thru. For instance: there has been at least a dozen million and five million dollar hotels mentioned that have not been built or even started. Land has been sold in Florida that will take many years to reclaim. We are bound to have a big flare-back and Miami and Miami Beach are bound to suffer as a result of some of the exploiting schemes that have been carried on around Miami and further North...if you will check back thru your papers and look for statements that have not made good in the last two or three years, you will be amazed...

The city is literally flooded with "sharpers" who are pulling all sorts of schemes. The sales made at Miami are nothing as compared with the sales made thru the north."
Sincerely,
Carl G. Fisher [19]

Fisher was admonishing a man who was most likely making a significant profit from advertising revenue. It is reported the *Miami Herald* garnered more advertising revenue from a thirteen month period in 1925-1926 than even the *New York Times*. The *Herald* had more advertising business than any other paper in the world.[20]

Although Cox was the publisher of the *Miami Daily News* (formerly known as the Metropolis) it is reasonable to assume his paper was also making windfall profits from the crush of land sale advertising.

The reader will recall Fisher's own land sales during 1925 totaled over 23 million dollars in 1925, so it doesn't seem far-fetched our auto racing oriented subject would call up Jack Prince and say, "Let's build one of your wooden race tracks down here in Florida."

While the race track lay in ruin it was reported hundreds of souls lost their lives and another 50,000 were homeless from hurricane damage.[21] Damage to the Fisher properties was estimated to be $400,000 of which half would be covered by insurance. [22]

Fisher's sales manager, Pete Chase said in a letter to Carl,

"The reports of our recent storm printed throughout the north exaggerated actual conditions greatly...the chief property damage consisted in tiling blowing off roofs and rain damage caused

Of the many upscale shops on Lincoln Road, Lincoln Motor Car Co. provided this car lover's delight showing the potential customer their wares in their barest and fully dressed forms. [2]

by awnings breaking holes in windows...There were three deaths." [23]

Consequently, conflicting reports abound on the effect of everything from the hurricane to how badly the Binder Boys affected real estate sales. We do know Carl's hotel chain consisting of the Lincoln, Flamingo, Nautilus, King Cole and Boulevard all opened for the winter season. The hurricane may have blown some common sense into Florida as the ensuing years would prove with falling real estate prices. Then again, common sense has not been a term encountered by this reporter in years of research regarding Carl Fisher's attitude toward making things happen. He was a builder and a doer, a catalyst who knew he could provide underwater spark. He saw the positive when the rank and file shook their heads in their usual nay-sayer fashion. He wrote to his now Paris-based wife:

"Dear Jane:
Don't worry about the hurricane. It will prove to be the greatest blessing to Miami Beach in the long run. Miami Beach will be more beautiful and bigger than ever before. After we get rid of this shyster boom trash there will be only hurricane proof structures allowed to be built. Miami Beach will ride all tides of time and change and coming through this storm will only make her the winner and the gainer in the end. As old Jess Andrews said, "Nothing much happened to Miami Beach- but a hell of a lot happened to the weather." [24]

Fisher's vision of transforming the dull tan sand he viewed many years prior into a vibrant city had proven his tenacity and creativity beyond question. If he could take an insect infested swamp and transform it into a place that made one's eyes smile, he wasn't about to allow a little storm upset his vision. Besides, he wanted to do it all over again up there on the tip of Long Island where rolling hills were already in place. He wouldn't have to create the land. This time he would wag his finger around and tell the builders what he wanted. He knew his judgment was sound. When Carl Fisher built, people bought. "What the hell was there to worry about, anyway? christ-on-a-bicycle, let's clean this damn place up and get on with it".

Ultimately, the site of Carl's wooden race track would yield to another recreational past-time as it was transformed into the Presidential Golf Course located east of the present I-95 and NE of 19th St. [25]

Panoramic view of Fisher's Fulton-By-The-Sea track. [2]

Chapter 10
Problems of A Promoter

"What the hell do I care about money?"

Carl had been on his way back from Montauk when notified of the hurricane so his mindset was on creating the new development on Long Island. It was evident he liked this business of developing land and his inner creativity seemingly wouldn't allow him to bypass the visions he loved to describe.

He would initially create an area called Bay View Colony on Manhasset Bay where he had purchased a home. Carl had gone to Long Island in 1922, presumably to escape Indianapolis' humid summers that created havoc with his hay fever.[1] The Bay View development was small on the Fisher scale as it was to have included, "forty-five restricted home sites and recreational facilities managed by a private club". [2]

Before long, the old adage "you meet who you are supposed to meet" came into play and Carl hooked up with a real estate salesman who drove him as far out on Long Island as one can go to have a look at, at not much of anything really. The landscape revealed bare rolling hills, hemmed in by sandy beaches. Ultimately Fisher and friends bought 9,632 acres that would have accounted for ninety square miles of living space. Carl was thinking of "The Miami Beach of The North" as has been described in writings on

Scenes of the hurricane that visited Miami Beach in 1926 and its aftermath. [2]

the area.

Prior to Fisher's discovery of the area another millionaire, one Arthur W. Benson had envisioned the countryside as the perfect setting for lovers of the outdoors, especially ones interested in Benson's passion for hunting and fishing. Benson's plans had begun in 1879 and he forged ahead by bringing in the man who had won the bid to design New York's Central Park, Frederick Law Olmstead. The new village did include spacious cottages, stables and a club-house, all amenities his upper class friends expected.[3] Carl did not have to contend with the Indians living on the land as Benson did and as noted, the land was in place, he didn't have to dredge it up from ocean bottom muck. Benson pumped enough effort in the landscape to construct at least seven cottages and formed The Montauk Association. Continued growth must not have been a priority for the developers and by the turn of the century many of the houses were uninhabited.

The description given in the *East Hampton Star* touted the area when it reported:

"There are several miles of ocean shore front, the land formation being high rolling hills, different from that found anywhere else on the eastern coast." [4]

For the Montauk caper Carl decided to share the wealth and invited several of his automotive oriented pals to pony up the 2.5 million dollars it took to secure the property. He had continuing correspondence with buddy John LaGorce who said to him:

"Why do you need to make more money? You have more than you need now. Why can't you take things easy?"

Fisher replied,

"Damn your soul, who said I'm building Montauk for the money? What the hell do I care about money? Miami Beach is finished and there's nothing left for me to do there but sit around in white pants looking pretty like the rest of you goddamn winter loafers. Hell Jack, I've got to build something. I just have to see the dirt fly." [5]

As you can see, Fisher called John LaGorce, Jack. And thus it was that our bicycle-dealing, balloon flying, race car driving, bootstrap-pulling subject came to direct a fellow named Walter A. Kohlhepp to do the following:

While holding a map of his new-found playground Fisher said, "Walter, I want the first hotel to be built here, on this high point overlooking ocean sound and lakes. The second hotel should be located here on the lake front and the third on this point on the opposite shore.

"Rename this lake, the largest on the property, Lake Montauk to replace that unpronounceable Indian name and cut a channel through from Block Island Sound to Lake Montauk, build jetties, and make Lake Montauk a modern land locked yacht harbor. This island in Lake Montauk is about thirty five acres in area. Put the yacht club and pier on it.

"This area is best adapted to the construction of the first golf club-but put the club house and the first tee here for it is the high point affording an excellent view in every direction.

"Layout the business district here, locate a village of 100 comfortable homes over here, pave this area for residential estates and build at least twenty high-grade houses here.

"Build a big bathing pavilion here, so that it will be accessible for bathing in the surf and in the more sheltered waters of the lake, put a series of tennis courts here and the polo fields will fit into this flat valley already leveled off by nature.

"Fifty miles of roads should go in at once, with a boulevard skirting the lakes and the golf course, weaving around the hills and through the valleys. Build twenty miles of bridle paths and lay out a half mile gentleman's driving track." [6]

Walter Kohlhepp was described as being Carl's Chief Executive.

"Oh yes", Fisher said as an afterthought, "there used to be sheep on this land when the Indians inhabited it. That must have been a wonderful sight. Put a thousand sheep out to grass in the spring." [7]

While press agent Steve Hannagan compiled the above quotations, we can't promise they came as stated, but we don't doubt their veracity.

The blasting began on schedule to cut the inlet through from Long Island Sound to Lake Montauk. Fisher was determined to have Montauk become a passenger port for New York travelers. He and George LeBoutillier, president of the Long Island railroad wanted to see a deep water port serving ocean liners, that would save trans-Atlantic passengers a day of travel time. Fisher had long proposed such a facility for Miami Beach but his plan was thwarted by the man you'll recall was responsible for the town's first bathing beauty contest, Chamber of Commerce president, E.W. Sewell. [8]

While the dirt was flying at Montauk Carl was forced to concern himself with the same in Miami Beach. He had to have been funneling revenue from the Florida Beach to his new lollipop in Montauk, but this time he had investors to satisfy. Internally, the stress of meeting obligations on both waterfronts must have been considerable and the concerns found their way to paper as he wrote to friend LaGorce: "we have a great deal of money due and overdue" and noted he was more interested than ever in selling the Indianapolis Motor Speedway. [9]

Tranquility and her twitchy sister anxiety would

America's Ace of Aces, Captain Eddie Rickenbacker. [1]

quiver in Carl's daily affairs from the day the hurricane hit: Where am I going to get the cash to pay for....pay for all that dirt to keep on flying? The 1927 season at Miami Beach saw a decline in revenue and Carl had promised investors the Montauk development would be introduced to the public with the opening of his two-hundred room Montauk Manor Hotel and land sales would start. Carl's home life had not been ideal for quite some time as he was mentally and physically separated from Jane.

The formality of their divorce was finalized in 1926. He had written to Winnie Hussey a cousin.

"Jane has been visiting in Miami...but we have

definitely decided to separate as soon as the legal papers can be arranged. We just don't get along together as we should and we are not having any fuss over the matter." [10]

A month earlier his attorney Frank Shutts had advised Carl he could obtain a French divorce easily because, "the French Court will grant divorcee decrees upon the general proposition that two people do not want to live together any more." [11]

We cannot put a precise figure on either Fisher's fortune at the time of the hurricane or how much it was affected but undoubtedly he was cash strapped. Carl knew "The Greatest Race Course In The World" his Indianapolis Motor Speedway was a parcel of land that could be turned into spendable revenue if he could locate a buyer and by July of 1927 he had penned a letter to the man who was known as America's Ace of Aces for his aerial exploits in the Great War, the previously mentioned Captain Eddie Rickenbacker. The man who had piloted the Fisher-Allison-owned Prest-O-Lite Maxwell race cars had distinguished himself admirably during the conflict. His race car driving days were now far behind him and he was again reaching toward the skies climbing America's business ladder. Fisher wrote to him:

"You are the only real life looking customer at this time who understands the business and could handle the proposition and there is no reason why, if we have not sold it, you should not continue to see if you can get together a bunch to buy it." [12]

Rickenbacker's fortunes, and his fame, had advanced and contracted since his return from the war. He had seen the automobile manufactured with his name on the radiator shell die, and in May of 1927 his status as America's number one aviator was eclipsed when

Rickenbacker poses with his Spad that was to carry him to many Distinguished Service Cross medals. [20]

By 1914 young Eddie Rickenbacker had won enough respect as a race car driver to be trusted with an entry in the Indianapolis 500. He finished tenth after a seven hour grind. [4]

Rickenbacker's 94th Aero Pursuit Squadron used the Hat In The Ring logo on their aircraft and it was transferred to the radiator shell of the car that would bear Rickenbacker's name. The vehicle was named an official PaceMaker at The Indianapolis 500 [2]

Charles Lindberg successfully flew nonstop from Long Island's Roosevelt field to LeBourget field in Paris in 1927. [13] Rickenbacker would go on to a distinguished career in aviation with Eastern Airlines while Lindberg would spark controversy over his political commentary about the respect and credibility of what would become Adolf Hitler's Third Reich.

But in 1927 Carl Fisher knew nothing about Rick's airline ambitions or Adolf Hitler's coming quest for power. He had dirt that needed wings and Rickenbacker was the only live wire he had found. Previously he corresponded with two-time (1921-23) Indianapolis 500 winner Tommy Milton about purchasing the track

"If you are sure you're through with racing as a

driver, why don't you buy the Speedway? Jim and I haven't had any fun out of operating the track since our fight with the legislature.

"So far our only offer has come from a group which wants to use the land for a real estate development."

Milton replied,

"I don't know a single thing about the responsibilities of a promoter. But if the Speedway is no longer fun for you, I'm sure it would be an even bigger headache for me." [14]

Fisher's "fight with the legislature" was the result of a bill that made it through the Indiana Legislature in

1923 banning all "commercialized sports" from being held on Memorial Day, the date the Indianapolis 500 was run. Days after the bill passed Governor Warren McCray vetoed it. The legal hassles coupled with his time consuming Miami Beach development caused Fisher to declare he would entertain offers to sell the track and if he did not receive a reasonable offer from someone who would continue the facility as a race track/proving grounds, then he would enter discussion to transform the facility for other purposes.

Word spread throughout the automotive industry and the end result was Fisher did not sell the track and racing continued. He did however, turn management responsibility over to Jim Allison. [15]

Sale of the track to Eddie Rickenbacker (and

presumably a group of General Motors investors) was consummated. The base selling price of the Speedway to the Rickenbacker group was $650,000 in 1927. Final price with interest was $672,690.92 [16] You could buy a nice four bedroom home in California for less than $3,000 then and an apartment would run you about $40.00 per month for a two bedroom in Syracuse, NY. The 1927 Model T Ford, in its last year of production could be driven home for less than $300 ($265 for a roadster, $290 for a Coupe). A new Buick cost $650, Chevrolet was $490 but there were many other makes in the $3,000-$5,000 range. Gasoline was .15 per gallon, while seven pounds of potatoes were a quarter.

Rickenbacker's fame (he was lauded coast to coast for downing 26 enemy aircraft) and attendant respectability among financiers were the foundation for his ability to attract the financing to buy the Speedway and of course to launch a vehicle named after him. The most definitive biography on Rick as he was known to friends, comes from historian W. David Lewis who spent 15 years researching his boyhood hero.

Lewis tells us in his *Eddie Rickenbacker; An American Hero*

"In The Twentieth Century Rickenbacker was, "defensive, dogmatic, concealing his feelings of cultural inferiority behind a crusty, abrasive and overbearing manner. His arrogance was a defensive mechanism." [17]

Rickenbacker had worked his way up from apprentice mechanic to successful race car driver to become the most famed air ace of WWI. He would prove to be a good custodian of the Indianapolis Motor Speedway but in the end he too considered selling the land after WWII for purposes other than racing. Former Indy 500 winner Wilbur Shaw became de-

Captain Eddie progressed steadily after his successful tenure as race car driver then fighter pilot to an executive role in the aircraft industry. This photo depicts one of the DC-1's in his Eastern Airlines fleet. [2]

termined to preserve the track after WWII and ultimately convinced Terre Haute, Indiana businessman Tony Hulman to purchase the property and continue the "500". The Hulman family has operated the track since 1946. [18]

Although Carl had a place for his share of the revenue from the sale of the track, it appears from a letter written by "Pop" Myers to him in December of 1927 Fisher had personally rewarded Myers for his service. Myers wrote:

"Dear Mr. Fisher

With the final payment by Rickenbacker on his contract, it would appear that my relations with you, at least as far as the Indianapolis Motor Speedway is concerned, are at an end.

With the parting of the ways came to me a feeling of extreme regret because my association in various capacities with this institution over a period of almost eighteen years I can truly say has been a very pleasant one I could not permit this occasion to pass on without expressing to you my appreciation of your having given me the opportunity to carry on this pleasant work during this period.

At the same time I want to express to you my very sincere thanks for the substantial financial reward resulting from the sale."

Signed T.E. Pop Myers [19]

Myers offered his help in the future to Fisher and remained a close friend. We found a letter in the Florida Fisher Files from The Montauk Yacht Club listing Myers as being Chairman of the establishment.

Fisher's personality enabled him to maintain close relationships throughout his life and none better exemplified this trait than the one he had with his first wife, Jane.

We have to recall the pillow seen in Carl's home that read "A Woman Is Just A Woman, But a Cigar is A Smoke" when we look at this 1927 photo depicting Carl and his new wife, the former Margaret Collier. Carl is holding a cigar with one hand, his lady with the other. [2]

She says in her biography about a trip to Miami Beach:

"Not with any idea of being Carl's wife. That was over; but there was between us as great a friendship, I believe, as ever existed between a man and a woman.

We still shared all interests. Only the physical love was gone. All else that had been remained." (20)

Each of these partners went on to marry others, Jane married twice more while Carl married his secretary Margaret Collier in 1927. The minister for the ceremony was the husband of another of Carl's inamoratas, Ann Rossiter. [21]

The mood in Miami Beach after the hurricane was one of resolve, and looking toward the future for prosperity. The Florida boom was over by 1927 and the following year seemed tepid in comparison to the flurry of activity that had gone on for the prior several seasons.

A meteorological service informed Carl about another impending hurricane about to hit South Florida and he wrote back:

"I would like to ask you if you can figure out through your horoscopes, telescopes or any other

kind of scopes just what other pest can hit us at Miami Beach. We have had the "Binder Boys", we have had inflation, deflation, we have had mosquitoes, shortage of building supplies, thousands of bankers trying to loan money, thousands of bankers trying to get out from under loaning money, hurricanes, tornadoes, cyclones, whirlpools, water spouts, water shortage, too much water both fresh and salt and non-drinking, lots of good liquor and a lot of bad liquor, bootleger wars; and now you talk to us about a Tidal Wave or some sort of somersault which the ocean is going to turn which will knock all the clothes props out of the back yard.

"Between you and me: I have had everything happen to me down here except, like the nigger who was going to be shot at sunrise said, "I have had everything happen to me that could happen except pulling the trigger on the final scene" [22]

While the terminology used by Carl in the above letter is abhorrent to us today, the description used was commonplace for the day. Fisher continued to be an advocate for the rights of blacks.

Judge A. Frank Katzentine
December 19, 1931
Congress Building
Miami, Fla.
"Dear Frank:
I enclose you a statement from a colored boy who works here on the Beach. He has been hauling three servants back and forth to the Beach to work, in his Ford car. It is a great accommodation for these people to be hauled over here and back to town. Of course they divide up the expense.
I know that that indiscriminate jitnies (sic) are no good, and that there should be some control of them, but no law can be made to stick, that will fine a

workman under these conditions. This has been tried in other courts and will not stick, and while I don't want to buck the law and have an argument, I do think this fine should be remitted, and this boy should be given a license to haul these employees to and from the Beach.
The young man works here at the Maren Apartment, 1543 Michigan Avenue, and if you wish him to, he can come down and have a talk with you."
Yours, C.G. Fisher [23]

Jane tells of the time one of Fisher's black workmen fell into a vat of hot tar and she and Carl transported the poor soul to a local hospital only to be tuned away with the admonition, "We don't treat niggers at this hospital." The incensed Fisher vowed to "put that goddamn place out of business" Jane also reported Fisher gave generously to negro institutions.[24]

Carl's personal servant Galloway, whom he had hired away from employment at Pop Haynes' restaurant in Indianapolis, wrote Fisher a thank you note in penmanship worthy of a greeting card, and said:

"Thank you from my heart, also for the consideration you have shown me for at least 20 years."

In the note Galloway thanks Fisher for the check he had received,

"for it filled my heart" and noted, "no more investments for me. You hit the key note." [25]

We get the impression Fisher went along with the segregation mores of the era but did not treat

blacks as second class citizens.

During Fisher's Miami Beach building era, the Jewish in America were socially prosecuted. Henry Ford's newspaper the Dearborn Independent was distributing copies of a manifesto decrying the Jew; resorts in the Catskills and Adirondacks

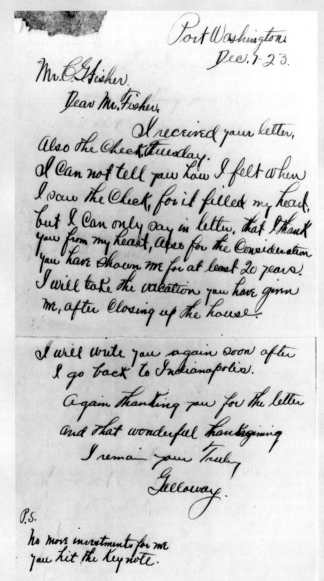

Copy of the letter from Galloway, his long-time servant. [2]

barred the Jew. Covenants were included in real estate transactions banning Jewish ownership.[26]

It was not uncommon for Carl to receive correspondence such as the following:

"Dear Mr. Fischer: (sic)

One of the best friends I have on earth, Mr. Wm Lewin is staying at Miami beach at 849 West Avenue. He is the first person I ever played golf with in my life, and he is anxious to make some connection so that he can play golf at the Beach.

I realize that on account of his nationality there may be some objection but if you can possibly get him the courtesy of your golf club I shall be everlastingly grateful to you.

Sincerely yours,"
Victor J. Miller
Mayor of Saint Louis [27]

Fisher seemingly divided his personal feelings regarding the Jewish as his own real estate contracts included the aforementioned covenants but Carl could claim many satisfied Jewish land owners who had purchased from him and could count many influential friends of the Jewish faith. The aforementioned, Julius Fleishmann, heir to the yeast fortune of the same name, was a continuing supporter of Carl's projects and brought a stable of polo ponies to Miami Beach. His correspondence with Fisher can be viewed as one friend to another. [28]

Mitchell Wolfson, a Miami Beach Mayor reported:

"He (Fisher) found there were others on the Beach who were his contemporaries...who were very much opposed to me because they didn't think they'd want a Jewish member on the council. Mr. Fisher had quite a fallout with some of them as a result of supporting me, but I would think that I owe my election more to Carl Fisher than to almost anyone else...At the time there were not sufficient Jewish votes on Miami Beach to elect someone like myself." [29]

Consequently, while we cannot judge Carl as being dedicated to social reform, he did display an enviable sense of fairness. We also have no reason to not believe Jane Fisher's (fawning) accounts of her husband's largesse as she tells in her biography. She recounts tales of Fisher supplying funds to rebuild a black women's college; giving $10,000 to Sergeant Alvin York, "bravest hero of WW 1" for a school, providing a church for Miami Beach and later supplying a carillon (bells actuated by a keyboard) to his friend Father Barry, an Irish-Catholic priest who enjoyed movies and boxing matches with Fisher; Barry unsuccessfully tried to convince Carl to concern himself more with spiritual and religious affairs to no avail. [30]

By 1927 Carl had been hit in his left eye by a tennis ball that left it useless. He was gaining weight and remained a regular consumer of alcohol. For a time he would continue running on all cylinders, but his tank of finances was beginning to sway toward the E side.

Chapter 11
The Dirt Stops Flying

"I myself lost about twenty-five million, but am still able to eat, up to this evening."

The reader will recall Fisher's admonition to his construction supervisor from Chapter 5 when Carl said....*"Lincoln road is going to be the American Rue de la Paix"* [1]. Carl's vision became reality that remains to this day.

A handsome brochure in the Florida Fisher Files was located that features Carl's Lincoln Building and listed 22 stores on Lincoln Road whose pedigree could have landed them on any of the best streets in the world. Among those listed were: Elizabeth Arden's; Chrysler Motor Salon; General Motors Salon; Packard Motors Salon; Madam & Moghabghab; Sak's Fifth Avenue; Bonwit & Teller. [2]

He had already proven his formula successful and was now trying to clone his efforts for Montauk. He had said to himself previously, *"Hell any fool can see this jungle turned into a fabulous city,"* when he began making the dirt fly in Florida. The same thought pattern had to exist him when he surveyed Montauk. The land was already there, it was beautiful and all you had to do was plop in a big hotel, build some fabulous looking homes and cottages and the

Fisher's brochure described the above scene: "When your thoughts bend northward to lands of ever-changing seasons, another Carl G. Fisher creation beckons to you from the easternmost tip of Long Island, New York. There beautiful MONTAUK MANOR of early English Tudor-design, surveys nine hundred acres of playground between the waters of the Atlantic and Long Island Sound. The many forms of outdoor recreation are eclipsed by incomparable deep sea fishing." [2]

place will sell itself. A self-seller again.

On June 1, 1927 Carl introduced his stunning Montauk Manor, a 200 guest room facility built in traditional Tudor style. He had spent over one million dollars on the hotel and drew 3,000 cars and 10,000 people for opening day ceremonies.[3] A emotional description of The Manor was provided in a brochure that told of:

....proud Tudor gables rising from a lofty hill overlooking the Sound, with a vista of sea and green, rolling knolls to the south...gay, gracious, suave. Friendly and warm, yet with a formality bred of good taste....

Good taste came naturally to Fisher and while he wasn't a culinary connoisseur (as noted he was a steak and potatoes man) he could recognize upscale quality and didn't pinch pennies delivering it to upscale customers. He had George LeBoutillier, the previously mentioned president of the Long Island railroad serving as toastmaster for the opening festivities, adding credibility that the line would soon serve this outer most tip of Long Island.

A $100,000 terminal would be built and service to Pittsburgh was planned.[4] Montauk Manor represented class, upper class. Montauk Manor had been built by someone who knew how to satisfy the discriminating.

He built the Carl G. Fisher office building on Montauk, a duplicate of the Lincoln Building in Miami. Today it sits unoccupied begging passer-bys to look upward slightly and wonder why its there. The force that created it met obstacles not seen in Miami Beach.

Although Montauk's fat, rolling land brought the viewer's eye a sense of tranquility, the bucolic,

A section of the spacious ballroom featuring ceiling tapestry. [2]

Guests tour the first golf course. [2]

Manicured gardens surrounded by stone fencing attest to the craftsmanship evident at Montauk. [2]

The classic beauty of 1920-30's vehicles had to add to the ambiance of the Montauk Manor. [2]

pastoral countryside did not serve as a barrier for the inclement weather often experienced. The differences between weather in Miami Beach and Montauk are those of chalk and cheese. There are only a few months per year when Montauk residents can go out and comment on how lovely the day is. There was established competition on Long Island for real estate investment that didn't exist in Miami Beach. The competition Carl experienced in Miami Beach, notably from Mizner's Coral Gables development, probably helped Fisher more than it hurt him as Mizner reaped the benefit of extensive advertising, and thus Carl's project only a few miles away also had to be a beneficiary.

Carl would scramble to keep the development going and encounter bright spots along the way as land sales and building continued, slowly. Traffic was so heavy during 1927 that East Hampton residents approved expenditure for a new road. [5]

One need only to read a few of the letters Carl wrote in 1928-32 to sense the end of his Montauk activity was inevitable. He told George LeBoutilllier that two million dollars worth of land sales were necessary to "take care of minimum figures," for the coming year.[6] George was used to receiving more promising correspondence such as the one Carl wrote to him just before the opening of Montauk:

"Dear Mr. LeBoutillier:
April 18, 1927
We have a present for you at the house from Cuba. Incidentally, there are twelve bottles of Usher's Green Stripe which a friend of mine bought for me in Scotland nine years ago.....Please divide it up with Mr. Atterbury and tell him that the last railroad president I was out with drank a full quart of this Green Stripe in one evening with no bad results except that he had steam coming out of his nose for three days.

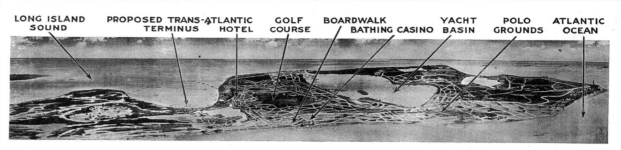

LONG ISLAND SOUND — PROPOSED TRANS-ATLANTIC TERMINUS — HOTEL — GOLF COURSE — BOARDWALK BATHING CASINO — YACHT BASIN — POLO GROUNDS — ATLANTIC OCEAN

Montauk Beach, Long Island, N.Y.

JAMES C. WILLSON & CO.
130 SOUTH FIFTH STREET
LOUISVILLE, KENTUCKY
INVESTMENT — SECURITIES

Above and below: Mother Nature provided Carl Fisher with the canvas to create his visions. Montauk Beach, Long Island, N.Y. provided the expanse of land that was to become Carl's "Miami Beach of The North". [2]

Photos right and below: European flavored dwellings set amidst thoughtful landscaping created an air of tranquility appreciated in any era. [2]

Workmen toil to create a channel for the yacht basin. Note there are three men with shovels and three wearing ties. [2]

Carl's Montauk customers had to be provided with proper parking places. We believe the ship in the foreground is Carl's Shadow K. [2]

After drinking a lot of White Mule for the last two years and then going on a beer diet, it (sic) just my tough luck to dig up some of this old time Scotch. We brought this old Scotch from Nassau about nine years ago and hid it on Dat Key and it has only been recently we had opportunity to get a man to deliver it to us.

Yours, Carl G. Fisher [7]

Fisher's mention of White Mule tells us he was using moonshine, the legendary concoction that results in a drink that is excessively high in alcohol content.

It is evident Fisher did not spend all of his efforts toward his real estate ventures as proven by letters in his files. In fact, he was hop-scotching around with so many un-related activities one can get the feeling that during his promotion of Montauk his focus was far too wide for an efficient executive His interest rambled from a magnificent trailer known as the Aero-Car, to ice-cube trays, giving advice to the president of Hudson Motorcar Co. to divorce and diesel-engines.The diesel engine adventure appears to be a lengthy one consuming much of Carl's energy and cash.

A good example of his varied interests lie in the Aero-Car, the uniquely attached travel trailer that set the standard of the day.

The trailer was towed behind a conventional automobile in an unconventional manner. Imagine if you will, taking the trunk off a vehicle, then bolting the spare tire flat on the trunk's floor. This cushioned device can now serve to hold a gooseneck shaped bracket that attaches to the trailer behind it. Today, we see multitudes of pick up trucks so equipped with such a gooseneck attaching device, also called a fifth wheel, but without the usage of the spare tire as a mounting bracket. The gooseneck arrangement provided for a better ride than a standard trailer hitch because the attaching point of the trailer was located directly over the tow vehicle's suspension rather than being hung from the rear bumper.

When aviation pioneer Glenn Curtiss designed the trailer for his own usage, he came up with the new mounting system and was convinced to market the plot. He referred to it as his "motorized gypsy van" and "motorbungalo" and decided on the name Aero-Car. [8] Spelling of the vehicle is seen in varied forms. The name Aerocar had already been used on the American public back in 1907-09 as being "The Practical Car Built By Practical Men". The original Aero-Car automobile was backed by coal baron Alexander V. Malcomson who had been one of Henry Ford's original backers, a venture in which he ultimately lost control. Malcomson wanted to promote larger vehicles than Ford had in mind and Malcomson ultimately sold his interest in the firm back to Henry Ford. [9]

Fisher was so enthused with the trailer he also saw it as being a successful self-propelled vehicle and corresponded with the Auburn Automobile Company, E.L. Cord's automobile producing empire that was known for its front-wheel drive vehicles, the Auburn and Cord. The firm also produced "The World's Finest Motorcar" the Duesenberg.

The author feels E.L. Cord's name in the history of the automobile is one to be revered and study of his accomplishments is a must for any serious automotive historian. Griffith Borgeson's "*Errett*

Loban Cord" book published by Automobile Quarterly tells the complete story and features marvelous photos.

H.L. Briand of the Auburn firm wrote in part to Carl:

"April 18, 1929
Dear Mr. Fisher
.....Should we be able to seriously consider building a Front Wheel Drive power unit for you I will drop you a line and we can arrange for some of our engineers to come down and work out with your engineers the requirements and specifications." [10]

When Carl received a glowing report from

Arthur Brisbane, one of the most influential men in American journalism he penned a letter to:

"The Stockholders of the Aero-Car Corporation
Tuesday September 4, 1928
Ten years ago I heard one of American's greatest business men say that Arthur Brisbane could look through a brick wall. At least, the fact remains, that Arthur Brisbane's editorials are read by probably more American people than the editorials of any other writer.

Yesterday Mr. Brisbane had an hour's ride in the Aero-Car. He made the following suggestions and criticisms.

First, that he wanted an Aerocar as quickly as he

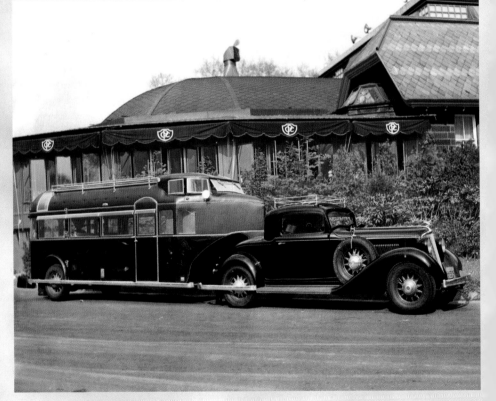

Glenn Curtiss and Carl Fisher pose next to one of the earliest Aero-Cars

Later versions of the Aero-Car featured progression to more luxurious models. The finely crafted interior displayed is spacious. [2]

could have it delivered. Price was not mentioned and it was not a part of the consideration., Mr. Brisbane having faith in the fact that the people who are back of the Aerocar would deliver the car properly and that the price would be satisfactory.

He further stated that the man who owned an Aerocar owned a private car which was the equal, if not much better than a privately owned railroad car.

My. Brisbane said that he could save the best part of an hour or hour and a half going to his business and being able to transact business going into town, also on returning from the city he could save time and when fatigued he could have a good rest, which is hardly possible in any other type of road transportation.

Signed
Carl G. Fisher [11]

In our current era of around the clock television and internet activity, it is difficult for us to connect with Brisbane's popularity. In an August 16, 1926 story that featured Brisbane on the cover, TIME magazine stated Brisbane''s "Today" column "vies with weather and market reports for the size of its audience, probably beating both. It is said to be read by a third of the total U. S. population. Obviously this is an exaggeration, but half that many would be some 20 million readers."

Brisbane is credited with the statement that has been delivered to journalism students in one form or another: "*If you don't hit the reader between the eyes in your first sentence of your news column, there's no need to write anymore.*" [12]

Obviously Brisbane's endorsement of the streamlined trailer was a plum in the firm's marketing basket. Had Fisher been able to marry the successful

front wheel drive system to the Aero-Car he would have created the nation's first Winnebago. Another self-seller.

We have seen the Fisher fingers in the automotive manufacturing pot previously and watched the result as his Empire automobile company floundered. Once again, his passionate drive and sales pitches did not culminate in the introduction of a successful Aero-Car business.

Besides, Glenn Curtiss had too much money and too many other business interests to devote an appreciable amount of time to the success of the product. Curtiss was a long-established friend of Fisher's (he had an aviation school in Miami Beach at one point) and they did share some kindred spirit. Curtiss' achievements are legendary in the annals of aviation history. The powers that be actually name him as holding the nation's first public flight in 1908, even thought the Wright Brothers flew in public at Kitty Hawk, N.C. five years previously. Nevertheless, Curtiss earned his wings through his own aerial accomplishments and set speed and distance records, was the first to establish a flying school, built the first successful pontoon aircraft and is lauded as being the father of Naval aviation. His company produced 6,000 Curtis "Jenny's" for WWI.

He too was a Florida land developer and is credited with having the guiding hand in Hialeah, Miami Springs and Opa-Locka communities.

The photo of him we like the best is in front of his G.H. Curtiss Bicycle Shop in Hammondsport, NY. Curtiss entered the world of wheels just as Carl did, but he progressed to motorized bicycles and became America's first motorcycle champion. He set records at 1, 2 and 3 miles and by 1907 was proclaimed the "Fastest Man In The World" when he rode a motorcycle at 136.36 mph. His motorcycle manufacturing company was making very good profits when as employee Harry Genung recalled, "*We had a front row seat in the motorcycle business when aviation came along and pushed the business out the back.*"[13] Curtiss' motorcycle was initially sold as the Hercules and later his own name. It should be noted Curtiss also divested himself early on of his harness making business, sensing its bleak future.

Curtiss' Aero-Car was most likely, the lightest and most comfortable travel trailer of the day. It contained aircraft construction technique and was therefore superior to anything else (of which there was very little) on the market. His unique system of attaching the trailer to the tow vehicle, provided an ease of ride heretofore not experienced. In order for the reader to appreciate the staggering importance of ease-of-ride in a moving vehicle we submit the case of Billy Durant.

Durant was a young cigar salesman who hitched a ride in a buggy with an un-conventional spring attachment. Normal buggies bounced the passengers up and down. Durant's ride gave the passenger a wave motion effect. Billy said, "*This thing is a self-seller.*" He bought the patent rights and built the world's largest carriage corporation, Durant-Dort Carriage Co. Durant had the same exclamation about self-selling when he took his first ride in a car to become known as the Buick, the vehicle Durant used to found General Motors.

Automobile manufacturers have been waxing eloquently about the cloud-like ride you will experience in their vehicles ever since Billy Durant hopped in that buggy.

Fisher probably experienced an ah-hah moment when he took a ride in the Aero-Car but his enthusiasm wasn't enough to make the project successful.

Curtiss died in 1930 at age 52. It is doubtful he would have wanted to invest any significant time in the Aero-Car operation as he already had more money than he knew what to do with and enjoyed his own land development projects. He said to a friend, "*I have so much money that when I think about it, it gives me a headache.*"

A man named Wally Byam proved Curtiss' and Fisher's idea to be sound when he introduced the Clipper travel trailer to American in 1936 from his new Airstream Trailer Company. It featured aircraft

G.H. Curtiss Bicycles was the launch pad for Glenn Curtiss' wildly successful career. [17]

construction just like the Aereo-Car and is still being manufactured to this day in trailer and self-powered recreational vehicle form.

Carl had a history of scattering his efforts far from the main goal and could not discipline himself to pass up what he thought to be a potential successful venture.

A letter found in the Florida Fisher Files finds Carl ranting to his friend "Boss" Kettering of General Motors tells us Fisher too was enamored with the manufacture of a refrigerator before Billy Durant brought the idea to GM. where it became the Frigidaire.

Carl said in part:

June 11, 1929
"My dear Ket: (sic)
When are you going to get out some small Frigidaires that look like music boxes or bureaus and have a nice mahogany finish instead of coffin white?

Another thing (you will notice I am one of these nuts who has not enough business of his own to attend to and can always horn in on other people's affairs). Here is a new thought that won't cost you a nickel and some day you or some of your engineers are going to settle the question of taking the cubes out of the Frigidaire without making it necessary to go into the bathroom, turn on the hot water, then go back and take an ice pick and hammer and thaw or cut or knock out the ice from the little containers.

I just happen to think that the first ice machines in this country were made by the Isco Company in Detroit. You folks have not improved a nickel's worth on the construction of this tray for the cubes over the ones we first built in Detroit fifteen years ago.. Henry Joy was the chief Engineer; Albert Gowan and myself were the promoters and put up most of the cash—a good part of which remains "up".

Sincerely,
Carl G. Fisher" [14]

Kettering replied in part:

June 18, 1929
"My dear Carl:
I am sending abstracts of this letter to Mr. Biechler of Frigidaire.
We have been working on both of the things you mention. I think the boys have gotten the ice cube business fairly worked out.
I think you are right in your point of view relative to the appearance of these jobs.
Yours very truly,
C.F. Kettering" [15]

It appears as though Fisher had designs on becoming a refrigerator manufacturer and lost money in the process.

The reader may recall Joy was the president of Packard and Gowan president of the cement company that donated extensively to Fisher's Lincoln Highway plan.

Part of Carl's personality is described in one of the more descriptive sheets of paper found in the Florida Fisher Files. It is not dated or signed, but we suspect it to be the work of a female black cook named Danny. Jane tells us:

"Danny adored Carl, but her temper was as stormy as his. The scenes between them were Wagnerian, and after every upheaval Danny quit and was rehired in a reconciliation scene equally stormy. After one thunderous leave-taking, Danny scribbled on the kitchen wall a message for whatever cook might follow.
"This is the way Mister Fisher orders his meals:

'Goddammit to hell, why in jesus name don't I get my goddam breakfast?" [16]

The sheet we found was titled "Cuss Words by Carl G. Fisher at bridge Thursday night from 10:15-11:00. It contained Carl's usual barrage of goddam, jesus christ, What The Hell, For The Love of god, Dammed Card System, etc. and so on into the night. [17]

Carl found time to chastise friend and fellow Montauk investor Roy Chapin head of the Hudson Motor Car Company in a detailed diatribe concerning the plating on the firm's vehicles.

November 8, 1928
"Dear Roy:
There is something very radically wrong with the nickel-plating on your cars. We have two Hudsons in service that have had less than five months' service and as far as the nickel plating is concerned they look like they are ten years old. No amount of washing or polishing will keep them up. In fact the radiator, bumpers, nuts that hold the tire clamps, and all the nickel plated parts including the lamps are terrible. We haven't a single complaint to make regarding the operating nor the excellence of the car itself, but your nickel plating is rotten.
Yours,
Carl G. Fisher" [18]

Carl went on to explain the plating on his Studebaker and Graham-Paige cars were superior to Chapin's product and both were over four years old.

Carl could jab at Roy Chapin's product from one friend to another. Chapin was a Montauk investor and constant correspondent with Carl. When notified the Chapin family had a son Carl wrote:

(Date not legible) 1926

"My dear Roy:

I notice you have a son named Dan.

All boys named Dan should be red-headed, freckle face, inclined to have pug-nose, wide behind the ears, and just all around boys. After they are eighteen or nineteen years old, and their family have gone to the "poor house", kids of this description generally step out and amount to something. Do not let him have any chicken bone until he has at least reached six months.

Best regards.

Yours,

Carl G. Fisher" [19]

While Carl's thoughts were rambling from Montauk, to Aero-Cars, Fridigaires, nickel plating on Hudsons and red-headed young men, the nation was about to be rocked by the most devastating economic downturn in the country's history. There seemed to be no central theme to Fisher's business activities while he was promoting Montauk, but the entire world would center its focus on the most financial street in the world: New York's Wall Street.

Between October 23 and October 31, 1929 some days have become known as Black Thursday, Black Friday, Black Monday, Black Tuesday. Nearly 70.8 million shares of stock were traded in eight market sessions. These sessions accounted for more trading than had ever taken place in any single month prior to 1928. Both the Dow-Jones and the New York Times combined averages fell over 50 points (over 40 percent of value) to mark what is known as the Great Wall Street Crash of 1929. Nevertheless, the market did bounce back in the coming months and the Dow regained 74 percent and the Times average gained 63 percent of what had been lost. Prices went back to those comparable at the end of the record setting 1928 year. The Great Depression itself is said

not to have started until the autumn of 1930.

The question scholars have been debating for decades is what effect the stock market crash had on the economy, and the market itself.

"The disagreeable truth...is that most responsible students of the events of 1929 have been unable to demonstrate an appreciable cause-and-effect linkage between the Great Crash and the Depression." [20]

The social and economic circumstances surrounding the market crash and ensuing Great Depression have been subjected to scholarly study outside the scope of this book. Theories range from under consumption to contraction of investment to decline in foreign trade to institutional dysfunction to problems with the gold standard.[21] Although Carl never had an appreciable amount of money in the market, (we found no documentation proving he did) the same cannot be said for his Montauk investors. The giddiness and nothing-but-blue-sky attitude that defined the Roaring Twenties were to be replaced by high unemployment figures, the likes of which had never been seen in the US previously. Soup lines and tent cities would dot our landscape for the next several years, and study shows our country did not come out of the Depression completely until the manufacturing necessary to win WWII emerged.

Thus Carl Fisher was trying to sell bicycles to people who didn't have legs. His Montauk community was designed for that small segment of the population who control the wealth the rest of us are after. Most of the wealthy were still almost wealthy after the stock market crash but Carl couldn't find enough of them to share his vision of sheep grazing on Montauk's bulbous green pastures.

Reading of the machinations Fisher went through in an attempt to continue the Long Island development is a cheerless circumstance. Throughout his career Fisher had never been so reduced to seeking funds to

finish a project, and he entered a circumstance that had to be degrading for him.

Carl Fisher had walked through the fire a long time before he ever heard of Montauk, or the beaches in Florida. He knew sales acceptance and rejection from the time he was a boy selling magazines, books and bicycles. His formula of delivering at least, if not more, than you promised brought satisfaction. It was evident to all who visited, the Fisher spirit was being injected into the flying dirt at Montauk. The improvements and buildings he constructed at Montauk are simply beautiful. .

Although the Long Island Forum gave a glowing report of the July 4, 1930 activities at Montauk, land did not sell. Fisher had convinced fellow Montauk Beach Development Corporation investor, Representative Fred Britton of Illinois and Chairman of House Naval Affairs Committee, to use his considerable influence to hold training maneuvers for the U.S. Atlantic Fleet at Montauk. Britten loved the idea and said it would be the first time observers could see the action from the shoreline. [22] The maneuvers were held successfully and they brought some interest and publicity to the Long Island real estate, but buyers were scarce.

The report to stockholders said, *"there was very little, if any, public interest displayed in the purchase of real estate during the past two seasons."* [23]

Carl was watching his Miami Beach development gain in national stature as his close pal John Oliver LaGorce wrote a 12,000 word story that dominated the January 1930 National Geographic magazine. Titled, "Florida-The Fountain of Youth", The prestigious publication known for its bland golden-yellow covers borrowed a line from Fisher's favorite pillow by sub-titling a paragraph: "But A Good Cigar Is A Smoke" while it reported the sunshine state produced 600,000,000 cigars annually.[24]

In the year America produced some of its most enduring automotive designs 1932, the Montauk Development Corporation defaulted on its financial obligations of 3.7 million dollars.[25]

Our adventurer who had gone from strength to strength in each of his life's endeavors, was knocked out of his dirt-floor arena. We can hear him saying, *"Well jesus christ. For god's sake. damnit the hell anyway, Montauk can be a fabulous community, how in the hell can this happen?"*

When we recall from Chapter 6 Fisher had offered $50,000 out of his pocket in 1918 to help build a plane to cross the Atlantic his financial fall by 1932 is dramatic.

By December of 1932 Carl was offering his own Miami Beach home for sale in which, "I have over $300,000 invested in this property and would make you a price of $185,000 in order that I might clean up the mortgage and taxes on the property." [26] Carl was writing to Charlie "Cast Iron Charlie" Sorenson, Henry Ford's production man who was highly respected throughout the auto industry.

Carl's toy-box had always included mechanical devices, (mostly motor-boats) that held him in awe. His interest in speedboats and yachts never flickered and he was a believer in the Diesel engine (invented by German Rudolph Diesel) as power-plant for not only his beloved water-craft, but as an industrial mode of power The diesel engine utilizes a light fuel oil and does not use a spark plug ignition as the regular internal combustion engine does. The diesel relies on the heat of highly compressed air for ignition. In Fisher's time development was still experimental, but the diesel held the promise of high horsepower and great reliability.

It seems only reasonable Fisher would have invested in the diesel engine because the original concept was to replace the steam engine for industrial

A duplicate of this building in Miami Beach was seemingly a magnet for success, so Carl had one built at Montauk. [2]

usage. One of Rudolph Diesel's Munich Polytechnic Institute's professors was a Carl Lind, who had been credited with making the first ice-making machines. Lind showed Diesel the steam engine was woefully inefficient as it turned only about ten percent of the heat contained in the steam to useful energy.

Diesel was fascinated, as Carl Fisher surely would have been with "a bicycle pump like apparatus at the school made of glass that permitted one to see how, whenever the pump was operated, the air thus compressed, became heated and would ignite tinder."

Diesel later worked in plants utilizing Lind's ice making equipment and called upon his own creativity to perfect a process to make clear ice cubes, thus providing him with a patent appreciated by bar and restaurant owners. Eventually he perfected the process of using heat (generated by compression) within the engine to create combustion of kerosene, and thus the diesel engine was born. [27] We found no record of him having been a bicycle racer.

Another man named O.D. Treiber had convinced Fisher his own version of the diesel engine would be superior to anything on the market in terms of horsepower vs weight. In modern day vernacular, Carl Fisher was a gearhead, he loved mechanical apparatus, especially if it made vroom-vroom sounds.

We remind the reader when Carl Fisher was 26 years old in 1900, steam and electric power was favored in about three-quarters of the vehicles manufactured and the remainder were gasoline operated. In the ensuing years from 1900-1930 the gasoline engine became standard for automotive use. Diesel fueled engines were termed "oil burning engines" in the Thirties era and diesel technology was not perfected.[28]

No less an entity than what was the world's largest and richest corporation, General Motors saw the possibilities of efficient diesel engines and had directed one of Carl's close acquaintances, the aforementioned "Boss" Kettering to research the diesel industry. Correspondence between he and Fisher shows Kettering was interested in the Treiber diesel Carl was promoting.

"You would be surprised to know the tremendous interest there is in railroads, street car lines, bus lines, and all other power company plants in connection with oil burning Diesel motors," Fisher wrote to Kettering. [29]

Kettering and the other engine-oriented souls at General Motors most likely knew a lot more than

Carl Fisher did about the potential of the diesel. Fisher had again recognized a good thing and had sunk about $225,000 into Treiber's operation. He was concerned Treiber's lack of business expertise might well force him out of business before he completed Fisher's own boat engines. Kettering and GM were initially anyway, very interested in Treiber's designs. [30].

Further correspondence between Fisher and Kettering continued as Carl expressed concern over Treiber's business ability. [31]

Carl's long time friend Caleb Bragg, the Yale educated boy racer who had beaten famed Barney Oldfield in a match race at the fast Playa Del Ray board track, and who had previously been the fastest qualifier for the 1913 Indianapolis 500, and who was also a three-time Detroit Gold Cup winner in his "Baby Bootlegger" boat (1923-25) had interest in the Treiber Diesel.

He wrote to Carl:

October 8, 1928
"Dear Carl:

I had quite a chat with Kettering on the way home and agree with him that it would be a mistake for us to attempt to put diesel engines in the fishing boats, primarily because it would be foolish for Treiber to build a lot of these motors until one had been constructed and thoroughly tested which, of course, would make the delivery of the balance of the motors too late for use in the fishing boats.

Secondly, the fishing boats will prove to be of considerable sales value to Montauk next year and we should do nothing which would jeopardize their delivery.

Kettering spoke very highly of the new light weight-Winton Diesel and I am enclosing their circular showing this motor, and advise you have a further talk with Kettering before permitting Treiber to build

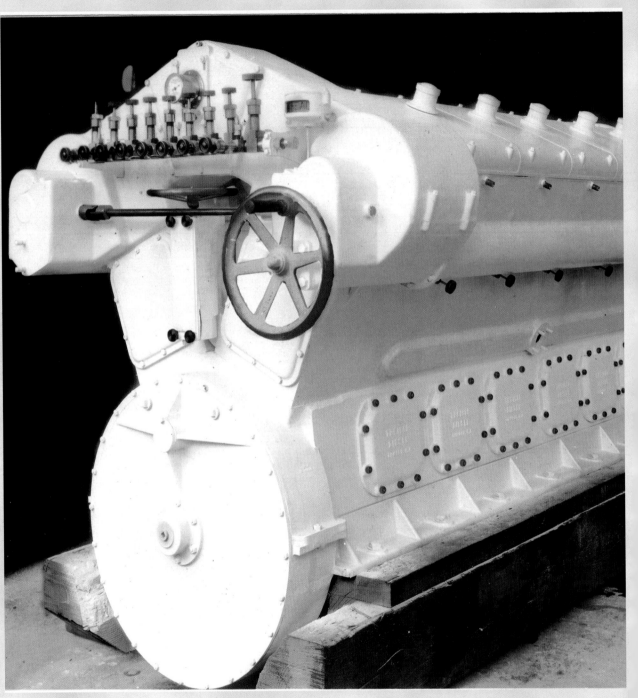

Carl Fisher and a man named O,.D. Treiber hoped the above diesel engine would become a mainstay in the industry, but the power plant did not meet expectations. [2]

any quantity of these motors, as they may not prove to be as satisfactory as the Winton motor and besides that, he is without their sales organization, which would make it pretty difficult to sell these motors in competition with Winton.

Yours sincerely,
Signed :Caleb" [32]

Caleb Bragg and a man named Victor Kliesrath were successful manufacturers of a vacuum operated "Booster Brake" system for trucks and heavy equipment and Bragg evidently had some interest in Montauk.

Ultimately the old bicycle and automobile manufacturer we met in the early part of this book, Alexander Winton won as GM purchased his firm in 1930 and later merged it with The Cleveland Diesel Division of General Motors. Winton had produced a superior diesel engine that out-performed the Treiber Carl had invested in.

Kettering wrote to Carl, *"From my standpoint, the present Diesel engines that Treiber is building I would not have as a gift."* [33]

Consequently General Motors terminated its involvement with Treiber only weeks before the stock market crash. If Kettering wasn't impressed the deal was dead. [34]

General Motors went on to develop very successful diesels used in varying forms over the coming decades and became a leading force in the industry.

A fellow Hoosier farm boy named Clessie Cummings furthered Carl's case for the reliability of the diesel engine when he entered his diesel-powered car in the 1931 Indianapolis 500 and saw driver Dave Evans finish 13th, having gone the distance using only one tank (35 gallons) of fuel. [35] Next time you hear a big truck backing off with the familiar braaaapppp sound, you can thank Clessie for his invention of the compression release engine brake, otherwise known as the Jake brake.

Fisher was floundering about looking for investors in the diesel project and wrote to pal Tommy Milton,

"There is a tremendous demand for diesel engines and I think Treiber is one of the best posted engineers in this business......If we could only keep him locked up in a cage where he would do all the designing work and submit to some real engineers to build, then we would be going." [36]

Milton proved to be a friend through all circumstances. He used positive language with Carl after Montauk's failure. He said it had been, "a privilege to buy any of the stock and also that had normal times prevailed it would have been just as good an investment as Miami Beach was. He told Carl *"not to assume moral responsibility"*. [37]

* * * * * * * * * *

While Carl did not flaunt his wealth through his own personal street transportation, (as we have seen he drove plebian Hudsons, Studebakers, Graham-Paige and R.E.O.'s) or clothing, (all descriptions of him usually note he *"always wears some kind of floppy hat"*) he liked the usage of money. His boating interest are financial self-indulgence and the Treiber diesel incident was yet another he would have to swallow with no return on investment. Carl had seen the future regarding diesel power but the best he could say about his promotion was, he wasn't wrong.

In the same year he offered his home to Cast Iron Charlie Sorenson (1932) Fisher was forced to write:

I am hard up as hell for cash. We are having a very poor season here, and not making any sales. Do you know somebody among your friends who will buy "Smoke of the Forty-Fives"?

Carl owned a painting by Charles Russell whose proper title was "Battle of the Forty-Fives". He was writing to one R.F. Garland and offering to sell the original Remington, plus a duplicate of *"Selecting A Polo Pony"* that *"is a better picture than the original."* Fisher explained he refused $15,000 for the original, "and when I thought I was very rich I presented it to the Detroit Athletic Club." [38]

Correspondence relating to our subject's financial demise reveals the unsettled tone born from frustration. He wrote to Claude Mercer:

Oct. 5, 1934
"Dear Claude:
Your letter of October 1st is received and I am glad to hear from you and to know you are getting along as well as you are.

As to the depression, do you know of anyone it did not leave an imprint on? I myself lost about twenty-five million, but am still able to eat, up to this evening.

Yours,
Carl G. Fisher" [39]

Precisely how Fisher could have lost twenty-five million dollars is impossible to detail. Evidently his investment in Montauk was a phenomenal drain and the development faltered. Carl must have experienced guilt feelings as he had attracted several investors who had faith in he and the Montauk project.

His generosity continued as long as he had means. There were regular payments to relatives, he assisted his servant Galloway's daughter with tuition that continued his long tradition of donation.[40] After 1930 he turned down requests and replied to a request for a hospital donation: "it has been necessary to borrow money to take care of our own obligations, so I am in no position to make a donation at this time." [41]

His second marriage did not produce a happy union. All that's left to research the marriage has been preserved by Carl's second wife Margaret Collier. She did make a valuable contribution to the Fisher legacy as she donated everything from, old photographs, business correspondence, stubs, income-tax forms, auditors' reports, personal letters, newspaper clippings to the collection housed in the Historical Association of South Florida. Authors Polly Redford, Jerry Fisher, Mark Foster and this reporter have all plowed through the letters from mistresses, bankruptcy proceedings, telegrams from the elephant trainer, divorce papers, advertising copy, medical records, orders to bootleggers, Lincoln Highway Association meeting reports. Thus we journalists have to credit Margaret for her preservation effort.

Among the letters to and from her we see she did not replace Jane.

One of Carl's rants sounded a death knell for the union: He was warning her about a financial business deal she was about to enter.

August 3, 1935
"Dear Margaret:
You are no more fit to carry on a deal than is a dead cat-against the people you are dealing with. Take this or leave it but from now on cut me out and row your own canoe and we will split. You go your way and I will go mine.......I would like ½ of the furniture and my office stuff and then we will split. Dont (sic) think I'm sore but I am tired of being a dray horse....

As a young lady, Jane Fisher was provided with means enough to spend $86,000 in a Paris jewelery emporium. Here she poses forty years onward with a painting made during her golden era. [14]

Yours,
Love, Skip"

Carl noted how lonely he was and wanted a *"no noise, no publicity"* divorce. Margaret had a pre-nuptial agreement with Carl and he said she was *"well fixed for life if you have any brains".*[42]

A couple of weeks after Carl wrote the above letter, Jane informed him her own third marriage had gone sour. She said: *"I thought what I wanted was a "good man"-he did not drink or smoke and was a Christian Science Healer—he bored me to death— I'd much rather have him get drunk and beat me than be so dammed good—soooo (sic) I told him to pack his things and take his children and go back where he came from."* [43]

Bankruptcy proceedings for the Carl G. Fisher Co. were completed in 1934. Carl maintained some income and an office from his Bay Shore Company but control of his properties passed to others. The Collins family, who had first seen Carl gazing at their father's half-finished bridge to nowhere, would run the Boulevard, Nautilus and King Cole Hotels. [44] Carl could spend even more time reading from now on.

Judging by the astonishingly long lists of book orders Carl sent to the E.P. Dutton Co. at 681 Fifth Avenue in New York, we know he was a prolific reader. Copies of Memorandums listing over forty separate titles (in one order) are located in the Fisher Files. On a continuing basis Carl was ordering significant numbers of books for his own use and when he came across something he liked he would have copies sent to friends. The list of people he sent books to reads like a Who's Who of America.

Carl may have been in an adventuresome mood when he placed an order for two books: *"Bring 'Em Back Alive"* by noted big game hunter Frank Buck

and *"Al Capone, The Biography of A Self Made Man"*. His previous book order had stated: "RUSH-Would like two of the latest and best books on Psycho Analysis."[45]

It is reasonable to believe Carl wanted to know all he could about celebrated gangster Al Capone as the Chicago mob boss had descended on Miami Beach. As it turned out, beer barons swapped money and Capone found himself ensconced in a Spanish castello on Palm Island previously occupied by Clarence M. Busch of the Anheuser-Busch (Budweiser) family.[46]

Carl told his hotel detective Mike Glenn to research Capone's activites in Miami Beach. The one page typed report outlined not only Capone's holdings, but named city officials who were involved in gambling activity.[50] Capone's home was declared a public nuisance because of its known criminal inhabitants and Big Al was put on trial. The *Miami Daily News* said during Carl's testimony Capone *"sat for five minutes and glared at the witness with all the ferocity of an infuriated beast."* [47]

Miami Beach prosecutors were unable to convict Capone of a crime and ultimately it took the federal government's Internal Revenue Service to have him removed from Florida as he was sent to prison for income tax evasion.

Fisher had kept the gambling rooms out of his Miami Beach hotels. Although he patronized

Fisher was able to spend the last years of his career doing business from the attractive Alton Beach Company office. [2]

The City of Miami Beach did not welcome Al Capone and his friends as valued members of the community. Efforts to run him out of town were unsuccessful. [2]

the bootleggers and in the strictest sense could be considered one himself, he did not follow the lead of the wealthy Henry Flagler who was known to have built *"discreet high-toned"* rooms for his upscale clientele to wager in. [48]

Fisher had to face the fact the Miami Beach he had come to love was changing after the land rush subsided. The director of Miami Beach's exclusive Surf Club, Alfred Barton, who served in his post for four decades said of the Thirties:

"The social life of Miami Beach was just whipped cream on top of the cake. Because the real Miami Beach, as I look back on it now over the years, was certainly the theatrical, gangster, middle class....The

gangster element was so predominant here during those years that Twenty-third Street was the hangout for every known gangster in America." [49]

The gamblers remained in Miami Beach and Carl Fisher would continue to go to his attractive Alton Beach Company office throughout the Thirties. Fisher may very well to have loved *"shooting craps with his friends at The Shadows for a thousand dollars a throw"* [50] but he must have experienced indignation when his own bedroom in The Shadows was turned into a designated room. Jane says, "Final triumph of the gambling interests was in Carl's bedroom. A roulette wheel was standing where his bed once stood under the

pictures of Lincoln and Napoleon! [51] Jane had visited their original Beach front home after Carl sold it and became depressed over what the new owners had turned it into.

The kind of gambling Fisher liked best was when he decided to invest in that which he knew was a good thing. The self-seller. After all, if he had not gambled on the risky proposition of inserting acetylene into metal bottles that made his Prest-O-Lite fortune, he would have never had the capital to build Miami Beach in the first place. Carl's money was all gone by the mid-1930's, but the spirit of creativity doesn't know about money and still visited him regularly.

Chapter 12
Another Fortune On The Way

"I cannot get out of my head at all the fact that this marvelous material of silica sand goes to waste."

The February 14, 1925 edition of the *Miami Life* newspaper headlined *"Can We Afford To Lose Carl Fisher?"* The lead story centered upon Carl's continuing struggle with the Miami Chamber of Commerce over the sale of a three acre parcel of ground at the bay entrance Carl wanted to use for a deep water seaport. The newspaper article chided Chamber President Ev Sewell stating: "Do you think we better leash Ev up for a time..." Sewell had long opposed Fisher's plans and was seemingly the only obstacle in the way of providing Miami and the Beach with the deep water port.

The paper said, *"Does anyone have to be reminded that Carl Fisher is the outstanding developer of Florida today; that he is one of the most dramatic city builders in the United States; that his name is linked throughout the north with Miami's development more than that of any other person?.... We'll go further and assert that more credit is due him for the list of notables now at Miami Beach than both chambers combined."* [1]

A few years later the April 13, 1929 edition of

Miami Life

PUBLISHED AT 610 N. E. SECOND AVENUE, MIAMI, FLORIDA, BY MIAMI LIFE, INC.

Vol. 2. No. 5.
February fourteenth

Edited by Wen R. Phillips

Five Cents a Cop
One Dollar for Six Month

Can We Afford to Lose Carl Fisher?

T BEGINS to be apparent that the four years' warfare waged by E. G. Sewell upon Carl G. Fisher's development of Miami Beach harbor has reached a rather grave crisis, one serious enough to alarm all Miamians who give a tinker's dam about the future.

KNEE LENGTHS
is one of MIAMI LIFE'S most interesting features

You will find it on Page Eight

vindictiveness—are well known. But we can't understand the attitude of the level-headed directorate and membership of the Miami Chamber of Commerce. Their mesmeric leader seems to have deprived them of reason, sense of justice, or appreciation of Fisher's status in Miami development Does anyone have to be reminded that Car

In the mid-1920's Carl Fisher was considered a valuable asset to the Florida economy and gained headlines over his proposed development of a deep water harbor for Miami Beach. [2]

SATURDAY EVENING, APRIL 13, 1929.   21

SPEEDWAY CITY, WHICH CARL G. FISHER DREAMED OF TWENTY YEARS AGO, MAY YET BECOME "HORSELESS CITY" DEVOTED TO MOTORS AND AVIATION

Fisher's visions for the future of Speedway, Indiana as a "Horseless City" were recognized twenty years after he expressed them. [2]

the *Indianapolis News* headlined, *"Speedway City, Which Carl G. Fisher Dreamed of Twenty Years Ago, May Yet Become "Horseless City" Devoted To Motors And Aviation"* Reporter William Herschel was recounting a conversation he had with Fisher, as best as he could recall back in 1909, about the future. Fisher said, *"Wouldn't it be a great idea to build a horseless city just opposite the Motor Speedway? Make it an industrial city devoted to motorization of all traffic. Put it down as a rule of the municipality that all horses be barred from its confines. Do everything by motor."* [2]

The book you are reading was written in large part on Main Street in Speedway, Indiana flanked by the original Allison Engineering Company to the north, where Fisher and Jim Allison housed their Indy 500 cars and its natural enormous outgrowth to the south. The Allison Engineering buildings cover acres of Speedway, Indiana property today.

Now, however, in the mid 1930's there were no more headlines telling of Carl Fisher's vision.

His stature was so diminished that by 1933 he had written, to old friend and associate J.N. Lummus:*"I am very frank to tell you if you will give me $50,000 for the furniture and the "K" you can have them and I will be glad to make a deal with you".* [3]

After his bankruptcy Fisher was able to draw $50,000 annual salary from the Bay Shore Company, but as the Depression continued it was decreased to $10,000.[4] Although his real estate fortune was gone he continued to seek another Prest-O-Lite.

In reality, Carl had a history of dabbling in inventions. He received a patent dated June 26, 1928 for an Electric Switch Attachment. The device clamped on the spokes of the steering wheel and contained five toggle switches to run, well, to run some of the things you didn't need a switch for, such as the horn.[5] The application noted, ""Important

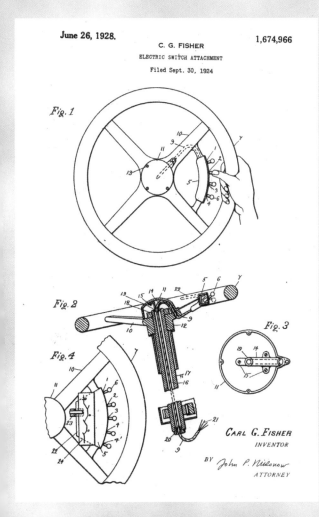

Evidently, Carl must have believed his Electric Switch Attachment would make for safer driving. [2]

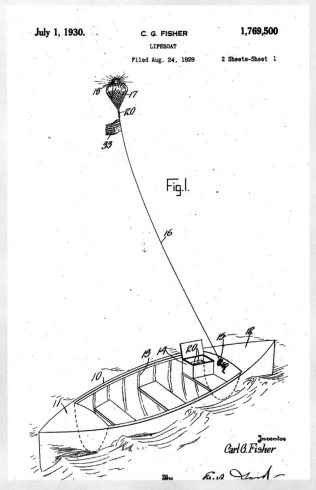

July 1, 1930.

C. G. FISHER

1,769,500

LIFEBOAT

Filed Aug. 24, 1929

2 Sheets-Sheet 1

Carl's signaling device for lifeboats may have been a desirable product, but like his other patents failed to reach success in the marketplace. [2]

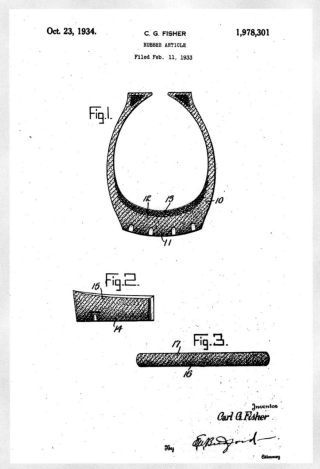

Fisher firmly believed his patent on mixing silica sand with rubber could revolutionize many standard products. Here we see an automobile tire, rubber heel for a shoe and rubber belting. [2]

advantages of my switch mounting is that the switches can be easily operated by the driver's thumb without releasing his grip on the wheel."

We wish Fisher had lived long enough to witness drivers cradling the left side of their head with a palm nearly concealing a cell phone while their right hand guides the vehicle. To his credit, we have seen the inclusion of buttons on steering wheel spokes in modern day vehicles so the basic idea did have merit.

The following year on August 24, 1929 Carl's patent application was submitted for a "distress signal apparatus to be used in connection with the life boats." Carl's days as a balloonist may have triggered this invention which utilizes a small balloon tied by rope to the distressed lifeboat to act as a signaling apparatus. The complex unit incorporated a valve to control a catalytic agent that would presumably serve to keep the balloon aloft. He noted in the patent

application his term "life-boat" would include "air planes, and all craft for which the invention may be appropriately adapted."[6] Presumably, the lifeboat occupants would have to have dry matches to light the unit. Simultaneously he was working on patents for a "collapsible rubber pontoon, steel spring rubber covered boat."[7]

While the steering wheel switch may have commanded the use of a banjo player's fingers, Carl's patent "on the mixing of silica sand with rubber in various quantities as necessary to prevent slipping of rubber heels, rubber soles, belting, rubber hammers, or wherever rubber is used where it would be desirable to use a material that mixes perfectly with the surface. It presents a much longer wearing surface and also an adhesive quality that cannot be found in rubber alone" [8] sounds as though it may have had excellent potential. Carl noted in his patent application, "*I have found that automobile tires made of my new rubber composition have been run ten thousand miles after which they showed less deterioration than tires made from any other material.*" The patent was granted October 23, 1934. Alas, your reporter could not locate any modern day products which utilize a silica sand and rubber combination.

Clearly, Carl most assuredly did not invent the inventions for which he was receiving the patents. We found no sketches, drawings, or correspondence relating to the development of these products in his files and assume he was searching for another Fred Avery, the man who sold him the patents that fathered Prest-O-Lite. Fisher must have been hoping Albert T. Bremser of Westmont, N.J. was his man. A patent issued Feb. 11, 1936 listed Mr. Bremser as having issued fifty-two percent patent ownership to Carl G. Fisher of Miami Beach, Fla. for their patent on a Solar Operated Refrigerating System. The first sentence of the patent application reveals its usage: "*My invention provides a system of cooling by utilizing the heat energy of the sun's rays.*" [9] This one may have been a dud as no correspondence was located promoting it.

The most entertaining of the lot is also described in the first sentence of the patent application, which was granted on Nov. 8, 1938 and states:

"*This invention relates to improvements in models for use in connection with the display of merchandise in store windows, show rooms, show windows or other*

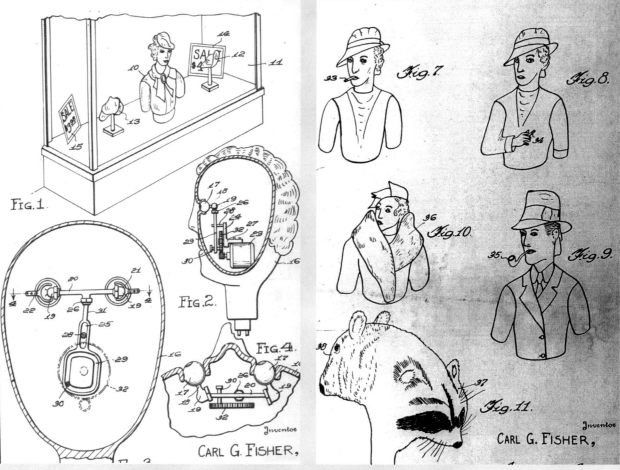

CARL G. FISHER,

The action-oriented Fisher was convinced potential customers would look twice at a store window model whose eyes followed your path. [2]

places where merchandise may be displayed." The accompanying illustrations show us Carl had invested in a mannequin style head that featured "a head with moveable eyes mounted in sockets therein, said eyes having operating attachments there on extending back into the head".

The plot contained within the dummy's head was to be operated by an electric motor that would "impart a slow rotary motion".

Consequently, we assume the passer-by would be compelled to stop and look at the model because

it was rolling its eyes at you and moving them left to right as you walked by. The invention said the mechanism "*will give the eyes both a vertical and a lateral movement and will also give them somewhat of a rolling motion.*" [10] It is safe to surmise prospects of Carl's moving-eye gizmo did in fact roll their eyes when the invention was presented.

Fisher put the most effort into the silica sand and rubber combination. After a discouraging letter from U.S. Rubber products he wrote to pal Tommy Milton:

"Don't forget that the Prest-O-Lite gas tank was dropped and kicked around the whole world for ten years, "because" and just "because", and it was perfected into what, I think, was quite a success (if you will pardon my modesty on the subject) by people who were not engineers." Carl had previously told Tommy, *"You are supposed to be an engineer, and if you are an engineer worth a damn, think these points over and see what you can figure out. I don't just exactly know, of course what combination will eventually be worked out that is practical for the use of silica sand as a wearing material, but I do know there must be some place where it will fit the job...I cannot get out of my head at all the fact that this marvelous material of silica sand goes to waste.(11)*

Tommy's replies provide some insight into their mutual friendship.

"Your liver may be turning into a "hunk of coal" but it hasn't affected your mental processes to any visible extent."

Tom, as he signed his letters continued,

"You will be interested to learn that I have taken a small office in a good building and we are going ahead as fast as we can. By the end of the year I expect to have a sample in operation and if the gadget (it really isn't a gadget) is all I expect it to be I will buy you a rubber laboratory in which you can make your own experiments with silica. Once I have that matter settled, one way or another, I will devote some time to your silica, marine balloons and hotel refrigerators. In the meantime please be patient and charitable. If my scheme turns out okay it will be bigger than Prest-O-Lite ever was-and that's no hay." (12)

We do not know what project Milton was working on that caused his high hopes.

In the end, and the end was near, Carl wrote to Tom,

"In sending you the patents and making a gift of them to you, I am doing so with the idea that you may be able to promote them, as I am not able to do so.... and you are under no obligations to me for future payments of any kind."

A registered letter assigning six of Carl's patents to

A mid-1930's photo of Fisher in one of his usual floppy-brimmed fedoras seemingly depicts a man who has hope for the future. (2)

Milton was sent on November 30, 1938 from attorney A.J. Sterman.(13) Carl gave away the patents and the hope that went with them.

Tom Milton had been hearing of Carl's promotional schemes for years. Fisher had directed his attention toward inexpensive prefabricated housing back in 1933 and imagined he could build a business that would rival the Johns-Manville Company. Tom read the houses were, *"practically indestructible, and certainly fire-proof, vermin proof and proof against the continuous sunshine"* (14)

Carl had envisioned simple low-cost housing would find a ready market.

Fisher's houses were to be built out of sand and coral rock building blocks with concrete floors and asbestos shingles for the roof. At the time there was no knowledge available on the dangers of using asbestos.

As we know, Carl did not come to rival the Johns-Manville Company and his housing proposition fell by the wayside.

Out of the multitude of names in industry Carl became friends and corresponded with, one is curiously missing, that of Powel Crosley. Crosley had actually worked for Fisher's automobile dealership(15). Crosley was so enamored with becoming a race car driver, and manufacturer he was termed as "one of the boys" by Ernie Moross, Barney Oldfield's publicity manager who had gone to work for Fisher promoting the Speedway.(16) Crosley rose to become known as "The Henry Ford of Radio" by 1923(17) and went on to successfully manufacture a wide variety of products ranging from the Shelvador refrigerator (first refrigerator with a shelf in the door) to aircraft, to the tiny Crosley automobile that made its debut at the Indianapolis Motor Speedway in 1939 a few months before Carl's death.(18)

Crosley's name from the 1920's onward was as familiar to Americans as the president of the United

A voracious reader, Carl looked bloated as he takes in the day's news toward the end of his life. [2]

States. Powel Crosley, aided by his devoted brother Lewis, was a man known for buying and partnering inventions as he too was always looking for the next big thing to sell. It seems only fitting Fisher would have known Crosley but why their their paths never crossed still remains a mystery.

Carl had mentioned to Tom Milton his liver was turning into a "hunk of coal" and so it was.

By the mid-Thirties Carl was diabetic, became an insulin user and he continued to ingest alcohol regularly.

Letters in the Fisher Files abound recounting his deteriorating physical condition. To pal Barney Oldfield he wrote:

"I am not doing so well these days-I mean my health. I go up to the hospital every seven days and they bore a hole in me with a fence auger and let out about 18 pounds of excess fluids. In the olden days they called this dropsy; nowadays they call it cirrhosis of the liver. The operation isn't all that painful and I am out flying around in a couple hours afterward. [19]

Oldfield had previously told Carl he was considering writing a book and Fisher made the following suggestion:

"I think one of the best little anecdotes you could mention in your book would be the time you broke the Speedway record with the old Christy at Indianapolis. Our bet at that time was a plug hat; but if left out the fact that you had a few drinks, I believe the story would be flattened considerably. Of course, if you have tried to dodge the fact that you were drunk a good deal of the time, or at least in a hilarious mood a good part of the time, you not only fly in the face of Providence, but you spit in the eye of a great many of your friends, who, if they weren't pretty tight at the time, were just getting over being tight, or were making preparations to be tight later on in the day."

Carl also told Oldfield:

" .....but the real kick of a lot of these stories is the use of some profane language. I think "Hell-Fire" and "Gott-Dam" and Begeeses," if spelled phonetically out to pass in any story because they put horse-radish or tobasco sauce in a story that a whole paragraph won't explain." [20]

Carl's left eye problem is graphically illustrated in this photo taken about a year before his death. [2]

Oldfield himself was promoting to the end as well. We discovered a brochure touting "Barney Oldfield's Country Club" in Van Nuys, California that featured the expected amenities of swimming, dancing, cocktails, barbecues, etc.

Barney talked of taking his trailer to Florida to visit Carl, but it didn't come to pass. The next time he visited Carl was to serve as a pall bearer at his funeral.

Carl Fisher's luminous journey through this life on earth came to an end on July 15, 1939 in St. Francis Hospital, having died of a gastric hemorrhage. [21]

The flags in Miami Beach flew at half mast and someone dressed Carl in get-up he would have never put on himself. He lay in his casket wearing a tuxedo, a rose in the lapel and wearing his horn-rimmed glasses. A floppy hat was not part of the attire. After he turned to spirit he probably said, "*Kee-rist-on-a-bicycle, put some clothes on that guy he can live in.*"

Later on in 1941 a small monument would be erected in his honor that included a bust of Carl, complete with appropriate hat. The inscription reads, "Carl Graham Fisher-He carved A Great City Out of A Jungle."

In March of 1951 Jane Fisher was on radio station WMAQ saying, "*I must confess, as I stood there watching the darkies swinging their axes on trees that forty years before natives were stripping off bark for the tannic acid the mangrove trees contained, I too felt Carl Fisher was having impossible dreams.*" [22]

Of course there have been Carl Fishers in every decade of recorded history who have had impossible dreams, men who wanted to make the dirt fly. For the most part Carl achieved his goals and when we consider from whence he came and the height he had risen, some at his funeral were probably saying:

"I'm sure glad I knew you Skip, you left a lot behind for us to enjoy."

Looking more dignified in death than he usually did in life, Fisher's funeral featured decorum and dignity he would have appreciated. [2]

The Carl Fisher memorial at Alton Road and 50th Street proclaims: He Carved A Great City From A Jungle [2]

Chapter 12

Carl Fisher: His name is not known to many,
but his accomplishments are enduring. [4]

Historical Background Section

History: Chapter 1
Rolling Over The Land

Chariots shall rage in the streets, they shall jostle one another in the broad ways; they shall seem like torches, they shall run like the lightnings.   Nahum: circa 612 B.C

"Oh, you're all skinned up Carl. Did you fall off that confounded contraption again?" Carl Fisher's mom asked."

"Yeah, we were racing and I hit a chuckhole. Threw me right over the handlebars. I'm ok, but I think I bent the front wheel."

Carl Fisher undoubtedly had many a spill from atop his two-wheel contraptions while he was growing up. It's safe to say the first thing Carl Fisher was, was a bicycle man. By the time he was ten years old in 1884, the bicycle was commonplace in American and around the world. Carl had discovered it was a lot of fun to glide on two wheels. We doubt he gave any thought to its invention.

We have lived with the wheel for so long we can't remember a time when it wasn't a part of our daily life. When you were a kid you had a tricycle. Maybe you started out on one of those plastic bodied Big Wheels. It had handlebars and pedals and a little seat made just for you. Your mom or dad couldn't ride it and no one had to teach you what to do. You hopped on and you were mobile, even though you didn't know what mobile meant. You scurried up and down the driveway, and the sidewalk out in front of your house was just perfect for an adventure.

Later on you could see that the 'big kids' had bicycles that had just two wheels and they could go farther and get there faster. So you got a bicycle, and maybe in the beginning it had four wheels, two training wheels out back. Then came the day when the training wheels were taken off and you were just like everyone else, you could get from here to there all by yourself, probably as long as you stayed out of the street where the big, fast and dangerous wheels were.

Back in the 1800's kids used to roll hoops of steel from here to there with a stick. But not all kids back through time had wheels to roll, or ride. Where did the wheel come from? How long have we been using it, and why do we call it a wheel in the first place?

The origin of the word 'wheel' comes to us from the ancients and according to archaeologists the earliest usage was around 8000 BC. in Asia.The oldest wheel discovered comes from Mesopotamia from the 3500 BC Era. We have clay pots excavated from Southern Poland dating to 3500BC that depicts a wagon. Egyptians were known to have spoked wheels by 2,000 BC while similar specimens date to India in 1500 BC

The word wheel traces its roots to the English

A proper looking gentleman named Elwood Haynes poses with his creation designed to replace the horse. Haynes became known as an important metallurgist. [5]

just cutting the log does not yield a piece of wood with enough structural support in all directions to support weight. It cracks. Man had to figure out that many boards pieced together in the form of a wheel was the solution. Or, as cartoons have depicted, man had to fashion a wheel from stone.

Historians point us to the fact that even developed civilizations such as the Maya and Aztec did not utilize the wheel. There is no evidence to prove people in the Western Hemisphere used the wheel until they came into contact with the Europeans.

We USA settlers literally rolled over the native American Indians and told them: "We're taking this land, go somewhere else." Our native Americans utilized the bow and arrow and at the risk of stereotyping, it is this writer's opinion our native born simply did not develop the tools necessary for their own defense. It is evident the land was more peaceful without the use of wheels.[1]

Once the wheel was more or less perfected man dreamed of gliding over the earth's surfaces with as little effort as possible. Consequently, mankind took a long, arduous route in developing means of propulsion that included steam, electric and gasoline power.

Throughout the world we knew how to manufacture a steam engine in the 1800's, and our knowledge of manufacturing to precision tolerances was advancing. Making a wheel and axle suitable for a horse going ten miles per hour was one thing, but more precision was necessary once we replaced the horse with an engine that propelled the vehicle. [2]

The claim of "America's First Car" comes from Kokomo, Indiana where an inventor named Elwood Haynes became the center of attention on July 4, 1894 when he drove down Main Street in his carriage without a horse in front of it. Haynes' name is respected throughout the metallurgical world as being the inventor of Stellite, a fabulous wear resistant

hpeo, as well as the Proto-Indo-European *kweklo* which evolved from the root K which means to revolve, move around. the Greeks used the word *kuklos* and in Sanskrit *chakra* was used to describe the round device that has so transformed mankind and his ways. Yoga practitioners know a chakra is the energetic center of the body at which a number of channels meet, and use varying meditation systems for their chakras. The Latin *rota* lets us know where rotate came from.

While some animals can roll, there are no wheels in animals or plants that are visible to the naked eye. Although man made the wheel, not all cultures did. The oldest wheels uncovered are very new in the scheme of things.

The chronology of mankind tells us it was a very long time before we utilized the wheel. Since it was easy to see a log rolled, our first inclination is to believe we can merely take a slice off a log, bore a hole in it, insert an axle and make a cart. However,

History: Chapter 1

Charles Duryea in 1894-95 in the vehicle that won the nation's first automobile race (Chicago) held in November of 1895. This is the prototype of the 1896 Duryea production vehicle. [1]

steel which still enjoys widespread usage today and is a staple in the aerospace industry. [3] Haynes' claim of first on the road has been successfully challenged to the tune of a couple of years.

Automotive historians will be quick to point out Charles E. Duryea of Springfield, Massachusetts and his brother Frank operated their own gasoline-powered vehicle in 1892-93. Today you can see their vehicle in the Smithsonian Institution. Ranson E. Olds is credited with a similar vehicle in 1895 and thus the mighty Oldsmobile was born. [4]

The evolution of the automobile happened in a virtual eye-blink of time when we consider the very earliest traces of Homo erectus, the first true man, are dated about 1.3 million years ago. The Neanderthal Man lived 100,000 years back in time and we Homo sapiens are 40,000 years old. [5]

The best chronology I have uncovered pertaining to the evolution of self-propelled vehicles is contained in the appendix of Arthur Pound's "*Turning Wheel, The Story of General Motors Through Twenty Five Years*", 1908-1933 and is to be considered valuable reading for any automotive historian.

Studies of the ancients teaches us Hero of Alexandria proposed use of steam power as early as 150 B.C. Leonardo daVinci's fertile mind gave us a wheeled vehicle sketch in his Codice Atlantico (anno1500). [6]

By late in the 1800's the use of steam was changing the face of the world through railroads, steamships, and industrial machinery. Many believed steam would rule the world of the horseless carriage. Others tied their dreams to electric power. Nevertheless, our now familiar internal combustion engine became the premier power-plant.

The internal combustion engine and its origins have naturally been the subject of the debate of who-was-first. The development of the self-contained

Henry Ford's first vehicle has been aptly termed a Quadricycle. [(6)]

engine traces its roots to the mid 1800's and by the turn of the 20th century this new power-plant had been developed sufficiently to be a reliable source of power. It had significant competition from its steam and electric counterparts. Precise accuracy notwithstanding, out of 4,192 automobiles in the U.S. In 1900, 1,691 were steam-powered, 1,585 electrics and 936 were gasoline engined. Eleven car companies advertised in Auto Topics in January 1901: four each powered by electric and gas while three were pulled by steam. [(7)]

The state of automotive development in 1900 was enjoying the fruits of labor from the world's current inventions and of course from the many mechanically minded souls who had been experimenting for over a century. The old country, specifically Germany and France were ahead of we Americans in automotive technology as we entered the 20th century but it wouldn't take us long to catch up.

Although the new 1899 American built Packard looked like a carriage to be pulled by a horse, it featured a three-speed forward and one speed reverse transmission, thereby depicting our knowledge of not only gearing, but materials as well. As can be imagined, once at least two vehicles were side by side, one driver surely said, "*I think mine is faster than yours.*"

Thus the first international automobile race, held from Paris to Lyon was staged in 1900 to compete for sportsman Gordon Bennett's trophy. The winning vehicle, a Panhard-Levassor averaged 38.5 mph. The French at this time were at the forefront of automotive technology. [(8)]

Proponents of the electric vehicle perked up in 1900 when they learn Thomas Edison has developed a nickel-iron battery and a man named Junger believes his nickel-cadmium battery will prevail. Then one Charles Palmer notched a point with a breakthrough in gasoline refining technology, using high pressure and heat to decompose crude petroleum. The steam locomotive is brought to its highest level of development through research done by England's G.J. Churchward. The electric arc steel-producing furnace is introduced by Paul Heroult and is heralded as a significant development in preventing contamination thereby making cleaner steel possible. Heroult's method of using the electric arc canceled the use of solid, liquid or gaseous fuel thereby preventing contamination of the steel by impurities. [(9)]

By meandering through development of steam, electric and gasoline we can see the advances in steel production affect all our methods of propulsion. As one industry matured another could prosper, or falter. This era prior to and during the cultivation of the motorcar is a romantic one as we sought to harness the road, and the sky. Fortunately images were now preserved thanks to Nicephore Niepce (1765-1816) who played a key role in inventing photography when he discovered a silver-chloride coated plate could retain an image. A sunbeam reflected off an object and passing through a small hole in a dark box projects an inverted duplicate image on the opposite wall of the box. Niepce projected onto the described plate and gave us photography. He should also be credited with giving us an early form of the bicycle as we shall see in the next chapter.

Photographs of the turn of the 20thth century could now be taken by anyone as Kodak introduces its new Brownie camera in 1900 and the Browning company introduced its Model 1900 handgun, a pocket model. Now we easily take a photograph of a man with a gun. Within a few years Carl Fisher would utilize photographs of females that would raise many an eyebrow.

The aviation-oriented Wright Brothers, Wilbur and Orville who had been experimenting with kites and gliders since 1896, flew their first un-piloted glider at Kitty Hawk, North Carolina Their quest for manned flight would be achieved in 1903. Carl Fisher would go on to become close friends with the Wright brothers as he became an early day supporter of flight. During this era another inventive soul took a piece of wire and bent it in such a fashion it would hold a few sheets of paper together as the paper-clip was invented.[10]

Most of the men we are reporting on in this book were born between 1860 and 1875 and they had the proverbial front row seat for the dawn of the automobile. For those whose interests lay in things mechanical, the Industrial Revolution that had begun in the mid 1800's provided a marvelous fertile field for their inventive minds. The value of manufacturers output rose from two billion dollars to nine from 1860-1890. The nation was being criss-crossed by railroads: there were five transcontinental trunk lines

The Stanley brothers, Francs E. and Freeland O. and their first steam vehicle, a most compact unit. Their creations were among the finest steam-powered cars made. [1]

by 1893 and mileages on rails were doubling and re-doubling every few years. [11].

However, the idea of self-propelled vehicles, whether on the ground or in the air was as foreign as outer-space travel to most of the world's population. Any report of a carriage making its way without a horse gained full attention of the general population.

Those who believed the steam engine would ultimately become the power-plant of choice continued their quest as did those who felt electric driven vehicles would triumph. Each made significant contributions and to a degree each succeeded. We already trusted steam power for our locomotives and anything else was suspect. It was agreed that with an internal combustion engine you could literally be sitting on top of an explosion. Fact of the matter is, thousands of explosions per minute were necessary to make the gasoline engine work.

Baker Electrics

A luxurious **motor** car refined to the point of utmost simplicity. Free from fads or frills of construction which interfere with unfailing operation. A highly efficient electric, backed by fifteen years of sound engineering.

"Baker Service Follows Every Baker"

THE BAKER MOTOR VEHICLE COMPANY, CLEVELAND, OHIO

Canada: The Baker Motor Vehicle Company of Canada, Ltd., Walkerville, Ont.
Builders also of Baker Electric Trucks : Branches or Dealers in Principal Cities

There were at least 46 U.S. Manufacturers of electric vehicles between the late 1890's and 1940. The Baker was one of the more successful and produced cars from 1899-1916. [1]

The Stanley brothers in the U.S. along with Abner Doble were responsible for constructing technologically advanced and quiet steam-powered automobiles. Steam engines in automobiles did reach an admirable level of sophistication and were user-friendly, but our wheels would ultimately be powered by gasoline engines that inhaled the clean air we breath while exhausting deadly carbon monoxide.

The electrics provided quiet and reliable transportation for relatively short time periods before their batteries would have to be recharged. As I write now in the year 2010, I cannot suppress a sly smile after reading the latest electric vehicle promises to go forty miles before needing a recharge. The electric vehicles produced a century ago were actually providing a very useful service to the public, most especially when you consider the short distances required by most.

As we now know, the internal combustion power-plant proved to be the most efficient. Steam and electric proponents continued their quest well into the 1920's with varying degrees of success. Our hybrid vehicles of the 21st century pay homage to these early creators. Aircraft enthusiasts will recall that as recently as the 1960's Bill Lear (of Lear jet fame) was working on a steam-powered vehicle.

Brief History of The Internal Combustion Engine

Dutchman Christian Huygens worked in the 1670-80's period and also attempted an internal combustion engine utilizing gun powder. The principle of containing an explosion in a cylinder was brought to life when one Allessandro Volta built a pistol utilizing a mixture of marsh gas and air ignited by an electric spark back in 1777. [12] One of his pupils, a Denis Papin is believed to be the man who created the idea of converting reciprocating motion to rotary when he invented the crank pin and connecting rod system.

(13) The lineage continues to a Swiss named Isaac de Rivaz who was granted a patent in 1807 for a gas-air engine. Rivaz's device is said to have been a single cylinder contraption that was ultimately mounted in a carriage. (14)

The early inventors up through about 1825 used inflammable gases and were not producing true internal combustion engines. Englishman Robert Street (who obtained a patent to utilize a liquid fuel in 1794), Frenchman Philippe Lebon (credited with realizing vapors had to be compressed before igniting, 1799) and American Peter Cooper were among the first experimenters. Michael Faraday was able to extract benzene (gasoline) from coal which is said to be the first liquid fuel suitable for engine use.

The creative cloud that has engulfed Italy for centuries provided Luigi De Cristoforis with imagination enough to see him produce a working power-plant based on the theory of internal combustion (1841). Eugenio Barasanti and Felice Matteucci developed Cristoforis' idea far enough to obtain a British patent in 1854. A few years later craftsmen from Zurich named Eschel and Wyss continued research and achieved a measure of success. (15)

The complete theory of what is known as the four stroke engine was outlined by Alphonse Beau de Rochas in Paris in 1861, but who never built an engine. Rochas clearly described the four-stroke cycle in a handwritten, lithographically produced pamphlet in 1862 and received a French patent.

The four-stroke engine can be described as a pump with rotating force. A piston and rod assembly contained in a cylinder are connected to a rotating crankshaft that has a U bend in it. When the crankshaft is rotated the rod connected to it moves the piston up and down, within an air tight cylinder. Consequently the four strokes include: intake, compression, combustion and exhaust.

Stroke 1, the piston goes down the cylinder and sucks in fuel. Stroke 2, the piston compresses the volume inside the cylinder as it goes to the top. Stroke 3, the fuel in the cylinder is ignited and forces the piston down, spinning the crankshaft, thereby making power. Stroke 4, the piston rises and pushes out the exhaust gases. Then the piston starts its downward travel once again for another cycle. Two stroke engines were invented, but for our purposes we are concerned only with the four-stroke. As is easily imagined, making the air/fuel mixture ignite at precisely the right moment became critical and mechanically oriented souls around the world worked to perfect power-plants.

Jean Joseph Etiennc Lenoir, was a Belgian who received a patent in 1860 for an engine that utilized illuminating gas along with a mixture of air ignited by an electric spark. While Lenoir's engine actually represented an adaptation of the principles used in a steam engine, it had no compression and ultimately proved to be inefficient. Nevertheless, Lenoir's name became famed after he installed an engine in a boat he ushered up and down the Seine. It was later proven Lenoir had actually constructed an automobile that traveled 14 miles in three hours. Lenoir's accomplishment's became the subject of a spirited controversy as the Austrians claimed Sigfried Marcus's 1877 efforts earned the rights of who-was-first. The Automobile Club of France settled the claim in January of 1900 with a detailed, documented report stating the Lenoir vehicle had in fact accomplished the feat in 1863. Lenoir himself said the vehicle was underpowered but nevertheless, self-propelled. (16)

The work of Nikolaus August Otto of Cologne bore fruit enough by 1861 to be called the most successful four-stroke engine of the times. Otto and partner Eugene Langen used coal gas. Sigfried Marcus is credited with constructing the first four-stroke engine to use Faraday's principle (to use the

gasoline he discovered) in 1875. Otto and Langen set up a shop appropriately titled Gasmotorfabrik deeutz and noted historian automotive Jan Norbye calls the Cologne based operation a "great value as a training ground for automotive engineers." Its staff included Gottlieb Daimler and Willhelm Maybach, names that would become synonymous with high quality craftsmanship in the horseless carriage industry. Norbye says Daimler can be considered as the world's first true automotive engineer. (17)

Daimler and Karl Benz, working independently of one another (in fact they never met each other face to face) each developed highly successful gasoline engines and each prospered. Their designs were copied for many years.

By and large, the Europeans were ahead of their American counterparts in terms of automotive development. By the mid 1890's the previously mentioned Duryea and Elwood Haynes along with Henry Ford, Charles B. King, Alexander Winton and Ransom E. Olds had all built their first, primitive gasoline driven cars based on the Otto-Langen design. At first blush, it does not sound as though the Americans were far behind the Europeans, but we have to consider our pioneers used imported technology.(18)

When Count Albert de Dion and engineer Georges Bouton were able to achieve a production engine capable of reaching 1,500 rpm in 1895 it was evident the self-contained power-plant was a mechanical innovation that had come into its own.

Through the engineering skills of Daimler and Maybach some 2,000 engines were sold through 1885 and numerous licenses for manufacture were issued. It is estimated in approximately 1890, 1,900 licenses were granted for the Daimler engine. One licensee found success in an unrelated industry, William Steinway, founder of the Steinway & Sons piano company who originally brought out a twin

ONE OF THE LUXURIOUS LENOX BROUGHAMS BODY BY BRUNN.

THE AUTO CAR EQUIPMENT COMPANY

MANUFACTURERS GASOLINE AND ELECTRIC VEHICLES BUFFALO, NEW YORK

The stagecoach era was not far behind this "Luxurious Lenox Brougham" that left its driver to battle the elements. [1]

cylinder engine before turning his attention back to the piano.

Meanwhile the aforementioned Karl Benz's creation saw its way into a three-wheeled tricycle that would etch his name into automotive annals. It is generally agreed that with the introduction of the Daimler and Benz machines, the basic tenants for the invention of the automobile had been completed.

Lest they be forgotten, the efforts of Italian Bernardi in the 1890 period proved to be prophetic. Bernardi made great strides with his removable cylinder head, rocker valve operation and constant-level carburetion. His vehicles did not enjoy great success and the reason given is simply the Italian economy was not ready to develop the industry. The Italians may have been a little slow out of the starting gate, but Enzo Ferrari would come along a few years hence and provide the world with an automobile to be remembered.

Historians estimate there were about 350 motor vehicles on the road in France in 1895 and about 75 in Germany of which Karl Benz was responsible for making 135 self-propelled units. [19]

Most wheels were still being turned by horse and pedal power at the turn of the twentieth century but it would not be long before the world would experience a wheeled-vehicle surge that would ultimately change the face of our planet such as mankind had never seen. A successful farmer may have been using a steam powered tractor at the turn of the century but by 1910 he would have heard of, and could well own a new Model T Ford automobile. Then he could drive to town, and visit the next town. The automobile mobilized the society and created a lasting romance we continue to savor.

Carl Fisher was like many other young men who fell in love with things that rolled on wheels and his fascination would ultimately carry him from buying and selling bicycles to erecting facilities that would host the world's fastest automobiles. The wheels he loved would provide him with capitol enough to build another facility that would host the President of the United States as well as luminaries from around the world. In-between times he was responsible for giving us roads that were the finest of the day.

Carl Fisher's world was one of wheels and engines that made his ears smile. His journey began while pushing a pair of pedals so we'll take a look at that device.

Chapter 2
Pedal Power

"Why Carl, that machine is all beat up. What are you going to do with it?"
"I'll fix it and sell it, Mom."

Carl Fisher's main interests until middle age were bicycles, females and automobiles. He was enchanted with the bicycles of his day and followed the natural progression to automobiles. Again, I think it will be educational to present at least a rudimentary history of the progression of wheeled transportation, (namely the bicycle as that is the vehicle upon which Fisher built his first business success) to help you better understand the era he grew up in.

The study of the automobile's ancestry inherently includes that of the bicycle and of course to a degree, the airplane and locomotive. The continual cross-pollination of these mechanical marvels naturally attracted the same type of inventive mind and the ever-present challenge for perfection. The world had been using carts pulled by horse and oxen for

The original 1816 Draisine built by Baron von Drais.[13]

An artist's rendering of the inventor astride his creation.[13]

thousands of years, but it took us a very long time to discover we could put one wheel in front of the other and actually glide over the land. Carl Fisher felt the exhilaration of balancing atop two wheels and it was this love affair that put him in business.

The idea of inserting two wheels in between a beam that would hold them upright was not utilized until more than a thousand years after the birth of Christ. We could not figure out how to ride atop one wheel and probably believed it impossible, until someone invented the uni-cycle.

It wasn't until 1816 that Karl von Drais, known as alternately as Baron Drais bolted together the device instantly recognizable as the forerunner of the bicycle. Karl von Drais was an inveterate tinkerer who had the duty of patrolling miles of forest paths for his employer, the Duke of Baden. In order to make his journeys more palatable he concocted what is known as the original Draisine that shows considerable forethought.

The beam of wood connecting the wheels incorporates a dip in it to carry the rider along with vertical rests fore and aft of the seat in order to aid pushing the machine.

We assume after von Drais straddled the machine and walked it thorough several paces, he would discover that it could not only roll easily in a forward motion, but could be balanced with practice. Consequently, on downhill grades, he would have been able to coast. It is reported he negotiated the road from Karlsruhe to Schwetzingen in one hour astride his machine, a journey that normally took a man walking, four hours. [1] Karl von Drais had contrived a device that would alter mankind's mode of transportation.

The bicycle! Our skinny frame, skinny tired vehicles that are now as much a part of our landscape as the roads upon which they travel became the single most important device in Carl Fisher's life as an adolescent and well into his teenage years.. He and his friends the world over began their journey through life on and because of the bicycle. Baron von Drais and his like-minded brothers of the world had no idea of the importance of their creation.

As is to be expected, there exists another claim of first-on-the-road by the supporters of the Chevalier de Sivrac who say the Frenchman preceded the von Drais machine in 1790. Drawings exist showing

This 1818 hobbyhorse utilized a pad for the rider's chest. [(18)]

J.J. Lawson's Bicyclette from 1879 is considered to be the first sprocket and rear-wheel chain driven machine. [(18)]

A copy of the graceful 1839 MacMillan rear-driven bicycle . [(18)]

the Sivrac machine, called a Celerifere did in fact exist prior to the von Drais device. However, the Celeriferes were constructed in the forms of animals (think of hobbyhorse) and did not feature a steerable front wheel. In January of 1818 Karl von Drais was actually granted patent protection "for his invention of a tread machine".

It has been discovered Nicephore Niepce, a Frenchman also introduced a "Celeripede" at about the same time the von Drais machine appeared. The Draisine, as it came to be known became the vehicle to which all others are compared. Niepce was yet another creative soul who is recognized as the man who simultaneously invented photography and photogravure.

To this reporter, it seems only fitting that von Drais, who had acquired the moniker of "Professor of Mechanics" and who literally bankrupted himself in the quest for new mechanical contrivances, was honored by a monument in the form of a school in 1891 in his native city of Karlsruhe. that displays not only the original machine but a bas-relief of the vehicle along with a flock of birds, evidently included to depict flight over the land. [2]

From the period of 1816 onward there appeared a variety of two wheeled vehicles called hobby horses and velocipedes, all meant to be propelled by the rider shuffling his feet along the ground. In England they were referred to as "dandyhorses" after "the foppish men who rode them".[3] Both men's and ladies' models were available. One Denis Johnson, an English Cartwright saw the possibilities

It was a lucky young man whose parents could afford a mini-high wheeler. [1]

explosion within a cylinder to perfect the internal combustion engine, nearly two decades passed before pedals were added to the budding bicycle. Tricycles had incorporated cranks as early as 1820, but it took a town blacksmith to construct the first workable pedals.

Kirkpatrick MacMillan of Pierpont, and Dumfriesshire of Scotland put together a curvaceous machine supposedly in 1838-1840, that linked the rear wheels, via rods linked to pedals. The MacMillan machine was ingenious for its day inasmuch as the blacksmith also incorporated 'rake' to the front forks (leaning them backwards) which allowed the front

of the machine and made improvements to patent his creation in 1818 as well. Although he called it a Pedestrian Curricule the public utilized such terms as Hobby Horse; Swiftwalker; Patent Accelerator; Bicipede, Velocipede, Bivector.[4]

Books detailing the history of the bicycle are chock full of grin enhancing prints depicting properly attired ladies and gents shuffling their two wheelers about.

As we learned in chapter one, while inventors were struggling with the problems of containing an

A boneshaker with pedals attached directly to front wheel hub. [1]

A typical high-wheeler popular from 1870 on. [1]

Will Robertson of the Washington Bicycle Club rides a Star down the steps of the U.S. Capitol. The Star was a very stable machine. [1]

wheel to stabilize the machine to such a degree that it was as easy to balance as a modern day bicycle. MacMillan's machine may have spurred on fellow countryman Gavin Dalzell to construct a somewhat updated version in 1845.

The appearance of the Dalzell machine was challenged by a James Johnston who said Dalzell merely copied the earlier MacMillan [5]. Clearly, the who-was-first-trophy in all manner of mechanical devices seems to prove that many like minds were working simultaneously throughout history.

Researcher David Herlihy has compiled a scholarly work in his " *Bicycle The History*" published in 2004 and those interested in two-wheeled-locomotion will find this book to be invaluable. Herlihy points out the term bicycle was not in common usage until the 1860's and was preceded by our aforementioned names such as draisine and velocipede (from the Latin meaning fast foot).

For our purposes in we are not going to detail the year-by-year development of the bicycle. Once pedals were added to the front wheel it became evident

Progression of the two wheelers is depicted here from right to left. [1]

the machine would enjoy wide acceptance. The velocipedes, (also known as boneshakers) dominated throughout the 1860's and then the regal looking high-wheelers (known as ordinaries) emerged as the mainstay of the industry. The public's imagination was fueled by competition not only between human participants, but crowds turned out to see a bicyclist run against a trotting horse. Enthusiast clubs formed and the world became a smaller place for bicycle riders. [6].

While incarnations appeared in the form of both pedal and leverage arm operated three-wheelers (never very popular in the USA) our two-wheeler would ultimately become a world-wide staple. Front wheels grew in diameter sometimes reaching sixty inches in diameter with a trailing rear wheel of no more than sixteen inches leading to the term of "Penny Farthing" to describe the machines for the disparity in diameters.

Carl Fisher began his bicycle riding career on a towering high-wheeler that had a small step affixed to the left side of the frame to allow the rider to mount

and dis-mount. The rider would push the machine forward, mount the step, hop onto the seat and and then catch up with the spinning pedals on the front wheel to keep the vehicle in motion. Of course the rider had to reverse the tricky procedure to dis-mount. Nevertheless, Fisher and his friends were so smitten by being able to glide over the landscape nearly as fast (and sometimes faster) as a horse that wheels would become part and parcel of their lives.

Carl Fisher would go on to register a mark on the world of wheels that lasted for generations to come.

By 1891 the safety bicycles were purchased by over 150,000 Americans and became an integral part of the world's road system. [1]

A pack of healthy young men on their safety biciycles head into a turn on a midwestern fairgrounds track.
Although Fisher was not in this photo, he was an active bicycle racer himself. (13)

Acknowledgements

This book is the result of 15 years worth of part-time research and 50 years' interest in the world of wheels in general. Thus the job of crediting all those along the way who have aided in one form or another its total content becomes impossible.

To begin I have to go back and thank one of America's most loved race car owners, J.C. Agajanian for his efforts in introducing me to the professionals who attended an Indy car race at Continental Divide Raceways in 1968, and I owe thanks to Bill Kenz and Roy Leslie of Kenz & Leslie V-8 Service in Denver, Colorado for giving me my first introduction to craftsmen who were dedicated to the sport of speed. My good friend Sam Jameson shared his Floyd Clymer Indianapolis 500 Annuals with me and sparked my interest in the famed 500 Mile race. Life long friend Duane Helms supplied most of the mechanical knowledge necessary for the construction of our first race car that helped seal my interest in auto racing.

Along the route I met Butch Wilson, a fine auto racing oriented craftsman who encouraged me to further my education as did a well to do man named Vic Breeden who supplied me with a beautiful 1937 LaSalle Coupe to drive to college and challenged me to become articulate. Wilson introduced me to one of the twentieth century's most beloved and successful drivers, Dan Gurney who set an example for gentlemanly conduct in the sport.

I have to thank the hundreds of race car drivers, car owners, mechanics, sponsors and members of the news media, including writers and photographers who contributed to my publishing company I encountered during my 30 year auto racing publishing career. Each in their own way assisted my continuing success. College provided me with a life long friend, Art Fein, who assisted me in the production of Speed Wheels newspaper when we were college seniors. Al Bloemker of The Indianapolis Motor Speedway saw my potential and allowed me to publish my Indianapolis 500 Yearbook and Dr. Harlen Hunter who furnished part of the necessary capital to produce my first 500 Yearbook and race car collector, auto racing promoter and banker Don Smith who provided continuing loans to continue my publishing activities. Photographer Jim Chini provided not only magnificent photographs for my early publications but knowledge of the industry as well.

For the specific compilation of material for this book I have to acknowledge, in no particular order: David White, Kettering University; Ann Lawless of the American Precision Museum; The Krishnamurti Archives; Andy Clark of the Sloan Museum; The Scharchburg Archives; Dr. P. Christian Kleiger Senior Curator of History, Oakland Museum; The Free Library of Philadelphia; Pat McGeehan at National Geographic; Kay Webster of the Elwood Haynes Museum; Prudence Doherty, Bailey Howe Library, University of Vermont; Chicago Historical Society; The Wheelmen; The Walter P. Chrysler Boyhood Home & Museum; Richard Leisenring, Jr, Curtiss Museum; London's Science Museum; Muskingham County Library, Zanesville, OH for assistance concerning the fatalities caused by Fisher's auto racing accident; Dawn Hugh, Historical Museum of Southern Florida who guided me through the vast Fisher Files, Carillon Historical Park, Dayton, OH; Smithsonian Air & Space Museum; Patzetta Trice of Allison Transmission Division of General Motors; U.S. Patent Office; Larry Kinsel, General Motors Archives; Mary Michals, Illinois State Historical Library for assistance on Robert Ingersoll; Karen Rade, Montauk Library; Mark Patrick and Laura Kotsis, National Automotive History Collection, Detroit for their continuing assistance in my publishing efforts; University of Michigan Library; Iowa Department of Transportation; Indiana State Library; Susan Sutton, Indiana Historical Society for photographic assistance relating to Carl Fisher and the Indianapolis Motor Speedway; Ramsey Country Historical Society, St. Paul, MN for research on Tommy Milton.

I also want to thank: Jerry Fisher, author of The Pacesetter; Ron McQueeney of the Indianapolis Motor Speedway's photo department; Indy 500 statistician Donald Davidson's work was called upon frequently; John Darlington, Tom Rollings, John Blazier Indy 500 memorabilia collectors were again used for their well-researched assistance; Gordon Barrett automotive craftsman and historical researcher, who provided facts on Ray Harroun and Indy 500 car owner Lindsey Hopkins who knew Carl Fisher and shared his impressions of the man. My long-time secretaries Terri Gunn and Wilma Steffy gave their usual support and encouragement and without whom I could not have run a successful publishing company; Ron Smith who has made our photographs come to life and constructed the book itself. Fellow Vincent motorcycle enthusiast Gregg Max gave me invaluable assistance in final editing and proof-reading. Plus I owe a sincere thanks to the thousands of automobile racing fans who have purchased my books for over thirty years.

Photo Sources

1. **National Automotive History Collection**
   121 Gratiot Ave.
   Detroit, MI 48226
   313 628-2851

2. **Historical Museum of Southern Florida**
   101 W. Flagler Ave.
   Miami, FL 33130
   305 375-1492

3. **Indiana Historical Society**
   450 W. Ohio St.
   Indianapolis, In 46202
   317 232-1882

4. **Indianapolis Motor Speedway**
   Photo Shop
   4790 W. 16th St.
   Speedway, IN 46222
   317 492-8500

5. **Elwood Haynes Museum**
   1915 S. Webster
   Kokomo, IN 46901
   765 456-7500

6. **Henry Ford Museum**
   20900 Oakwood Blvd.
   Dearborn, MI 48124
   313 982-6001

7. **Carillon Historical park**
   1000 Carillon Blvd.
   Dayton, OH 45409
   937 293-2841

8. **Illinois State Historical Society**
   P.O. Box 1800
   Springfield, IL 62705
   217 525-2781

9. **Iowa Department of Transportation**
   800 Lincoln Way
   Ames, IA 50010
   515 239-1101

10. **Bailey Howe Library**
    University of Vermont
    Burlington, VT 05405
    8902 656-1493

11. **John Darlington**
    Private Collection

12. **Curtiss Museum**
    8419 State Route 54
    Hammondsport, NY 14840
    607 569-2160

13. **Carl Hungness**
    Private Collection

14. **Indianapolis Marion County Public Library**
    40 E. St. Clair St.
    Indianapolis, IN 46204
    317 275-4100

15. **Gary Doyle**
    Private Collection

16. **Dick Wallen**
    Private Collection

17. **Chicago History Museum**
    1601 N. Clark St.
    Chicago, IL 60614
    312 642-4600

18. **Science Museum**
    National Museum of Science & Industry
    Exhibition Road
    London SW7 2DD
    London, England

19. **Gordon Barrett**
    Private Collection

20. **Auburn University**
    Auburn, AL 36849
    334 844-4500

Bibliography

Borgeson, Griffith, *The Golden Age of The American Racing Car*, SAE, Warrendale, PA 1998

Bloemker, Al, *500 Miles To Go, The Story of the Indianapolis Motor Speedway*, Coward-McCann, Inc. NY, 1961

Catlin, Russ, *Automobile Quarterly*, Vol. 7, Number 4 (Spring 1969) *Who Really Won The First Indy 500*, pp. 382-385, *Automobile Quarterly*, NY

Catlin, Russ, *Automobile Quarterly*, Vol. IX, Number 3, (Spring 1971), *The Wooden Wonders*, pp.256-265, *Automobile Quarterly*, NY

Catlin, Russ *Automobile Quarterly*, Vol. XX, Number 4, (Fourth Quarter 1982), 54 *Bittersweet years of the AAA Contest Board-American Motorsport Goes Big Time*, pp 392-396 .In association with the Princeton Institute for Historic Research, Princeton, NJ

Collier, Peter & David Horowitz, *The Fords An American Epic*, Summit Books, NY ,1987

Curcio, Chrysler, *The Life and Times of An Automotive Genius*, Oxford University Press NY, 2000

Dayton, Duncan & Ken Burns, *Horatio's Drive, America's First Road Trip*, Alfred A. Knopf, 2003

Davis, Kenneth C., *Don't Know Much About History*, Avon Books, NY 1990

DePaolo, Peter, Wall Smacker, Thompson Products, Inc.

Cleveland ,OH 1935

Dees, Mark, L. *The Miller Dynasty*, Barnes Publishing, Scarsdale, NY 1981

Donovan, Frank, *Wheels For A Nation*, Thomas Y. Crowell Company, NY 1965

Fisher, *Carl G. Fisher Files Historical Museum of South Florida*, Miami, Florida

Fisher, Jane, *Fabulous Hoosier*, Robert M. McBride & Company, NY 1947

Fisher, Jerry, *The Pacesetter The Untold Story of Carl G. Fisher,* Lost Coast Press, Ft. Bragg, CA 1998

Fisk, Frederick & Marlin W. Todd,., T*he Wright Brothers*, Todd Fisk 2815 Moraine Ave., Dayton, OH 45406, 2000

Foster, Mark S, *Castles In The Sand The Life and Times of Carl Graham Fisher*, University Press of Florida, Gainesville, FL 2000

Fox, Jack C., *The Illustrated History of the Indianapolis 500 1911-1994*, 4th Edition, Carl Hungness Publishing, Madison, IN 1994

Freeman, Joseph S. *Automobile Quarterly*, Vol. 35, Number 2 (May 1966) *Fulford By The Sea: The Very Short Life of Miami's Board Track Speedway*, pp. 82-93, Subsidiary of Kutztown Publishing Co., Kutztown, PA

Giscard d' Estaing, Valerie-Anne, *The Second World Almanac of Inventions,* Pharos Books, NY 1986

Greeley, Roger E., *The Best of Robert Ingersoll*, Promethus Books, Buffalo, NY 1983

Gustin, Lawrence, *Billy Durant, Creator of General Motors*, Eerdmans, Grand Rapids, Michigan 1973

Harpur, Patrick, Editor, T*he Timetable of Technology*, Hearst Books, NY 1982

Hendry, Maurice D., Automonbile Quarterly, Vol. VIII, Number 3, (Spring 1970) *The Fred Moskovics Era*, pp.240-248, Automobile Quarterly, NY

Herlihy, David W., *Bicycle The History,* Yale University Press, New Haven & London, 2004

Hokanson, Drake, *The Lincoln Highway: Main Street Across America*, University of Iowa Press, Iowa City, 1988

Hopkins, Lindsay, Interview by Carl Hungness, 1973,

Horvath, Dennis & Terri, *Indiana Cars, A History of The Automobile In Indiana*, Hoosier Auto Show & Swap Meet, Indiana 2003

Katz, John F., *Automobile Quarterly*, Vol. XXIII, Number 3, (Third Quarter 1985) *Mister Fisher's Stoddard-Dayton*, pp. 228-235, *Automobile Quarterly*, NY

Kimes, Beverly Rae, *Automobile Quarterly* Vol. 6 Number 2, (Fall 1967) , *The Vanderbilt Cup Races*, pp. 185-204, *Automobile Quarterly*, NY

Kimes, Beverly Rae, *Automobile Quarterly*, Vol. VII, Number 1 (First Quarter 1974), *The Rise and Fall of The Empire Empire*, pp. 68-77, *Automobile Quarterly*, NY

Kimes, Beverly Rae, *Automobile Quarterly*, Vol. XV, Number 3, (Third Quarter 1977), *Willie K. The Saga of a Racing Vanderbilt*, pp. 312-317, *Automobile Quarterly,* NY

Kimes, Beverly Rae, Packard, *A History of The Motor Car & The Company*, CBS, Inc., NY 1978

Kimes, Beverly Rae, Clark Jr., Henry Austin, Editors, *Standard Catalog Of American Cars 1805-1942,*, Krause Publications, Iola, WI 1985

Klein, Maury, *Rainbow's End, The Crash of 1929*, Oxford University Press,Oxford & New York,2001

Kleinberg, Howard Miami: *The Way We Were*, Surfside Publishing, Tampa, FL 1989

Knauth, Percy & The Editors of Time-Life, *The Emergence of Man,The Metalsmiths*, Time-Life, N.Y.1972

Kollins, Michael , *Wheels,The Development of the Four Stroke Cycle Gas Engine*, pp. 6-8 Summer- Fall- 2003, pp.6-8, *Journal of the National Automotive History Collection*, Detroit Public Library

Lacey, Robert, F*ord The Men & The Machine*, Little Brown & Co., Boston, 1986

Leslie, Stuart, Boss Kettering, *Wizard of General Motors*, Columbia University Press, NY 1983

Lewis, David. W., *Rickenbacker, An American Hero In The Twentieth Century*, Johns Hopkins University Press, Baltimore, 2005

Lummus, J.N. *The Miracle of Miami Beach*: The Miami Post Publishing Co. 1944

McClure, Rusty with David Stern and Michael A. Banks, *Crosley Two Brothers and a Business Empire That Transformed The Nation*, Clerisy Press, Cincinnati, OH 2006

Minutes of the Annual Meeting of Active Members of the Lincoln Highway Association, Detroit Autromobile Club, December 30, 1918, Mimeograph copy Fisher Files Historical Museum of Southern Florida

Mr. Miami Beach, PBS American Experience Video, MDTV Productions, first broadcast February 2, 1998

Mulford, Ralph K. ,*Automobile Quarterly*, Vol.7, #4 ((Spring 1969) *Racing With Lozier*, pp.366-381, *Automobile Quarterly*, NY

Martin, Sidney Walker, Henry Flagler, *Visionary of The Gilded Age*, Tailored Tours Publications, Lake Buena Vista, FL 1998
Martin, John Bartlow, *Indiana An Interpretation*, Borzoi Book by Alfred Knopf, N.Y, 1947

May, George S., *R.E. Olds Auto Industry Pioneer*, William B. Eedermans Publishing Co, Grand Rapids, MI 1997

Montauk Beach Development Corporation, Report To Stockholders and Land Owners, May 23, 1930 Fisher Files, Historical Museum of Southern Florida

Norbye, *Jan Survey of The Gasoline Engine, Automobile Quarterly* Vol. 5, Number 1, (Summer 1966) pp. 86-90, Automobile Quarterly, NY

Palmer, Arthur Judson, *Riding High*, E.P. Dutton & Co., NY,1956

Pound, Arthur, *The Turning Wheel*, Doubleday, Doran & Co. N.Y. 1934

Prest-O-Lite Incorporation Papers, Sept. 6, 1904, Indiana State Archives, Indianapolis

Redford, Polly, *Billion Dollar Sandbar,* E.P. Dutton & Co., 1970

Reardon, L.F. *The Florida Hurricane & Disaster*, Arva Parks & Co., Coral Gables, FL 1986

Rickenbacker, Edward V. , *Rickenbacker An Autobiography*, Prentice-Hall, Englewood Cliffs, NJ,1967

Riggs, Spencer, *Automobile Quarterly*, Vol. 35, Number 2, ((May 1966) *Carl G. Fisher, Indiana's Best-Kept Secret*, pp. 66-81, *Automobile Quarterly, Inc.* Subsidiary of Kutztown Publishing Co., Kutztown, PA

Rollings, Tom & John Blazier *The Indianapolis 500* Yearbook, The Legendary Bricks of Indy, pp. 184-85 Carl Hungness Publishing Speedway, IN 1997

Roseberry, C.R. Glen Curtiss Pioneer of Flight, Syracuse University Press, Syracuse, NY 1991

Ruiz, Marco Editor, The History of the Automobile, Gallery Books, W.H. Smith NY, 1988

Scott, Bruce D., Indy: Racing Before The 500, Indiana Reflections, Batesville, IN 2005

Scott, Robert F., *Automobile Quarterly*, Vol. VI, Number 4 (Spring 1968) *A Sleeping Giant Awakes: The Invention of The Internal Combustion* Engine, pp.406-413, *Automobile Quarterly,* NY

Saal, Thomas F. & Bernard Golias, *Famous But Forgotten, The Story of Alexander Winton*, Golias Pub. Twinsburg, OH 1997

Sonnenburg, Paul & William A. Schonenberger, *Allison The Power of Excellence,* Coastline Pub. , Malibu, CA 1990

Shaw, Wilbur, *Gentlemen Start your Engines,* Coward-McCann, NY 1955

Wallen, Dick, *Board Track Guts, Gold & Glory,* Published by Dick Wallen, Lib. Cat. Card Number 90-090464, in November 1990

Weisberger, Bernard A., and the Editors of Life, *The Life History of The United States, The Age of Steam and Steel* Vol. 7, 1877-1890, Time-Life, N.Y. 1964

Weisberger, Bernard A., *The Dream Maker,* Little Brown & Co. Boston & Toronto, 1970

Winther, Oscar, T*he Transportation Frontier,* Holt, Rinehart and Winston, NY 1964

Woodforde, John, *The Story of The Bicycle,* Universe Books, NY 1970

Wright, Crocky, *The Nutley Velodrome,* Carl Hungness Publishing, Speedway, IN 1995

Newspaper Articles

"The Stylish Light Running Stearns Bicycle" ad for C.G. Fisher & Co., Bicycle ad Indianapolis News, July 5,1899,

"In The Bunch" ad for C.G. Fisher & Co. bicycle ad, *Indianapolis News,* 1909, Xerox copy, undated

"Prest-O-Lite People In More Humble Mood" page 1, *Indianapolis News,* June 8, 1908
,
"Frame Law To Bar Prest-O-Lite Plant" page 1, Indianapolis Star, June 8, 1908
"Balloon and Auto Sail Through Sky"

Indianapolis Star, October 31, 1908

"A Ballauto Trip—Fisher Went Away in the Air and Hiked Back on Land" Sioux City Iowa News, November 3, 1908

"Automobile As Balloon Basket Is Carried On Remarkable Ride" Los Angeles Express, November 14, 1908

"Fisher/Watts Wedding Announcement", Indianapolis News, October 23, 1909

"Fly-Fly-Fly Buy An Aeroplane" Advertisement for Fisher Aeroplane *The (Denver) Republican,* page 9, October 31, 1909

"Give Banquet To Honor Leading Business Men Citizens Praise Fisher, Allison, Wheeler and Newby, 150 At town Meeting" *Indianapolis News,* July 3, 1912

"Honor To Whom Honor Is Due" Indianapolis Star, July 3, 1912

"Singer Asks Half-Million" Indianapolis Star, October 6, 1912

"What We Are Doing At Alton Beach" Advertisement, *Miami Metropolitan,* December 31, 1912

" Fisher's Salary To Go To Roads" Indianapolis Star October 24, 1924

"Carl G. Fisher of Indianapolis Father of The Continental Road" Grand Junction (Colorado) News, July 16, 1913

"Gasoline Doomed If Zoline Comes" The Pittsburg Dispatch, November 19, 1914

"Zoline Fuel Test Is An Apparent Success" The Pittsburg Sun, November 20, 1914

"A Proposal For National Defense By Carl G. Fisher" Miami Herald, October 14, 1917

"Carl G. Fisher's Ideas On The Production of Airplanes" Indianapolis News, May 9, 1918

"A Open Letter To The People of Miami" Full Page Advertisement, *The Miami Metropolis,* January 14, 1919

" Oil 'Burners' To Run in Big Race" Knoxville (Tennessee) Sentinel, January 3, 1927

"24 Hour Contest Set for Autos" San Francisco (California)Chronicle, January 3, 1927

"American Night Fliers Prepare To Bomb The Hun" Public Ledger (Philadelphia) Magazine Section, September 8, 1918

"The Profit Made By One Woman at Alton Beach" Full page advertisement, *Miami Metropolis* March 8, 1919

"Can We Afford To Lose Carl Fisher?" Miami Life, Feb. 14, 1925

"A Blow To Narrow-Mindedness" " If Miami had followed the lead of Carl lFisher several years ago, not only Miami Beach but Miami today would have thirty feet of water and there would probably be no serious freight embargo throttling commerce of the city." *Miami Life,* October 31st 1925

"Will Miami Ever Have A Harbor? Miami Herald, November 7, 1925

"Warning Against Crooks Is Issued By Carl G. Fisher" Don't come to Florida and expect to become prosperous if you haven't been successful at home; don't come to Florida if you aren't a mechanic or workman with an occupation or unless you area

farmer ready to till the soil, etc"
Miami Beach Beacon, November 27, 1925

"*The Resignation of Sewell*" Everest G. Sewell, President of
The Miami Chamber of Commerce Resigns
Miami News, December 3, 1925

"*Speedway City Which Carl G. Fisher Dreamed of Twenty
Years Ago, May Yet Become 'Horseless City'* Devoted To Motors and Aviation" *Indianapolis News*, April 13,1929

"*One Man's Dream of A Horseless Industrial Center May Yet
Come True, Based on Construction of The New General Motors
Plant at Speedway*"
The Indianapolis News, September 21, 1935

"*Father of Miami Beach Lauded*" Credit for Growth of Charm-
ing Area Given Carl Fisher, *Illustrated Daily Tab*, Miami, Feb.
13, 1926

"*Carl G. Fisher Died In City He Made Rise From Swamps*,"
Miami Herald, July 16, 1939

Collections
Historical Association of Southern Florida, Miami Florida, Carl
Fisher Files
Marion Country Public Library, Indianapolis Indiana
Indiana State Historical Society
Detroit Public Library, National Automotive History Collec-
tions
Smithsonian Archives, National Air & Space Museum

Additional Sources
Address to the Conference of Governors at Colorado Springs,
Colorado, August 26, 1913 on the Lincoln Highway, Lincoln
Highway Association, 1913, Fisher Files, Historical Museum
of Southern Florida,

Hendry, Maurice D., *Cadillac Standard of The World, The Complete History, Automobile Quarterly Publications*,
Bonanza Books, Princeton Publishing, 1983

Huey, Edward G., *What Makes The Wheels Go Round?*
Harcourt, Brace & World, Inc. New York 1952

Kettering, Charles F. and Allen Orth, T*he New Necessity, The
Culmination of a Century of Progress in Transportation*,
The Williams & Wilkins Company. Baltimore 1932

Leif, Alfred, *The Firestone Story*, McGraw-Hill 1951

Roe, Fred Duesenberg *The Pursuit of Perfection*,
Dalton Watson Ltd. London 1982

Stoddard, Gloria May, Henry Leland, *The New England Press*,
Shelburne, Vermont 1983

White, Gordon, *Board Track Racing, Vintage Oval Magazine*,
May 2008

Radio Broadcast WQAM March 4, 1951 with Jane Fisher

Automobile Quarterly all editions from 1962 onward for
general automotive research

National Speed Sport News (National Auto Racing News)
all editions from 1934 onward for general automobile racing
research,

Indianapolis Motor Speedway Programs 1911-1939

Indianapolis 500 Mile Race Annuals 1946-1962, Floyd Clymer
Publishing, Los Angeles

Indianapolis 500 Yearbooks 1969-1997, Carl Hungness Publishing, Madison, IN

United States Patent Office for copies of Fisher patents

U.S. Department of Commerce

Footnotes

Please note the author has taken journalistic license in the quotes on pages 1, 10, 11, 12, 13, 17, 19, 23, 25, 58, 110, 157, 165
as being statements likely made. All other quotations in this book are taken from publications listed in the bibliography.

Chapter 1: The Greatest Race Course

1. Bloemker, *500 Miles To Go* pp. 60-65 Al Bloemker was a journeyman newspaper writer before becoming a publicity man and later vice-president of the Indianapolis Motor Speedway and has proven to be dedicated to accuracy. This title is considered essential for "500" historians. Bloemker also ghost wrote "Gentlemen, Start Your Engines," Wilbur Shaw's biography. Shaw is the man credited with saving the Speedway from being turned into a housing development after WWII and convinced Tony Hulman to purchase the plant and continue the "500. The Hulman family continue to operate the track.

2. Ibid., p. 45 Bloemker says Fisher was the 21st registered balloon pilot and Fisher himself has said 18 and 21, "My license number is 18" in a October 1, 1925 letter to General William (Billy) Mitchell. The letter to Mitchell outlined Fisher and Bumbaugh's harrowing 1913 experience in a national balloon contest. Fisher was writing to Mitchell after the September 1925 crash of the Shenandoah that was the worst aviation disaster to date as it killed 14 crewmen. Fisher and Bumbaugh encountered "spiral ascensions" that took them to 21,000 feet and descended so rapidly "we expected it to explode". Fisher was attempting to furnish Mitchell with knowledge to determine the Shendandoah's crash. Fisher Files HMSF

3. Scott, *Racing Before The 500* p. 22 Bruce Scott's book is a comprehensive 260 page work consisting of facts, photos,and stories, most of which have never before been published relating to activity at the Speedway and is highly recommended for any serious researcher of the track history.

4. Bloemker, *500 Miles To Go*, p. 48

5. Ibid., p. 53

6. bid., p. 60

7. Ibid., p. 14 We also located a well-researched four page story among the Fisher papers in Florida authored by one J. Douglas detailing balloon racing at the Speedway utilizing quotes from the Indianapolis newspapers of the era.

8. The Automobile, December 16, 1909

9. Bloemker, *500 Miles To Go*, p. 58 In the early days of racing most signal flags had an entirely different meaning than at the present time. Red indicated the start of the race and a clear course ahead; yellow,'stop immediately, the race is halted;" white, 'stop for consultation;" blue, "drive with care, danger ahead:" green, you are "starting you last lap".

Chapter 2: The Salesman

1. Foster, *Castles In The Sand*, p. 13 Mark Foster has also been through the complete Fisher Files at the Historical Museum of South Florida in compiling his accurate accounting of Fisher's life. His book lists precise box number location of correspondence.

2. Fisher, Jerry, *The Pacesetter*, p.3 One Carl's relatives, Jerry Fisher spent a monumental amount of time in ferreting out Carl Fisher's life story and for an in depth history of his family tree refer to his fine work The Pacesetter.

3. Foster, *Castles In The Sand,* p. 12

4. Fisher to John Hertz April 21, 1933, HMS Hertz was a major player in the famed Chicago Cab Wars of the 1920's and came away from the fray winner enough to launch his successful rental car business.

5. La Gorce to Fisher Oct. 30, 1929, Milton letter October 26, 1938, Fisher Files Florida

6. Ingersoll League Brochure, Fisher Files HMSF Also see The Best of Robert Ingersoll, edited by Roger E. Greeley, Promethus Books Buffalo, NY 1983

7. Greeley, p.86 Ingersoll stated: "My creed is this: Happiness is the only good. The place to be happy is here. The time to be happy is now. The way to be happy is to make others so." Other quotations taken from Ingersoll's speeches as appear in Greeley

8. Herlihy, *Bicycle The History* p. 160
9. bid., p. 161
10. Ibid., p. 166
11. Ibid., p. 217
12. *Second World Almanac Book of Inventions*, p. 17
13. Fisher , *Fabulous Hoosier* p.40 as well as in Jerry Fisher and Mark Foster works
14. Ibid., p. 37
15. Ibid., p. 39 Jane Fisher says he quit the railroad where he had been selling newspapers, candy, etc. to passengers at age 17 to open his bicycle shop.
16. Ibid., p.42
17. Ibid. p. 45
18. Herlihy, *Bicycle The History*, pp. 192-198
19. Bloemker, 500 Miles To Go, p. 18
20. Fisher, Pacesetter p. 1421
21. Ruggles to Fisher Nov. 13, 1925 HMSF Fisher replied to Ruggles on Nov. 15, 1925 stating: "I remember how hard it was to live in Chicago on twenty-five dollars a week."

Chapter 3: Presto
1. Lacey, *Ford The Men and The Machine*, p. 62 A scholarly work extremely well documented and highly recommended for any student of Ford history.
2. Horvath, Terry & Denise, A History of The Automobile In Indiana, Another love of labor book created by enthusiasts that preserves automotive history.
3. Martin, John Barlow, *Indiana An Interpretation* p. 117
4. Ibid.
5. *Fisher, Fabulous Hoosier p 30 We located a typed note (probably from the female cook Danny as mentioned in Fabulous Hoosier) noting Carl's "Cuss-words from 10:15-11:00 at bridge" that included, god-damn, Christ, Christ's sake, dirty little god-damn, what-the hell, son-of-a-bitch, Christ Almighty, For the love of God, Damn-dirty, dammed card system, and so on into the night".*
6. Ibid., p.8
7. Katz, John *Automobile Quarterly* Vol. 23, #3 pp. 228-231
8. Fisher, Pacesetter p. 37
9. Photocopies of newspaper articles in the Florida Fisher Files
10. Fisher, Fabulous Hoosier p. 11
11. Martin, John Barlow, Indiana, An Interpretation p. 120
12. Fisher, "*Fabulous Hoosier*" p. 16
13. Saal & Golias, Famous But Forgotten p. 19
14. Ibid., p. 15
15. Bloemker, "*500 Miles To Go*" p. 20
16. Fisher, *The Pacesetter* p. 23
17. Bloemker, "*500 Miles To Go*", p. 21, Oldfield also commented about his bicycle racing days to Fisher in a Dec. 20, 1938 letter to Fisher when requesting Carl write a story for Oldfield's upcoming book; *I won't ask you to go back to 1898, on the Newby Oval, when I was one of the "bottom" men in that triplet pile up."*
18. Fisher, "*Fabulous Hoosier*" p. 47 The James Gordon Bennett race was a product of the founder's name. Bennett was an expatriate living in Paris who is said to have loved the city, but who had fairly well worn out his high society welcome in New York City. He had inherited the successful *New York Herald* and its Paris edition from his father and became patron for daring sports and sponsored balloon and early automobile races.
19. Bloemker, *500 Miles To Go*, pp. 29-31
20. Kimes, Beverly Rae *Automobile Quarterly* Vol. 15, # 3 pp. 312-327
21. Fisher, *Fabulous Hoosier*, p. 54
22. Hargrave Aviation Pioneers website, aviation-pioneers.com
23. HMSF, Fisher Files Florida
24. Indiana State Library Incorporation Papers for "Presto-O-Lite"
25. Sonnenburg, Paul & Schoneberger, William A. *Allison Power of Excellence*, pp. 12-13 This is an officially sanctioned book produced by Allison Engineering and is considered to be the authoritative narrative on the firm. A typed sheet in the HMSF Fisher files has Jim Allison stating in part: "*...the only thing I got out of my eight years in school that has been of any value to me, was learning to read, write and cipher. I believe there is not a college in the world that can take the mediocre mind and make a brilliant mind of it. I believe that there are only small number of minds per thousand people of high average. I did not learn to speak English in school, but by conversing with educated people and reading books.*"
26. *Fisher, "Fabulous Hoosier" p. 57*
27. *Indianapolis News* June 6 & 8 1908
28. Prest-O-Lite advertisement undated
29. Fisher, *The Pacesetter*, p. 31
30. Ibid., p. 32 and U.S. Department of Commerce statistics
31. Blazier, John E. & Rollings, Tom *Indianapolis 500 Yearbook* 1997 pp. 184-185 This same yearbook contains in-depth stories relating to the badges worn by Speedway officials from its inception through 1997 as well as a feature listing books of interest to Indianapolis 500 fans throughout the years. The previous yearbook in 1996 features reproductions of the program covers used at the track from 1909-1997. Blaziere &

Rollings are both highly respected Indianapolis 500 historians who have preserved esoteric facts pertaining to the Indianapolis Motor Speedway.

32. Scott, . *Indy Racing Before the 500*, p.73
33. Ibid., pg. 74
34. Kimes, *Automobile Quarterly* Vol. 12, # 1 p. 72
35. Scott, pp. 125-130
36. Ibid., p. 162
37. Ibid., p. 71
38. Helck, *Automobile Quarterly* Vol. 5, #1 p. 55, Peter Helck was one of the pre-eminent automobile racing artists of his era and has been called the "Dean of American Motoring Artists" He also authored and illustrated T*he Checkered Flag* and *Great Auto Races* books valued by collectors.
39. Ibid. p. 56
40. Catlin, *Automobile Quarterly,* Vol. 7, # 4 p. 383
41. Ibid., p. 383
42. Ibid., p 385
43. Ibid., p.385
44. Mulford, Ibid., p. 375
45. Harroun, *Racing On The Rim* p. 71
46. *The Automobile* March 25, 1915,
47. Kimes, Beverly Rae, *Standard Catalog of American Cars*, p. 679 A massive work containing over 5,000 histories of automobiles from 1805-1942 utilizing over 4,500 factory photos. Invaluable research tool for automotive historians.

Chapter 4: The Coast to Coast Highway

1. "Fisher's Salary To Go To Roads" *Indianapolis Star* October 24, 1912
2. Fisher, *Fabulous Hoosier* p. 79
3. Fisher, *Pacesetter* p. 80
4. Collier, Peter & Horowitz, David , *Fords An American Epic*, p. 123 Another scholarly work by authors noted for their books on *The Rockefellers*

and The Kennedys, well documented. Contains quotations and truthful insight not usually found in works on the Ford family.

5. Fisher, *Pacesetter* p. 81
6. *World Almanac Book of Inventions*, p. 108 While Marconi received the original patents for radio broadcast, the Supreme Court of the U.S. reversed themselves in 1943 and awarded Nikola Tesla the rights. Marconi had utilized several of Tesla's previous patents. Tesla, the man who forever altered the transmission of electrical energy through is alternating current (AC) system created so many electrical technological breakthroughs a thorough study of his achievements is necessary to appreciate his importance to society. For example, he is basically responsible for invention of the new fluorescent light bulbs we currently use
7. Halberstam, David, *The Powers That Be* p. 14
8. Fisher, *Pacesetter* p. 82
9. Ibid., p. 86 Includes informative copies of additional letters from James Couzens to Carl as well as Carl's additional letters to Ford.
10. Ibid. p.92
11. Duncan, Dayton and Burns, Ken, *Horatio's Drive*, p. 19 Ken Burns produced another of his fine documentaries from the story line in this excellent , well illustrated work.
12. Ibid., p. 10
13. Ibid., p. 17
14. Ibid., p. 57
15. Ibid., p. 125
16. Ibid., p. 6
17. Ibid., p. 9
18. Martin, *Packard, A History of The Motor Car & Company*, p.23 Editor Beverly Rae Kimes
19. Saal, Thomas & Golias, Bernard Famous But Forgotten, p. 11 Two more automotive enthusi-

asts who have preserved important automotive history. The definitive work regarding Alexander Winton's career.

20. Martin, *Packard, A History*, p. 25
21. Ibid., pp. 36 & 49
22. Ibid., pp. 54
23. Hokanson, Drake, *Lincoln Highway*, p.9 Considered to be the definitive work on the history of the Lincoln Highway. Highly recommended.
24. Ibid., p. 11
25. Fisher, *Fabulous Hoosier*, p. 82
26. Ibid., p. 82 Jane had a misspelling of Batchelder's name and he was not secretary of the AAA committee, but Chairman. His participation of the Hoosier Tour was reported in the June 16, 1912 edition of the New York Times
27. Fisher, *Pacesetter*, pp. 99, 101
28. Ibid. p. 102
29. Ibid p. 93
30. Hokanson , *Lincoln Highway*, p. 18
31. Sulski, Jim Chicago Tribune, December 9, 1997
32. Hokanson, *Lincoln Highway* p. 13
33. Ibid. p. 19
34. Fisher, *Pacesetter*, p. 127
35. Ibid. p. 127
36. Ibid p. 130
37. Hokanson, *Lincoln Highway*, pp. 112-113

Chapter 5: Florida Discovered

1. Fisher, *Fabulous Hoosier* p. 20
2. Ibid., p. 21
3. Ibid., p. 21
4. Martin, Sidney, *Henry Flagler, Visionary of The Gilded Age*, p.47 This is the definitive biography of Flagler.
5. Ibid., p. 67
6. Ibid., p. 100

7. Ibid., p. 129
8. Redford, *Billion Dollar Sandbar*, p. 61 An entertaining, in-depth study of the building of Miami Beach by a researcher who was able to interview many of the original participants.
9. Ibid., p. 65
10. Fisher, *Pacesetter* p. 146
11. Ibid., p. 152
12. Ibid., p. 153
13. Bloemker, *500 Miles To Go* p. 98
14. Ibid., p. 105
15. Fisher, *Pacesetter* p. 157
16. Ibid, p. 157
17. Ibid, p 157
18. Kleinberg, , *Miami Beach; A History*, p. 33 Highly recommended for its historical accuracy.
19. Nash, *The Magic of Miami Beach* p.120 Highly recommended account by knowledgeable author.
20. Fisher, *Fabulous Hoosier* pp. 100-101
21. Ibid., p. 131
22. Nash, p. 108
23. Redford, *Billion Dollar Sandbar* p. 71
24. Fisher, Pacesetter p. 164
25. Lummus, *The Miracle of Miami Beach*: Miami p. 47 valuable and recommended work by one of the city's original builders.
26. Fisher, *Fabulous Hoosier* p. 130
27. Redford, *Billion Dollar Sandbar* p. 91
28. Ibid., p. 80
29. *Miami Herald* December 10,1913 Also see *Pacesetter* p.167 and Redford, *Billion Dollar Sandbar* p. 80
30. Ibid
31. Fisher, *Fabulous Hoosier*, p. 137
32. Fisher Papers HMSF
33. Gar Wood website www.garwood.com Wood became one of the most respected men in the world

of sport boating and was a life-long Fisher associate. Served as pall-bearer at Fisher's funeral.
34. Fisher, *Pacesetter* p. 180
35. Redford, *Billion Dollar Sandbar* p. 180
36. *The Pittsburg Dispatch*, Nov. 19, 1914
37. *The Sun* (Pittsburg) Nov. 20, 1914
38. Ibid
39. Fisher, *Fabulous Hoosier* p. 74
40. Ibid p. 75
41. Weisberger, *The Dream Maker*, p. 235 Recognized historian who has produce the most definitive work on Billy Durant. Well documented. Weisberger's historical knowledge of industry is an invaluable asset.
42. Fisher, *Pacesetter* p. 172
43. Ibid., p. 177
44. Redford, *Billion Dollar Sandbar* p. 92
45. Fisher Papers HMSF
46. Lummus, p. 66
47. Redford, *Billion Dollar Sandbar*, p.89
48. Fisher, *Fabulous Hoosier* p. 109
49. Ibid., p. 1ll
50. Fisher Files HMSF
51. Ibid.
52. *Miami Herald*, undated story in Fisher papers HMSF

Chapter 6: Citizen Soldier

1. Fisher Files HMSF: This story was printed in the Oct. 14, 19, 1915 Miami Herald
2. Ibid
3. Fox, Jack *Illustrated History of The Indianapolis 500* , pp. 40-44: For a detailed explanation of the founders involvement with race car ownership see Bloemker Chapter 9 Fox's book contains over 4,000 photos of Indianapolis 500 cars from 1911-1994 and is considered the easiest place to

reference driver statistics.
4. Bloemker, *500 Miles To Go*, p. 136
5. Fisher to Bumbaugh March 29, 1917, HMSF
6. Ibid April 9, 1917
7. Fisher to David Beecroft Nov. 22nd, 1917 HMSF
8. Bloemker, *500 Miles To Go* p. 139
9. Philadelphia Public Ledger, Magazine Section Sept.1918
10. Ibid.
11. Ibid.
12. Redford, Billion Dollar Sandbar, pp. 110-111
13. Telegram January 22, 1918 Fisher Files HMSF
14. Redford, *Billion Dollar Sandbar* p. 101
15. Ibid pp. 105-106
16. Fisher to H.H. Talbot, Jr. August 14th, 1918 HMSF
17. Redford, *Billion Dollar Sandbar*, pp. 111, 113,114
18. *Time Magazine* March 23, 1925
19. Fisher to Deering January 24 & 30th 1919 HMSF Fisher Files
20. Fisher to DePalma July 22, 1919
21. *Indianapolis News* August 20, 1919
22. Fisher, *Fabulous Hoosier*, p. 169
23. Ibid., p. 171
24. Ibid.,p. 172
25. Ibid., p. 173
26. Sonnenberg & Shonberger, *Allison Power of Excellence* p. 30
27. Ibid., pp. 20-21
28. Ibid., p. 22
29. Ibid., p. 74
30. Ibid., p. 21
31. Ibid., p.. 28
32. Fox, Jack *Illustrated History of The Indianapolis 500* & Scott, Bruce, *Indy Racing Before The 500* Figures provided were ascertained through

calculation of statistics contained in each book. Ray Harroun has eight wins from 1909-1911 for second place on the all time list.

33. The Timetable of Technology pp. 48-63
34. Fisher Files HMSF
35. Ibid.
36. Myers to Fisher, Jan. 6, 1919 Fisher Files HMSF There are numerous letters from Louis Chevrolet to Fisher making requests, and detailing his current activities. Louis is one of America's tragic auto racing figures. He and his brothers Arthur and Gaston were noted auto racing names in the first two decades of the century. He raced in six Indianapolis 500's, the first in 1915 in a Cornelian, a successful cycle car. A gifted natural engineer, he designed his namesake automobile for GM founder Billy Durant who went on to succeed with the name. He started the Frontenac auto company to manufacture cars, named after the 17th century governor of French colonies and partnered with the Stutz Car company, but the venture failed. His straight-eight engine entry in 1920 won the Indianapolis 500 with brother Gaston driving. Gaston was killed later in 1920 at the Beverly Hills board speedway. Chevrolet won again as an entrant in the 1921 '500" with Tommy Milton driving. Louis designed the Chevrolet 333 aircraft engine and partnered with Glen Martin to produce the unit for airplane usage, but the non business oriented Chevrolet did not stay with the company that ultimately became successful. His engine was turned into the Martin 4-333. He produced the highly acclaimed Frontenac cylinder heads for Model T Fords but went out of business with the introduction of the Model A. A former bicycle racer and manufacturer he was an extremely successful race car driver who spent the equivalent of three years convalescing from accidents between 1905 and

1920. He died broke in 1941. See *American National Biography*, Garraty & Carnes Oxford 1999; Entrepreneurs, *The Men and Women Behind Famous Brand Names*, Fulin, Joseph & Suzy, G.K. Hall 1985
37. Fox, Jack, *Illustrated History of The Indianapolis 500*, p. 48

Chapter 7: Attracting a President

1. Fisher to H.H. Talbot, Jr. Feb. 4, 1919 HMSF
2. Fisher to M. Hawley McLanahan March 24, 1920 HMSF
3. Fisher, J *Fabulous Hoosier*, p. 157
4. Redford, *Billion Dollar Sandbar*, p. 126
5. Ibid., p. 126
6. Ibid. , p.127 & HMSF
7. Fisher, p. 156
8. Fisher to LaGorce December 4, 1920 HMSF
9. Fisher, *Fabulous Hoosier*, p. 30
10. Fisher to Frank Stalnaker Oct. 1, 1920 HMSF
11. Thomas J. Pancoast to Carl Fisher September 23, 1920 HMSF
12. Accounting & Sales Sheets Fisher, HMSF
13. Fisher to Chas. Krom Feb. 15, 1921 HMSF
14. *National Geographic*, January 1921
15. Fisher to Senator Warren G. Harding Dec. 6, 1920 HMSF
16. Harding to Fisher January 12, 1921 HMSF
17. Rossiter to Fisher January 11, 1921 HMSF
18. Fisher to LaGorce January 14, 1921 HMSF
19. Redford, *Billion Dollar Sandbar* p. 132
20. Fisher, *Pacesetter*, p. 207
21. A. Batchelder to Fisher February 4, 1921 HMSF
22. Fisher, Fabulous Hoosier, p. 5
23. Fisher to R.E. Olds September 12, 1919, HMSF. See R.E. Olds, Auto Industry Pioneer, George S. May for a definitive biography of Olds.

24. Ibid., May 21, 1919
25. Fisher to W.C. Durant October 9, 1919 HMS
26. Champion to Fisher July 22, 1927 HMSF
27. Cost Sheets Flamingo Hotel, November 30, 1923 HMSF

Chapter 8: Dreams and Nightmares

1. Fisher to W.W. Atterbury April 26, 1927 HMSF
2. Fisher to his mother April 2, 1919 HMSF
3. Fisher to his father May 20, 1918 HMSF In another letter to his father dated March 22nd, 1919 Carl sent his father $100 and admonished him to repay a loan he previously encountered because, "a man who will loan you fifty dollars should be taken care of."
4. Fisher, *Fabulous Hoosier* p. 186
5. Ibid., p. 189
6. Ibid., p. 190
7. Ibid., p. 191
8. Fisher, *Jerry Pacesetter* p. 218
9. Ibid., p. 215
10. HMSF Fisher files
11. Allison, Michael M. to Fisher April 16, 1919 HMSF
12. Fisher to Michael M. Allison July 22, 1919 HMSF
13. Redford. *Billion Dollar Sandbar*, p. 141 & Fisher, Jan, 128
14. Fisher, *Pacesetter*, p.235
15. Bloemker, *500 Miles To Go*, p.154
16. Redford, *Billion Dollar Sandbar*, p.114
17. Fisher to Thomas Pancoast, Nov. 7, 1921 HMSF
18. Fisher, *Pacesetter*, p. 241, & Kleinberg, Miami Beach pg. 79
19. Ibid., p. 241
20. Redford, *Billion Dollar Sandbar*, p. 142
21. Ibid., p. 143

22. Ibid., p. 141 Redford has also listed the type of fauna utilized.

23. Ibid., p. 196

24. Unmarked newspaper ad HMSF Fisher Files. The list of luminaries who built homes in Miami Beach does not come from a single source and have been compiled from the Fisher Files. The conversation the author had with long-time Indy 500 car owner Lindsey Hopkins came in the mid-1970's as he related his feelings of embarrassment of being wealthy during the Depression while his fellow Americans were suffering massive unemployment: "I felt so sorry for all those out of work," he said, "and I was having extremely good fortune.".

25. General Hotel Ledger Sheets HMSF Fisher Files

26. Rogers, Oct. 11, 1925 Weekly Articles , HASF.

27. HMSF Carl Fisher Files

28. 1920'-30.com

29. Fisher, *Pacesetter*, p. 268 from Howard Preston's Dirt Roads To Dixie

30. Mazie Rattay to Jane Fisher May 5, 1922 HMSF

31. Fisher to Mazie Rattay, May 20, 1922 HMSF

32. Fisher to George L Denny, December 14, 1922 HMSF

33. Fisher to Mazie Rattay Feb. 22, 1923; August 6, 1923; August 23, 1923, December 10, 1923 HMSF

34. Foster, *Castles In The Sand*, p.221;

35. Fisher, Carl G. Separation Agreement November 24, 1926 HMSF

36. Fisher, Carl G. files, correspondence, newspaper clippings HMSF

Chapter 9: The Tide Changes

1. Fox, Jack *Illustrated History of The Indianapolis 500* p.44

2. Bloemker, *500 Miles To Go* p.145 The reader is referred to Al Bloemker's seminal work for a detailed analysis of this time period.

3. Ibid., pp. 149-150

4. Fisher to James Allison June 29, 1921 HMSF Files

5. Freeman, Joseph. F. *Automobile Quarterly* Vol 35. #2, pg. 91

6. Wallen, Board Tracks p. 29 Dick Wallen is a life-long auto racing fan, photographer and film maker who assembled knowledgeable writers to produce this definitive work on the board speedways that is profusely and beautifully illustrated.

7. Ibid., page 177,

8. Ibid., page 3

9. Ibid., p. iv Historians will remind us there was a very successful board speedway located in Nutley, N.J. originally constructed as a bicycle velodrome. It held Midget auto races in 1938-39 and saw lap times of under eight seconds. A book detailing the history of the track was published titled *The Nutley Velodrome*

10. Records Fisher Files HMSF

11. Fisher, *Fabulous Hoosier*, page 176

12. Borgeson, *The Golden Age of The American Racing Car*, p. 274

13. Catlin, Russ *Automobile Quarterly* Vol. 9 #3 p. 261,

14. Wallen, p. 420

15. Fisher, p. 233

16. Ibid., p. 207

17. Redford, *Billion Dollar Sand Bar*, page 150

18. Ibid., p. 152

19. Fisher to James M. Cox Feb. 1925, Fisher Files HMSF

20. Redford, p.162

21. Foster, *Castles In The Sand* p. 232

22. Fisher to LaGorce October 1926, Fisher Files HMSF

23. Fisher, Jerry *Pacesetter* p. 305

24. Fisher, Jane p. 236 The death toll according to an official Red Cross report on Oct. 9, 1924 listed 373 dead; 6, 381 injured and 17,884 families affected. Totals are for the nine counties surrounding Miami Beach, See The Florida Hurricane & Disaster, Reardon, 1986

25. White, *Vintage Oval Track Racing Magazine*, May 2008 p. 15

Chapter 10: The Tide Changes

1. Fisher, *Pacesetter* p. 272

2. Redford, *Billion Dollar Sandbar* p. 159

3. Fisher, *Pacesetter*, p 273

4. Ibid., p. 274

5. Fisher, *Fabulous Hoosier* p. 216

6. Hannagan, Steve, These quotations are from a press release located in the Fisher Files HASF

7. Ibid., p. 2

8. Fisher, *Pacesetter* p. 265, Fisher papers HMSF. The seaport was eventually constructed in 1965 half way between Miami and Miami Beach.

9. Fisher to LaGorce Oct. 8, 1926 HMSF

10. Fisher to Winifred Mussey March 12, 1926 HMSF

11. Shutts, Frank to Fisher Feb. 24, 1926 HMSF

12. Fisher to E.V. Rickenbacker July 12, 1927 HMSF

13. Lewis, David W. Eddie Rickenbacker, An American Hero in The Twentieth Century, Lewis gives us credible fact that Rickenbacker's own biography Rickenbacker is a modified version of his actual life's story. Lewis'

668 page work has received praise from aviation and historical experts.

14. Bloemker, 500 Miles To Go p. 170

15. Ibid., p.163

16. Myers, T.E. to James Allison December 7, 1927 HMSF

17. Lewis, p. 18

18. Shaw, *Gentlemen Start Your Engines* p. 280 The Hulman family still owns and operates the facility.

19. Myers T.E. to Fisher December 8, 1927 HMSF

20. Fisher, *Fabulous Hoosier*, p. 222

21. Fisher, *Pacesetter*, p. 312

22. Redford, *Billion Dollar Sandbar* p. 187

23. Fisher to to Judge A. Frank Katzentine, December 19, 1931 HMSF

24. Fisher, Fabulous Hoosier p. 30

25. "Galloway" to Carl G. Fisher December 7, 1923

26. Redford, *Billion Dollar Sandbar* p. 211

27. Miller, Victor J. to Fisher February 13, 1929 HMSF

28. Newspaper clipping dated February 1925 HMSF. Also noted in Pacesetter, p.260 Numerous letters from Julius Fleishmann are to be found in the Fisher Files, most relating making plans for upcoming polo seasons. It is evident Fisher and Fleishmann had a friendly relationship as Fleishmann gave Carl an invitation to his own golf course and corresponded with Carl regularly.. Reference:Letters, Sept. 8, 1921, October 23, 1923.

29. Fisher, *Pacesetter*, p. 262

30. Fisher, *Fabulous Hoosier* pp. 253-255

Chapter 11: The Dirt Stops Flying

1. Fisher, *Fabulous Hoosier* p 137

2. Brochure Fisher Files HMSF

3. Fisher, *Pacesetter* p. 314

4. Ibid., 316

5. Ibid., 315

6. Fisher to George Leboutillier April 18, 1927 HMSF

7. Ibid., April 18, 1927 HMSF

8. Roseberry, C.R. Glenn Curtiss p.444

9. Collier & Horowitz ,*The Fords*, 80, & Kimes, Standard Catalog of American Cars 18

10. H.L. Briand , Auburn Automobile Co. to Fisher April 18, 1929 HMSF

11. Report to Stockholders of Aero-Car Corporation HMS

12. *Time Magazine* ,August 16, 1926

13. Roseberry, C.R. p. 164

14. Fisher to Charles Kettering June 11, 1929 HMSF Kettering's notoriety later landed him on the cover of the January 9, 1933 TIME magazine.

15. Charles Kettering to Fisher June 18, 1929 HMSF

16. Fisher, *Fabulous Hoosier*, p.184

17. Copy of mimeographed sheet in Fisher HMSF

18. Fisher to Roy Chapin November 8, 1928 HMSF

19. Ibid., 1926 (date covered over with birth announcement) HMSF

20. Klein, Maury, Rinbow's End xii

21. Ibid ., xvi

22. Foster, *Castles In The Sand* p. 271

23. Redford, *Billion Dollar Sandbar* p.180

24. *National Geographic Magazine* January 1930 , p. 59

25. Foster, *Castles In The Sand* p. 272

26. Fisher to Charles E. Sorenson, December 15, 1932 HMSF

27. Grayson, Stan A.Q. Volume 12 # 3, p.256

28. Scott, Robert F. *Automobile Quarterly*. Vol. 6 #4 p.408

29. Fisher to Charles F. Kettering March 8, 1927 HMSF

30. Fisher to Henry B. Joy July 2, 1929 HMSF

31. Fisher to Charles F. Kettering August 9, 1929 HMS

32. Bragg, Caleb to Fisher October 8, 1928

33. Kettering, Charles F. to Fisher August 21, 1929

34. Wilson, Charles S. to O.D. Treiber October 4, 1929 Fisher Files HMSF

35. Bloemker, 500 Miles To Go , p. 179

36. Fisher to Tommy Milton August 18, 1930 Fisher Files HMSF

37. Milton to Fisher May 21, 1931 Fisher Files HMSF Milton may have lost significant investment in Montauk. He had become the first driver to win the Indianapolis 500 twice after victories in 1921 and 1923. Heralded as one of the greatest dirt track drivers of the era, his fame did not equal that of Barney Oldfield and Ralph DePalma as Milton was described as being reserved in his demeanor. His exploits are all the more admirable because his Minnesota draft registration for WWI notes his is "blind in the right eye." as did the *St. Paul Pioneer Press* in the March 19, 1922 edition. After his driving days were over he stayed close to the sport and drove the pace car in the "500" beginning in 1936 and was named Chief Steward in 1949. He too suffered failing health and had cirrhosis of the liver by the early 1960's. Scheduled for amputation of his right leg, Milton committed suicide on July 10, 1962. See *Ramsey County History Magazine*, Trimble, Steven, C. Vol. 42, 4, St. Paul, Minnesota .

38. Fisher to R.F Garland Feb. 18, 1932

39. Fisher to Claude Mercer Oct. 5, 1934 HMSF

40. Fisher, *Pacesetter* p.375

41. Ibid., p. 374

42. Fisher to Margaret Fisher August 3, 1935 HMSF

43. Fisher, Jane to Carl Fisher August 27, 1935 HMSF

44. Fisher Files HMSF

45. Memorandums of book orders in Fisher Files HMSF, July 10, 1930, Oct. 26, 1930 The vast range of titles Fisher ordered does not lead to conclude he had a continuing interest in any given subject

46. Redford, *Billion Dollar Sandbar* p. 192

47. Ibid., p.194

48. Ibid., p.196

49. Ibid., p.197

50. Fisher, *Fabulous Hoosier* p. 196

51. Ibid., p.225

Chapter 12: Another Fortune On the Way

1. *Miami Life* February 14, 1925 front page
2. *Indianapolis News* April 13, 1925 20,21
3. Carl G. Fisher to J.N. Lummus April 10, 1933 HMSF
4. Fisher, *Pacesetter* 383
5. Patent Application June 26, 1928 HMSF
6. Patent granted July 1, 1930 HMSF
7. Fisher August 28, 1929 to Lieutenant Alford. J. Williams, Jr. U.S. Naval Aircraft Station, Philadelphia, PA
8. Patent granted October 23, 1934 also see letter from Carl G.. Fisher to Mr. Art Williams Safety Air Transportation Co., HMSF
9. Patent granted Feb. 11, 1936 HMSF
10. Patent granted November 8, 1938 HMSF
11. Fisher to Thomas W. Milton October 17, 1938 HMSF
12. Milton to Fisher, October 26, 1938 HMSF
13. Stearman, A.J. To Thomas W. Milton from November 30, 1938 HMSF
14. Fisher to Milton February 12, 1935 HMSF
15. McClure, Crosley p.58
16. Ibid. p. 62
17. Ibid p. 169
18. Ibid. p. 337
19. Fisher To Barney Oldfield, December 13, 1938 HMSF
20. Fisher to Barney Oldfield April 25, 1939 HMSF
21. Fisher, *Pacesetter* 396
22. Copy of "*I remember When*" radio broadcast WQAM, March 4, 1951, HMSF

Historical Section

Chapter 1: Rolling Over The Land

1. Pound, *The Turning Wheel*, p.2
2. *Timetable of Technology* p. 11, By 1900 F.W. Taylor displayed at the Paris exhibition his new high speed steel cutting tools using tungsten and carbide which combined to produce a tool usable under extreme heat. Taylor's advance in technology can only be appreciated by those who need to manufacture steel parts to close tolerances which included anyone who wanted to manufacture an automobile.
3. Kokomo Indiana Brochure, Chamber of Commerce
4. Pound, p. 36
5. *Emergence of Man*, Chart, Perry Knauth & Editors of *Time-Life*
6. Ruiz, *History of The Automobile*, p.10 Excellent resource containing over 1500 color and black and white photographs detailing production, racing, land speed vehicles as well as technical innovations.
7. Donovan, *Wheels For A Nation*, p.63
8. *Timetable of Technology*, p.11 During this same year technicians were introduced to a new magnetic chuck (a holding device) had been developed which would greatly aid in finishing steel parts to a high and accurate finish.
9. Ibid., p. 10
10. Ibid., p.11 Also see *The Wright Brothers from Bicycle To Biplane*, Fisk & Todd p.70
11. Weisberger, *Age of Steam & Steel*, Vol. 7 p. 31
12. Ruiz, *History of The Automobile*, p. 14
13. Norbye, Jan P. *Automobile Quarterly*, Vol. 5, # 1. p. 86 *The Automobile Quarterly* "magazine" has been published since Spring of 1962 and must be considered as the premier automotive historical reference source in the United States. It has the most in-depth and lavishly illustrated articles ever published on the history of the motorcar. Produced in hard-bound book form it utilizes the world's most knowledgeable automotive writers. Photography and artwork are of the best quality obtainable.
14. Ruiz, *History of The Automobile*, p. 16
15. Ibid., p. 16
16. Scott, Robert F. *Automobile Quarterly*, Vol. VI #4, p. 411
17. Ibid, Norbye, p. 87

Chapter 2: Pedal Power

1. Palmer, *Riding High*, P.13 Also recommended is *The Story of The Bicycle*, Woodforde for illustrations and photographs.
2. Ibid., p. 14
3. Ibid., p.25
4. Ibid., p. 28
5. Herlihy, *Bicycle: The History*, p. 67
6. Ibid., p. 165

Index

Prest·O·Lite

INDIANA...

MIAMI BEACH

I Love to make